D0198296

SALES
MANAGEMENT

SALES MANAGEMENT

THE McGRAW-HILL EXECUTIVE MBA SERIES

ROBERT J. CALVIN

McGraw-Hill

New York   Chicago   San Francisco   Lisbon   London
Madrid   Mexico City   Milan   New Delhi   San Juan
Seoul   Singapore   Sydney   Toronto

5 6 7 8 9 0   DOC/DOC   0 9 8 7 6 5 4
14 15 16 17 18 19 DOH/DOH 1 5 4

ISBN 0-07-136434-X (HC)
ISBN 0-07-143535-2 (PBK)

McGraw-Hill books are available at special quantity discounts to use as premiums and sales promotions, or for use in corporate training programs. For more information, please write to the Director of Special Sales, Professional Publishing, McGraw-Hill, Two Penn Plaza, New York, NY 10121-2298. Or contact your local bookstore.

Library of Congress Cataloging-in-Publication Data

Calvin, Robert J.
    Sales management: the McGraw-Hill executive MBA / by Robert J. Calvin.
    p. cm.
    ISBN 0-07-136434-X
    1. Sales management.   I. Title

    HF5438.4 .C343 2000
    658.8'1—dc21   00-046462
                                                        CIP

CONTENTS

In memory of my father:
Joseph K. Calvin
My mother:
Pauline H. Calvin
And my daughter:
Amy E. Calvin

PART ONE

CREATING THE SALES FORCE

CHAPTER 1

People, Process, Technology, and Performance

THE PROCESS

Sale force management is a process; one step logically follows another. Control the pieces and you control the whole. In this book we will devote one chapter or a portion of one chapter to each of the pieces in the sales management process. For each piece we will build a model or a methodology, showing how marketing and sales management work together and how strategy drives tactics. As a sales manager or a student of sales management, you must understand not only each step in the process but the holistic system which these pieces create. You must understand and master not only the micros but the macros, not only the quantitative but the qualitative.

Some sales managers are inspirational motivators but don't understand the process for hiring salespeople. Others excel at coaching but don't understand the necessity for performance evaluations. Few people understand and implement the entire process. As a result, weak sales and sales management are the Achilles' heel of most old and new economy businesses. Most sales organizations need to be reengineered as you would a factory to increase capacity and productivity.

The sales management process/model involves the following pieces.

Strategy and Objectives

- Structure follows strategy.
- Tactics reflect strategy.

Hiring

- Job description, candidate profile, sourcing, interviewing, reference checking, final decision.

Training

- Product, competitor, customer knowledge.
- Selling skills.
- Field coaching, sales meetings, initial training.

Compensation

- Total dollar level.
- Fixed versus performance pay.

Organization

- Channel choice—Direct or indirect.
- Geographic, product, customer, or functional architecture.
- Territory boundaries—Deployment and sizing.
- Time management within territory.

Forecasts

- Bubble-up versus top-down.
- Format.
- Sales plan—Actions that drive forecast numbers.

Nonmonetary Motivation

- Different sparks light different people's fires.
- Recognition, usefulness, challenge, achievement, belonging, personal growth, leadership.

Sales Force Automation

- Systems applications.
- Ecommerce and the Internet.
- Implementation.

Performance Evaluations

- Results, activities, skills, knowledge, personal characteristics.
- Self-evaluation.
- Quarterly.
- Goal setting; development plan.
- Measuring productivity.

Hewitt Associates LLC asked sales and human resource executives at Fortune 100 companies to indicate the major sales management issues/challenges they face over the next one to three years. Of the 118 responses, retaining high-performing salespeople was cited as the top sales management issue by 80 percent of the participants, followed closely by recruiting high-performance salespeople (71 percent) and improving communication technology, reporting systems, data access, and sales automation (68 percent). The other major sales management issues cited were improving productivity (57 percent), restructuring the sales organization (56 percent), providing salespeople with better training and development (52 percent), and integrating ecommerce into channel strategy (43 percent).[1]

BASIC ASSUMPTIONS

This book makes three assumptions:

1. *A sales force is no better than its management.* A weak sales force reflects weak management. As a colleague of mine says, "When the fish stinks, it starts at the head." For the multitude of sales managers who complain about their salespeople, this can be a painful concept to accept.

2. *A sales manager's job is to get work done through other people.* His or her success depends on the success of the sales team. Often you can do the job better than each of your people, but you cannot do the job better than the group.

3. *A manager's job is to make heroes, not be one.* This applies to other functions besides sales.

BEST OF CLASS

Good sales management properly applied is the least expensive, most effective way to increase dollars of revenue and margins, market share, cash flow, return on investment, and net present value, as well as to beat the competition and make yourself a hero. Effective sales management is a great democrat for smaller firms. As the book shows, it costs no more to properly hire, train, compensate, motivate, and evaluate salespeople. Effective time and territory management, forecasting, planning, budgeting, and good communication and control are no more expensive than performing these same functions poorly. Sales drive profits and hide many sins.

---

1. Reprinted by permission of Hewitt Associates LLC, Copyright: Hot Topics in Sales Management and Sales Compensation 2000.

Ecommerce, the Internet, customer relationship management, and sales force automation are not silver bullets for success. They are part of the marketing and sales management process, which if properly applied, can improve sales force productivity and capacity. Successful ecommerce companies still rely on high-touch telesales/telemarketing and field salespeople. Computers don't replace salespeople; they make them more effective.

I am often asked at cocktail parties and on television talk shows what separates the best sales managers from the not-so-good. Each year as I journey through corporate America, I meet hundreds of salespeople and sales managers. The best sales managers have what I like to call the will to manage. They are willing to set standards, be critical, and sit in judgment. However, since most sales managers were promoted because of their record as a salesperson, it is not easy to set standards, be critical, and sit in judgment of their peers, even at a different employer.

The best sales managers realize they are agents of change and, as such they must manage change and change people's behavior. The twenty-first century will be even more turbulent than the 1990s. Rapidly changing competitors, products, technologies, markets, and customers make business a dynamic process where the future is a moving target. Sales managers are at the vortex of these changes. The best sales managers realize this is part of their job. The not-so-good complain about change.

The best sales managers don't whine about their salespeople. They work to change their behavior through nonmonetary motivation.

In addition, the best sales managers believe in what they are doing, which creates strong personal motivation and is passed on to salespeople and customers. They also delegate, set goals, and plan well.

KEY CONTROL POINTS

Every business and every business function has key control points. In the financial area these include dollars of contribution margin, capital expenditures, working capital needs, sales forecasts, and expense budgets. Write down the key control points in the sales management process for your firm or one you are familiar with. Which steps in the process are most important for the success of that business? Many sales managers say they include the job description, training checklist, salesperson development plan, sales forecast/plan, targeting, sizing, deployment, and performance evaluation. The key control points are an important concept which will vary by business. It will be different for managing the sales of telecommunication services and telecommunication equipment, and it will be different for sales of bakery products and refuse removal services.

The sales management process discussed in this book is equally applicable to telesales and field salespeople, consumer and business-to-business (B2B) products, full-time direct salespeople and indirect representatives, distributors, and brokers. The process makes the salesperson and the manager partners and increases sales force productivity, whether telesales, distributor, agent, broker, or full-time field person.

The marketplace demands that sales management and marketing work together to improve sales force productivity and implement the steps in the sales management process. In many companies, turf battles and organizational politics prevent this. Upper management must reinforce the need for marketing to devote 20 percent of its time to direct sales force support—for example, providing market, customer, and competitor knowledge to salespeople. Silos, where each department or function works independent of the other, create competitive disadvantages.

THE CHANGING LANDSCAPE

As mentioned, business is a dynamic process; the future is a moving target. Sales managers are agents of change and must manage change. The 1990s were turbulent, and the new millennium will accelerate the pace of change.

As a sales manager or a student of sales management, consider how the following changes will impact the sales management process, strategy, and tactics:

- *Shorter product/service life cycles* These shorter life cycles quickly commoditize products and services and make them more difficult to differentiate. In the twenty-first century, this trend will accelerate. Whether you sell semiconductors, medical devices, telephone services, or bakery products, successful services and products are and will be quickly imitated and improved on.

  A company's sales management strategy must reflect this through improved product knowledge and sales skills training, different recruiting requirements, and possibly a hybrid organizational structure. The companies which can reduce the time and steps between a customer's search and purchase will be the winners. You must compensate salespeople to compress the sales/buying cycle. (We will discuss this issue in a later chapter.)

- *Longer, more complex sales cycles* The number of steps from customer search to purchase is expanding. For example, in buying miniature transformers for insertion in a newly designed printed circuit board, customers expect vendors to do a needs assessment, have vendor engineering prepare customized specifications, submit samples which are used for demos and trials (betas), place a trial production order, and submit a final proposal. In selling a new variety of frozen muffin batter to a bakery, the salesperson must submit finished muffin samples for a taste test, deliver a trial batter order, show the baker how to use the batter, and train clerks on point-of-purchase sell-through. As recently as 1995 this was not necessary in either industry. However, the changing landscape demands a changing sales management strategy which drives new tactics. Sales managers may need to hire people with experience in this type of selling and train them on each step in their process, along with how to track the process. Sales cycles may be long, so performance pay might reflect progress from one step to the next. This might also necessitate organizing the sales force in teams.

- *Buying from experts and friends* In some industries the people who make buying decisions have become more knowledgeable and experienced, in others less knowledgeable and experienced. For example, the people involved in purchasing communication and navigational equipment for aircraft generally have a knowledge level equaling that of any vendor salesperson. Therefore, the salesperson differentiates himself or herself by being more of a friend than an expert, and the candidate-hiring profile should emphasize customer knowledge. Hospital personnel purchasing software for measuring efficacy or controlling costs probably will not be experienced or knowledgeable in this area. Such purchases might be a one-time or first-time event, so in this situation the salesperson must be more of an expert than a friend. Therefore, training should emphasize product knowledge over knowledge of competition or customers.

- *Group decision* In the twenty-first century, in order to spread the risk of major purchases, more decisions will be made by groups. For example, when a municipality buys catalytic converters for buses or a telco buys shielded twisted cable for data transmission, the purchasing decision will be made or influenced by engineers, purchasing, finance, and operations. This requires salespeople to be trained in multilevel selling. What are each group's needs and how will each group benefit from the purchase? Who is the decision maker and who are the influencers? Team selling may be required. Forecasts and plans may become more difficult. The candidate hiring profile might change.

- *Intense competition* Because of global markets and changing technology, competition in the twenty-first century will be even more intense. This drives the shorter product/service life cycles and commoditization mentioned in the first item in the list. The Internet, lower costs, availability of start-up capital, and greater speed of chips has allowed the proliferation of ants (small start-ups) to compete with the giants. Technology is the great democrat. World markets including the United States, will be impacted by the low-cost, highly trained, and efficient human resources in Asia, India, Russia, and Eastern Europe. To combat this, sales managers must use competitive grids to train salespeople. Who are the present and potential competitors? What are the competitive issues, and how does a customer choose between vendors?
- *Less customer loyalty* People who make buying decisions will become less loyal to a particular vendor in the twenty-first century. The CFO of a major hospital recently told me that unless he lowers the cost per patient day by 10 percent in the year 2001, he will be looking for a new position in 2002. The hospital's managed care customers demand this cost reduction. Access to the Internet provides instant competitive product and price information, further reducing customer loyalty.

  In the twenty-first century, salespeople must be trained to quantify benefits by demonstrating how much a particular feature can lower a customer's/prospect's costs, increase revenues, and lower capital expenditures or working capital needs. Whether you are selling paper stock to a printer or hand tools to a dentist, salespeople must be trained to demonstrate, quantify, and prove customer benefits. This allows a customer to rationalize his or her choice of vendors.

CHAPTER 2

Hiring the Best, Terminating the Rest

A CONTINUOUS PROCESS

What is the most important function a sales manager performs? The answer is hiring. No matter how good you are at training, motivating, evaluating, and planning, all that applied to mediocre salespeople produces mediocre results. Cast the play well and it becomes easier to direct.

Yet hiring is an area many sales managers have never been trained in and often have little experience implementing. How many times does a sales manager say, "I just can't improve this person's performance, so I must live with below-average results"? In the twenty-first century, you can't afford to live with below-average results, because effective sales organizations will create competitive advantages that differentiate one firm from another in a commoditized world.

This chapter talks about a hiring process which will increase the probability of hiring the best person and reduce the risk of hiring the wrong person. As you will see, each step in the process acts as a filter. The more steps you use, the lower your risk of failure. In its simplest form, the process involves preparing a job description and candidate profile, sourcing, screening, and making the final choice. Sourcing is where and how we look for candidates, whether through competitors, customers, or Web sites. Screening involves conducting phone and personal interviews; checking references; making credit, drug, and driver's license checks; testing; and making a final choice. Each step in a sales manager's hiring process should be driven by strategic corporate issues.

The vice-president of sales for a Fortune 500 company that employs over one thousand salespeople revealed that 55 percent of his salespeople are wonderful human beings, but they should not be in sales. Their skills, experience, and personal characteristics better suit them for human resources or information technology or operations. He said that 25 percent of the salespeople had appropriate skills, experience, and personal characteristics, but were misapplied. That is, they were good at selling products but were employed to sell services, or they were good at relationship sales but were being used for consultative sales. That left 20 percent of the sales force who produced over 50 percent of the revenues. "Just think," he said, "if we could expand that 20 percent, what our sales would be."

Hiring is a continuous process. You should always be looking for outstanding people, not just when you have a vacancy. The best way to interview a candidate is when they don't think it is an interview—at a trade show, for instance, or casually over lunch. When salespeople call on you to sell a service or product, evaluate them as a potential candidates. When a competitor's salesperson contacts you for a position, be sure to meet with him or her. Ask probing questions and be a good listener. Keep a file of qualified candidates. When a position is available, you will have a head start.

The president of a medium-sized Omaha-based meat processing firm was losing market share in this competitive industry. The firm employed ten regional sales managers who each managed ten salespeople. To improve market share, the company president insisted that each regional manager terminate and replace one of his or her salespeople a year, in addition to anyone who retired, voluntarily left, or was terminated for not meeting minimum performance standards.

Two years later, market share and revenues were on the rise. Five years later, the firm was an industry leader. There might have been many reasons for this, but one stands out. The new policy forced the sales managers to always be looking for better people. Letting 10 percent of the sales force go a year caused continuous improvement. The 10 percent were not top performers and were replaced by better people. The salespeople who remained were highly motivated to be part of a select team. The lesson is this: Use hiring to weed the garden and let the cream rise to the top. Rather than a reactive tool, use hiring as a proactive tool to improve sales force productivity.

COSTLY MISTAKES

Most sales managers have weak track records in hiring. We make the same mistakes continually and don't take corrective action. Most sales managers prefer salespeople who share their backgrounds, present a nice appearance, and do not threaten them. They hire people they enjoy. However, this natural selection does not necessarily result in the best sales force. First-rate managers hire first-rate people. Second-rate managers hire third-rate people. I attended a sales meeting where seven of the twenty salespeople were named Randy, fourteen were bald, and of the fourteen, ten had beards. Randy, the sales manager, was bald and had an attractive beard.

Being sales types themselves, many sales managers oversell the job when they meet Ms. or Mr. Perfect. They assure the candidate that competition is nominal, customers seldom complain, and paperwork is minimal. Overselling the candidate results in unmet expectations, disappointment, resentment, and high turnover. If the territory requires a great deal of prospecting or sales are declining, admit it.

Occasionally, after you have completed the steps described in this chapter, only a best candidate of those available will emerge, not an excellent candidate. Don't hire the best of a weak group because this will not solve your problem. A weak salesperson can prove more expensive than no salesperson. It proves less expensive to continue looking than to hire, fire, and look again.

Hiring requires planning, anticipating needs, and working within an appropriate time frame. Many managers hire reactively and under pressure. This increases the risk of failure. The hiring process takes 30 to 90 days. Having a mobile spare salesperson in training, on the bench, mitigates the time pressure. A 2000 study conducted by the International Association of Corporate and Professional Recruitment (IACPR) reports an average of 4.13 months to hire a qualified salesperson.

Ask any sales manager how many salespeople he or she has hired in the last four years, how many are still with the company, and of those how many he or she is happy with. The answers will surprise you. Industry averages are not meaningful because the range has such extremes.

A giftware importer selling to retailers which had 100 percent turnover in its 350-person sales force represents one extreme. Some territories turned over twice. Problems ranged from compensation to hiring to training. The cost of this turnover exceeded $2 million.

Hiring the wrong salesperson proves expensive because of the loss of potential sales (opportunity cost) and/or the loss and replacement of the person hired. You can easily spend $20,000 of time and out-of-pocket expense finding, screening, hiring, and training a new salesperson. Losing a new hire for whatever reason represents a nonrecoverable, nonproductive cost similar to a bad debt.

Termination also results in loss of continuity for the sales force and further reduces sales. Competitors target territories and companies with high sales force turnover. Customers must trust the salespeople they deal with, and continually replacing them destroys this confidence. A company with high salesperson turnover gets a bad reputation with customers, prospects, and potential salespeople, and, of course, lowers the morale of its current sales organization. In a smaller company, sales force turnover can also have a direct impact on unemployment insurance costs.

Hewitt Associates LLC asked sales and human resource executives at Fortune 1000 companies to supply their actual sales force turnover rates. Of the 116 responses, 18 percent of participants reported turnover rates of less than 5 percent, but the average actual turnover rate reported was 14 percent, the median was 12 percent, and the range was from 0 to 55 percent. Participants estimated the replacement cost per employee (turnover cost per employee) averaged $110, 400, with a median of $75,000.[2]

The basic techniques for reducing the risks of a bad hire and for reducing turnover are developing a realistic job description and candidate profile which reflect a firm's strategy, contacting appropriate sources for attracting candidates, and skillfully screening and selecting from those who apply. As we move into the twenty-first century, more skills and knowledge are demanded of salespeople, and, in return, they are demanding more from the organization, resulting in a more complex hiring process.

STRATEGIC DUTIES AND ISSUES

The job description is a list of anticipated duties. Where do you want the salesperson to concentrate? Does the job description target your most important customers, markets, and products? The candidate profile asks what experience, skills, knowledge, and personal characteristics these target customers, markets, and products require for success.

Target accounts, markets, and products are determined by dollars of present and potential revenue and income, cost to sell and serve, and probability of success. Some customers have high dollar potential for revenue and gross margin, but they take the margin dollars back by demanding costly services and/or a long, complex sales cycle. Activity-based accounting (ABC) can help you determine this. High-maintenance accounts might require "free" installation, training, design and engineering support. Export accounts might require special packaging and documentation. Customers and prospects that demand betas, trials, samples, demos, and teams are expensive to sell. Lucent may represent large potential revenue and income dollars for your business, but they have a three-year contract with a competitor. Your probability of success is low.

Industry publications, associations, and government statistics can be helpful in targeting markets. Revenue data is often available by SIC code, region, state, city, and zip code.

Some companies don't have targets, or they have incorrect ones. A home health-care provider thought their target referral customers were physicians, when in fact they were discharge social workers at hospitals.

---

2. Reprinted by permission of Hewitt Associates LLC, Copyright: Hot Topics in Sales Management and Sales Compensation 2000.

You would not hire the same type of salesperson to call on physicians as you would social workers. Clearly defining your firm's target customer will help you hire the most appropriate salesperson.

Another strategic issue to be reflected in the job description and candidate profile is whether you want salespeople to concentrate on new accounts or further penetration of existing customers. Where is the opportunity for growth better? Salespeople need to know this for proper time allocation. Opening new accounts versus penetration of existing accounts requires salespeople with different skills, knowledge, experience, and personal characteristics.

How does buyer behavior—a marketing concept—affect your target accounts, job description, and candidate profile? Are your target accounts making one-time or first-time purchases of your product/service (new systems), as with software or medical equipment? If so, salespeople need consultive sales skills and knowledge of long, complex sales cycles. Or are your target accounts making modified rebuys of the same product/service or existing system, in which case your salespeople need relationship sales skills and knowledge of negotiations (insurance or telco services). Or perhaps you sell a commodity (paper to printers) where salespeople are order takers and time management is most important. On the other hand, your target accounts might be most interested in a continual flow of new products/services, so selling skills are most important for new hires (pharmaceutical products to physicians). These issues need to be reflected on the job description and candidate profile. These buyer behavior issues also impact training, compensation, and organization of a sales force. Exhibit 2.1 illustrates the four quadrants of buyer behavior.

Similarly, if salespeople have a pricing window and negotiating price, and delivery and product/service customization is strategically important, it is imperative to list this as a duty in the job description and under desired experience in the candidate profile. You should also include pricing and negotiating skills in the training checklist (see Exhibit 3.1 in Chapter 3). If telesales is an important salesperson tool, put it in the candidate profile and job description.

Strategic management decisions concerning channel choice, team selling, sales force organization, telesales, and national account sales also should be reflected in the job description and candidate profile. If salespeople will be working in a hybrid organization selling through reps, agents, or distributors, this certainly influences the anticipated duties as well as the experience, knowledge, and skills you seek. If salespeople will be calling on national accounts in teams, state this as a duty in the job description.

Strategic decisions concerning deployment will influence territory size and the need for travel. Time away from home might be more appealing to

Exhibit 2.1

Buyer behavior; matching business-to-business sales.

NEW SYSTEMS BUYER

Inexperienced but real user; first time or one-time user.

Financial services, software, communication systems, consulting, law, computers, big ticket, high-tech. Heterogeneous product/service.

Long sales cycle, group decision, consultive sell, problem-solving. Strong product knowledge. Expert image. Partnership sales. Technical and application support. One-time purchase. Risk of failure. Highest total compensation for salespeople. High-percentage fixed pay.

ESTABLISHED SYSTEMS BUYER

Experienced real user. Modified rebuy.

Agriculture, horticulture, security systems, insurance litigation, printed circuits, subcontracting. Homogenous product/service.

NEW PRODUCT BUYER

Experienced users.

Feature/benefit selling.

Good closing skills. Low fear of rejection. Emotional appeal, pressure. Aggressively initiate customer contact; use probing questions.

Mid-level total dollar compensation

High-percentage performance pay.

Shorter sales cycle, group decision, relationship sell. Customer knowledge. Friendly image, purchase, and delivery needs. Great patience over a long period of time. Politicking, bargaining. Upper-middle or lower-upper total compensation for salespeople. Fixed versus performance pay 50/50. Increasing percent of customer's business, penetration.

COMMODITY BUYER

Experienced users with standardized product/service. Routine functions and rebuy.

Die castings, hardware, office supplies, injection molding. Homogenous products.

Route sales. Frequent sales calls.

Individual decision maker. Often delegated.

Relation sale. Price, delivery, availability, customer service, convenience.

Increasing share of customer's business.

Maintenance/penetration

Order taking. Time management. EDI. IT.

Small risk of rejection. Little personal involvement. High-percentage performance pay. Lowest total compensation.

Assess complexity of using a product/service and experience or expertise in its use or application. How does this influence hiring, training, compensation, and organization of salespeople?

some salespeople than others. If extensive travel is an anticipated duty, it might be helpful to look for people who are accustomed to it.

Most job descriptions and candidate profiles don't reflect these strategic issues. Your probability of hiring the right salesperson increases if you include strategic issues in the hiring process. Be sure the job description and candidate profile reflect shorter product/service life cycles; longer, more complex sales cycles; changes in the knowledge, experience, and loyalty of decision makers; group buying decisions; increased competitive pressures; and quantification of benefits.

JOB DESCRIPTIONS

Many companies have job descriptions for everyone in the firm except salespeople. Sales managers need a list of each salesperson's anticipated duties in order to train and evaluate them. As with any employee, salespeople need to know what is expected of them. Of course, job descriptions will vary depending on products/services, buyer behavior, type of selling, and company culture. Within the same company, salespeople selling different products/services, or with a different type of end user or with different levels of decision makers will have different job descriptions. Some sales managers write slightly different job descriptions for salespeople with the same title but different territory characteristics. A telesales person will quite obviously have a different job description than a national accounts manager. A route grocery store salesperson taking reorders for Mexican-style cheese will have a different job description from a salesperson selling Internet services to major corporations. In addition, each route grocery store salesperson may have enough variation in customer mix to have somewhat different duties. A new territory you are trying to develop may require more prospecting than a matured territory, where account retention and penetration is the primary task. The trend in the twenty-first century is toward more detailed and more customized job descriptions.

Exhibit 2.2 presents a job description. When creating the job description, be sure to include sales and servicing duties, planning, reporting, company relations, administrative chores, and housekeeping. Try to keep the job description to one page, or two pages at most. Review and revise it each year to reflect rapidly changing products/services, competition, customers, technology, and strategy.

Each year ask your salespeople to revise their job description, adding duties not listed and altering duties which have changed. Have them sign the job description, date it, and return it. Some sales managers ask their salespeople to rank each duty as to importance and note what percentage of their time is spent on each activity. The results may surprise you. If sales-

Exhibit 2.2

Salesperson job description.

OVERALL PURPOSE

Meet or exceed sales objectives of assigned territory by promoting and selling tires through professional sales techniques, product service, and long-term customer relationships.

MAJOR ACTIVITIES

- Meet and exceed sales targets; achieve maximum sales in assigned territory through dealer, affiliate, and other channels.

- Make at least 25 quality sales calls each week on dealers or fleet managers.

- Target A, B, and C accounts by present and potential dollars of revenues/profits, cost to sell and service, and probability of success.

- Allocate time and call frequency based on A, B, and C targeting.

- Make the appropriate number of calls on prospects versus customers. Identify potential growth areas, and open new accounts.

- Increase market share by calling on a large universe of diverse dealers to promote and sell tires, communicate special programs, present marketing/advertising programs and new products, handle and process warranties, prepare and conduct dealer training and educational seminars, collect competitive information, handle and resolve problems and complaints, and collect overdue receivables. Advise dealers on market conditions, wholesale, and end user accounts.

- Increase market share by calling on a large universe of diverse fleet accounts to sell tires, communicate special programs, conduct fleet inspections, monitor tire mileage, conduct educational seminars, handle and resolve problems and complaints including credit issues. Advise dealers on market conditions, wholesale, and end user accounts.

- Sell all products but concentrate on high-performance tires and value-added selling.

- Prepare written presentations, reports, and price quotations.

- Sell at transaction price approved for this type of customer.

- Negotiate delivery, availability, warranty, advertising, and pricing for discontinued items. Follow up on back orders.

- Maintain accounts receivables in compliance with objectives.

- Conduct customer education and product information meetings.

- Continually learn new product knowledge and acquire better selling skills.

- Keep abreast of competition, competitive issues, products, and markets for tires.

- Attend and participate in sales meetings, product seminars, and trade shows.

- Create customer sales programs.

TIME MANAGEMENT

- Work a 50-hour, five-day week.
- Do necessary overnight travel.
- See first customer by 7:30 a.m.
- See last customer at 3:00 p.m.
- Utilize laptops and cellular phones.
- Maximize percent of time in front of customers.
- Minimize travel time.
- Use customer service reps for follow-up and smaller accounts.
- Call on accounts in clusters. Work one section of territory each day. Use loops and cloverleafs.

E x h i b i t   2.2 (continued)

SELF-ORGANIZATION
- Plan each day, week, and month.
- Plan each call.
- Keep sales aids in mint condition.
- Dress neatly.
- Maintain a neat automobile.
- Present professional image.
- After each call fill in customer profile and daily planner.

ADMINISTRATIVE
- Maintain customer profiles and customer files.
- Submit the following in a timely manner: daily planner/call reports, sales plans, forecasts, expense reports.
- Communicate competitive information to corporate marketing.
- Complete and submit credit applications for new accounts.

- Use information technology to save time.
- Analyzing/monitoring data and reports.

COMPANY RELATIONS
- Comply with all company policies and operate within the expense budget.
- Work with, develop positive relationships with, communicate with, and coordinate activities with other employees in marketing, customer service, distribution, credit, accounting, human resources, engineering, national fleet, and finance departments.
- Communicate effectively; cooperate with your fellow salespeople and management.

---

people find this difficult, you should probably discuss it further or put it on the agenda for a sales meeting.

I work with twenty-five salespeople a year, coaching them during customer visits. At some point I ask whether their job description accurately reflects their duties. Eight out of ten times they reply they have no job description, and so I pull it out of my briefcase. Then they remember seeing it once. The annual review mentioned previously prevents this memory loss.

In a worst-case scenario, the job description can offer a defense in a law suit based on wrongful termination. The salesperson has acknowledged, by annually signing the job description, that he or she understands the anticipated duties. The lack of a job description and an annual review leaves an employer more vulnerable to litigation.

The job description can also offer a defense in a lawsuit brought for discriminatory hiring. Can you demonstrate that the person you hired has better qualifications for performing the anticipated duties than the people you did not hire?

A sales manager's most important function is hiring the best salespeople, and an important part of that process is the job description. When preparing a job description, always keep in mind that the job description must not discriminate based on race, gender, nationality, age, disability, or veteran status, and that all the duties must be job related. Have the appropriate person responsible for human resources review your job description, but do not have them write it. Also remember that the sales manager's feet will be held to the fire for poor hiring decisions, not human resources.

CANDIDATE PROFILE

Once you have developed the job description, it is time to translate it into a written candidate profile. Whereas the job description lists duties, the candidate profile describes the skills, experience, knowledge, and personal characteristics necessary for performing those duties. What do your most successful salespeople have in common? Similarly, what do your least successful salespeople have in common? Which of the skills, experience, knowledge, and personal characteristics are musts and which are wants? A must is, for example, hiring only candidates who have industry experience. A want might be a degree in engineering. The candidate profile forces you to learn from experience and not perpetrate the same mistakes.

Exhibit 2.3 gives examples of candidate profiles. Think of a candidate profile as your shopping list. Skills might include selling and computer skills, communications, and data analysis. Experience might include type of sales, industry, type of compensation, performance results, prospecting, national accounts, and type of customers. Knowledge might include understanding of customers, products, competition, and industry. Personal characteristics would include items such as confidence, enthusiasm, persistence, drive, passion, ability to be a team player, aggressiveness, desire, empathy, ability to accept rejection, honesty, initiative, and creativity. Most sales managers claim to keep this profile in their head but never write it down. Instead write it down, and review and modify it annually to reflect the changing job description.

The profile for a salesperson calling on hospitals and physicians with home health-care services will require very different knowledge, skills, experience, and personal characteristics than a salesperson calling on the same customers with medical devices or medications. Both these sales forces will have different candidate profiles than salespeople calling on tier-two auto firms for contract manufacturing.

Determining whether the candidate has these skills, knowledge, and personal characteristics is often very difficult. For example, what does past compensation tell you about the candidate? If he or she were successful in a 100 percent performance pay program, does that mean the candidate should be a team player or is confident, a self-starter, or would be successful at your

Exhibit 2.3

Salesperson candidate profile—musts and wants.

SKILLS	KNOWLEDGE	EXPERIENCE	PERSONAL CHARACTERISTICS
• Listening	• Tire technology	• Success in selling a business-to-business product	• Appearance
• Written and verbal communication	• High school degree	• Three years related experience	• Enthusiasm
• Sales	• Customers	• Sold premium product at premium price	• Self-organization
• Persuasion	• Markets	• Long hours	• Follow-up/ persistence
• Computer	• IT	• Large diverse customer base	• Sense of urgency
• Planning	• Bilingual	• Longevity in previous positions	• Team player
• Analytical	• Business management	• Industry experience	• Self-confidence
• Resolution			• Assertiveness
• Creativity			• Business judgment
• Learning			• Consistency
• Presentations			• Ability to develop new ideas
• Negotiations			• Self-starter
• Time management			• Ethics, integrity
• Technical aptitude			• High achiever
			• Money-motivated
			• Ability to accept rejection

firm? If a candidate's duties have not changed in five years, does that say something about his or her performance? We discuss techniques for determining this criteria later in the chapter.

Most sales candidates have taken many more interviews than you have given and many have become quite adept. Always remember, it is easy to be fooled.

The most unusual candidate profile I have encountered was for hiring a salesperson of precious gems for Central America. The position required a knowledge of Spanish, English, Arabic, and rare stones. Skills included self-defense, negotiations, and accuracy with fire arms. Experience included long trips and carrying large amounts of currency. Personal characteristics included the ability to stay alert on five hours of sleep a night. Needless to say, this profile quickly screened out inappropriate candidates.

SOURCES FOR ATTRACTING CANDIDATES

Finding the best candidate can be a challenge and often means looking in many places. Alternative sources for attracting candidates are as follows:

- Career ladders from within your organization
- Customers who can be referrals or candidates
- Referrals from your present salespeople in exchange for a bonus
- Suppliers and vendors
- Competition
- The corporate database
- Professional organizations
- Recruiters
- Media advertising
- The Internet
- Outsourcing firms and job fairs

Each of these sources has advantages and disadvantages which we will examine. What source or combination of sources you use depends on your job description and candidate profile. The Internet works well when you are looking for salespeople with technical skills. Customers are a good source when you are looking for salespeople involved in relationship sales. Each job search is different, but if in the past one source has produced better results, start with that.

Internal Career Ladder

Longer, more complex sales cycles and shorter product life have created a need for and scarcity of competent salespeople for the twenty-first century. A growing number of businesses deal with this by hiring from within and creating a career ladder from other functions/departments into field sales. Qualified people can move from engineering, design, or operations to purchasing, telesales, to field sales, or some other combination. In distribution companies there is a career ladder from the warehouse to truck driver to route salesperson. Some firms have academies or use outside seminars where nonsalespeople can learn selling and marketing skills as part of the career ladder. Financial institutions like to promote operations people into sales. A Christmas decoration firm finds that its best field salespeople come from the showroom staff.

The advantages of hiring from within are that the management knows the candidates, and the candidates know the products, customers, and competition. This saves recruiting and training time and reduces certain risks. The disadvantages are your firm may become inbred, and candidates may not possess the personal characteristics necessary for success in sales. Candidates may not be confident, enthusiastic, or able to deal with rejection. You may lose a good engineer and hire a mediocre salesperson. Internal candidates who are rejected may lose their motivation. To avoid the disadvantages, balance external and internal hiring, continually evaluate internal candidates, and quickly take corrective action.

Customers

Customers are an excellent source for sales candidates but cannot be used if privacy is important. You can hire customers' employees or use them as referrals. Customers understand market needs and have product knowledge, but again may not have sales skills or appropriate personal characteristics. If a customer employee becomes a candidate but is not offered the job, you may have lost a supporter. Unless you wish to lose an account, never hire a customer's employee without first asking permission from the employee's supervisor.

Often a customer's decision makers know of an appropriate salesperson who wishes to change employment. As sales manager, you should call customers who would be helpful and explain the job's requirements. Choose customers with whom you have a personal relationship and in whom you have confidence; they will be flattered. Tell customers that you are asking for their assistance because they will be dealing with the new salesperson.

The advantages of this source are that customers know salespeople and understand the job requirements. Customer decision makers network with many salespeople. In addition, they understand the job requirements and skills, knowledge, and characteristics necessary for success. The disadvantages are that customers might recommend a friend or relative who is down on their luck but not qualified, or they might want to be considered for the job themselves.

Firms which sell high-tech systems to the military primarily hire salespeople who have worked in government procurement. Food service firms have success hiring food and beverage managers. Many apparel firms hire department store buyers. These represent examples of using customers as a source for salespeople.

Current Employees

Current employees, especially your present sales force, often know qualified salespeople who might find the available position attractive. Offer a

$1000 bonus for referrals which result in hiring and an additional $1000 if the candidate stays for 14 months. Your salespeople have a wide network of associates; they understand the job requirements and usually want to recommend winners. Be aware, though, that when their referral is not acceptable, is an unqualified friend, or is hired and then later terminated, the salesperson may blame you and become angry.

Vendors

A sales manager always should be looking for qualified candidates. When an impressive vendor sales representative calls on you to sell printers, copy machines, software, laptops, or telephone or Internet services, get to know him or her. Use trade shows and associations as a way of meeting appropriate candidates. You can learn a great deal by watching people work a trade show or sell you their products or services. Keep a file of qualified candidates. One mobile home manufacturer and a storm window firm both have the greatest success hiring supplier salespeople because of their industry and customer knowledge.

Competitors

Snatching a salesperson from a competitor may look like a safe hire, but this approach is often risky. The advantages of hiring from competition is the salesperson's knowledge of customers, competition, and the product/service. Potential disadvantages are the salesperson's lack of credibility with customers, their inflexibility to your procedures, lack of loyalty to your firm, and bad habits they may have learned at the other firm.

Make sure you understand why the competitor's salesperson wants to leave, or else you may inherit someone else's troubles. He or she may not be performing or may be having personal difficulties.

Always interview candidates from competitors even if you have no openings. Ask probing questions and listen carefully. This can be a great source of market information. Mergers, reorganizations, and new compensation plans often make very qualified competitor salespeople open to new opportunities. Often, mature salespeople leave a competitor because their territory faces reduction or because the competitor desires a younger, less experienced, less expensive person. The right competitor candidate can bring captive customers, no bad habits, good product knowledge, and little need for training. In particular, hiring from competition has been very successful in the pharmaceutical industry. A European conglomerate which sells hand tools to U.S. dentists only hires from competition, as does a Midwest, family-owned firm which distributes fine papers to printers. Retailers shop the competitors' stores, not for products but for salespeople.

A large national apparel firm with several thousand retail outlets trains store managers in how to approach competitors' retail salespeople. The chain also insists that managers spend three days a month shopping competitors' stores for the right salespeople.

Corporate Database

Larger corporations keep databases of résumés received over the recent past. Generally, human resources keeps this underutilized file. Search the database for résumés of salespeople who meet your candidate profile. The corporate database is a larger version of your hiring file. In a large corporation, you may wish to consider a candidate from another division. Corporate human resources can help you find these candidates. At Motorola, Lucent, and General Motors, other divisions remain an important source of sales candidates.

Professional Associations, Schools, Military Discharge Centers

Professional organizations, schools, and armed forces discharge centers are excellent sources for salespeople. Most industries have professional associations, occasionally just for salespeople, which publish lists of available positions for their membership. Many groups have a local chapter in each state or major metropolitan area. Such associations range from the Men's Apparel Clubs in each state to State Health Care Associations to the Industrial Robot Division of the Society of Manufacturing Engineers. Be sure to list your job opening with the appropriate industry club or association.

Some software and pharmaceutical firms have found recent college graduates the best source for sales candidates. These firms require no industry or sales experience, but a candidate with a strong academic background in computers or life sciences. These firms prefer to train and mold younger salespeople. Colleges, universities, and technical schools have placement offices to assist recent and not-so-recent graduates. If appropriate, list sales positions with these placement offices and do on-campus recruiting.

A traditional furniture manufacturer in North Carolina arranges to hire interns every summer from a local junior college. Many of these interns later become permanent salespeople. The junior college has areas of study in interior design and business that fit the furniture company's salesperson profile. Banks and brokerage houses often hire previous summer college interns for sales positions after graduation.

As the armed forces downsize, well-trained people are being discharged from the military. An international conglomerate selling emission control devices to utilities worldwide hires only discharged military officers as salespeople. Selling a public utility requires understanding the decision-making process of large, complex, slow-moving organizations, and ex-military officers can certainly appreciate this. If appropriate, list your sales position with the local discharge office.

Recruiters

Recruiters that understand your industry and corporate culture and have a database of salespeople who match your candidate profile can be helpful. Look for recruiters who blend online sourcing with offline screening. Look for recruiters who have Web site job postings, know how to use online job boards, and blend this with email, phone, and in-person interviews. They can save you time in sourcing and screening candidates. Only use recruiters who provide legitimate references from your industry. Ask to speak with clients who have not been happy with their services. Don't use recruiters who will just make blind calls to your competitors and ask for a salesperson. Ask colleagues for referrals.

Negotiated fees range from 15 percent to 30 percent of the candidate's annual compensation, with a certain dollar amount paid up front and the rest based on performance. Negotiate a holdback to be paid to the recruiter after fourteen months of employment. After fourteen months you will know whether the salesperson meets your requirements. Put the fee arrangement in writing before the search begins.

Many recruiters dealing with middle-level salespeople lack professionalism. Their main interest is in making a match, but not necessarily a good fit. If you engage a recruiter, provide them with the job description and candidate profile, and agree on a realistic time frame. When candidates emerge, interview them immediately before they lose interest. Recruiters will coach candidates on what you are looking for and how to answer questions. Therefore, when using recruiters, you must vary the interviewing techniques.

A client of mine recently used a recruiter because she was planning to replace an underperforming salesperson but did not want the industry to know this. The recruiter, whose references were not checked, mistakenly called the salesperson who was to be terminated. As you can imagine, this resulted in a host of problems. Always check the recruiter's references and give him or her specific instructions on whom not to call.

Internet

With its wide reach, the Internet has become an important source for salespeople, and in the twenty-first century, it will continue to grow in importance. Your company's Web page should list employment opportunities in sales. In addition, employment opportunities should be listed on recruiting Web sites appropriate for your industry and region. Use a search engine to find the appropriate online candidate employment sites, and then key in on candidates who match your profile. General recruiting sites for salespeople include the following:

- www.thehrteon.com
- www.kforce.com
- www.headhunter.com
- www.monster.com
- www.careermosaic.com
- www.careerexchange.com
- www.bestjobsusa.com
- www.careerpath.com
- www.hotjobs.com
- www.careerbuilder.com
- www.salesseek.com
- www.salesjobs.com
- www.careercentral.com
- www.jobbanksusa.com
- www.salesclassified.com
- www. salesgiant.com

Online job boards and industry-specific communities of interest list candidates and contain classified ads by employers. Online job boards such as Headhunter.net and Monster.com produce large numbers of résumés in response to ads but require time to eliminate unqualified candidates. Professional recruiters who use online job boards can save their clients time and money.

The Internet provides a particularly appropriate source to look for technically based sales candidates. If you sell telephone services, software, chips, or medical devices, the Web is a must. Candidates are listed by specialty. For example, a printed circuit board assembly contractor found, and eventually hired, three salespeople from a two-hour Web search.

Job Fairs and Outsourcing Firms

Job fairs and outsourcing firms have become important sources for certain types of salespeople. Job fairs are organized by industry associations, or sometimes individual firms, to attract less experienced, younger salespeople. Retailers use job fairs, as do contract programmers. The fair is an open house to learn more about an industry or a company without actually making an appointment for an interview. A national electronic retailer with 250 stores insists that each store manager have an open house once a quarter. Each open house attracts at least six qualified salespeople, one of which is hired.

Although unemployment is low at the turn of the century, there is considerable movement from one company and industry to another. As one firm downsizes or one industry contracts, another is hiring and expanding. Outsourcing firms place professionals who are being downsized, many of them salespeople. List the sales employment opportunities with these firms.

Media Advertising

Media advertising for salespeople can be very effective if used correctly. The first issue is where to advertise; the second is what to say. Studies have shown that retailers, food service firms, and apparel manufacturers obtain the best results from local newspaper ads. The Sunday help wanted section generally pulls better than other days and sections, but depending on the job, the weekday sports or fashion page also attracts candidates.

Business-to-business firms generally obtain the best results in the classified "lines offered" section of trade or association publications. One day a week, or one week a month, the trade publication will specialize in employment ads or in your market segment. Advertise in the publications and sections which your target candidates read, and keep track of which media produce the best results. An agricultural seed firm primarily sources salespeople through their trade publications, as does an aluminum die-casting firm and a plastic injection molder.

Targeted radio stations can also source candidates. A Chicago-based Hispanic food manufacturer successfully hires salespeople from ads on the local Spanish-speaking radio station. This firm advertises its products on the Hispanic radio station and then adds a line or two concerning available positions.

Copy for print media employment ads should include company name, address, telephone number, and the person to contact. Ask candidates to write the sales manager directly if they feel qualified for the position. This humanizes the ad.

Blind ads do not produce qualified applicants. Salespeople hesitate responding to them because they may have been placed by their current employer. Blind ads also cause suspicion: What sort of employer won't divulge its name in an ad? If replacing a salesperson requires secrecy, rather than placing an unsuccessful blind ad, I suggest using other sources.

Your ad must contain an honest description of the position. If too much information is provied, qualified candidates might find something to discourage them from applying. If you include too little information, unqualified candidates are encouraged to apply. Remember that the ad's objective is not to hire and select the salespeople but only to produce qualified applicants. You will do the selecting from those who reply.

An honest description of the position states the product or service to be sold, type of selling, territory available, type of customer, what experience is necessary, and amount of overnight travel, if any. I would not include a compensation range, since this generally varies greatly depending on the applicant's ability. I also would not mention whether the territory contains established volume or requires pioneering. This information changes quickly and can best be handled in a personal discussion.

The ad should contain words accurately describing the job's non-monetary benefits such as *rewarding, steady, interesting, challenging.* Choose the words honestly. For example, a route salesperson's work is steady; a door-to-door salesperson's work is challenging.

Ads with creative copy attract attention and pull best. An effective technique for advertising in the Sunday paper involves asking the applicant to call you that Sunday. This requires your devoting that day to the project, but it produces results. If the ad is run outside your area code, it must specify a toll-free number or that collect calls will be accepted.

In addition to the copy already suggested, your Sunday ad might state:

> Don't write, but pick up your phone now and call me, Tom Brown, at this number. I am the sales manager of First Net.Com, and will be at my telephone between 9 and 5 today. I will tell you about the job opportunity, and you can tell me about your qualifications. I will not ask your name unless you wish to tell me.

The personal aspect of this ad plus the easy opportunity it offers for immediate response produces qualified candidates. Also, it allows people who are currently employed to call without fear that their employer will learn of their interest. Most companies have greater success hiring currently employed salespeople than they do unemployed salespeople. A variation of this idea involves asking candidates to call your assistant, having him or her do the initial screening, and then turn the most promising candidates over to you. As noted later, you and your assistant should describe the job but not the candidate profile. Use probing questions to determine candidate knowledge, skills, experience, and personal characteristics.

Certain advertising agencies—Nationwide Advertising Service Inc.; Shaker Advertising; Bentley, Barnes, and Lynn (BBL)—specialize in employment ads. In exchange for the 15 percent commission collected from the media, they will advise you on copy and choices of publication.

SCREENING AND SELECTING FROM THOSE WHO APPLY

Choosing the best candidate from a qualified group requires not only intuition and insight but also structure and technique. The probability of success can be enhanced and the risk of a bad hire reduced by following certain procedures. Because of time limitations, the temptation exists to take shortcuts in the selection process, but shortcuts only increase the risk of failure, forcing you to accept a mediocre salesperson or eventually seek a new one. Do it right, or do it again. Human resources, salespeople, and the vice president of sales can all help a sales manager in the hiring process. However, the sales manager must make the final decision and live with the results.

The steps used to successfully narrow the field include the following:

1. Conduct preliminary screening of résumés
2. Conduct telephone interviews
3. Request personal history forms
4. Conduct preliminary personal interviews
5. Check references
6. Continue interviews for finalists
7. Conduct testing
8. Make a job offer.

Not every job search requires all these steps, but as you can see, the process requires considerable time. The more time you make available to contact sources and screen applicants, the higher your probability of success. As mentioned, to maximize the available time for recruiting, try to anticipate hiring needs.

Again, the best sales managers set standards, are critical, and sit in judgment. Hiring in general and screening candidates in particular is a test of these skills. Candidates are selling themselves.

Reviewing Résumés

Begin the screening process by reviewing the résumés received and comparing them to the candidate profile. Eliminate those candidates who do not have the experience, knowledge, and skills listed as "musts" on the candidate profile. Look for employment gaps, job-hopping, weak written-communication skills, inconsistencies, misspelled words, and lack of completeness or accuracy. Be careful of candidates whose records show no improvements, such as a salesperson whose shipments and compensation have remained unchanged for many years or a salesperson who traded a good line with a top company for an inferior line with a second-rate organization.

Write a cordial letter to those people initially eliminated, expressing appreciation for their interest but informing them their fine backgrounds do not meet the position's requirements. The hiring process represents an opportunity for the company to make friends. Job applicants sometimes become customers, suppliers, politicians, managers, or repeat candidates. I know of many situations where an applicant originally rejected for one selling position was hired later for another. You should write rejection letters with this in mind and keep a file for future reference of all résumés received and notes taken from conversations.

Conducting Telephone Interviews

Call the remaining candidates for a telephone interview. Ask factual questions about their background, résumé, experience, knowledge, and skills. Why did he or she leave one employer for another? Does he or she have a formal education in molecular biology? Has he or she called on biotech laboratories? See if the candidate sells and persuades you to arrange an in-person interview. How does the candidate present himself or herself over the phone? This is an important part of most sales processes. Salespeople use the phone to sell appointments, take reorders, and resolve customer conflicts. If you are recruiting for a telesales position, give even more weight to the telephone interview.

The telephone interview will eliminate more candidates. Set appointments for an in-person interview with those you still have an interest in. Email or fax these people a short, simple personal history form to fill out and return before the interview. The personal history form asks the applicant for the following information:

- Name and address
- Educational background
- Employment history, with dates and responsibilities
- Outside interests

Although this repeats the résumé material, it often reveals conflicting information or provides more information. You also can see how quickly the candidate responds, whether he or she writes or types, how complete the information is, and whether the response is digital or snail mail.

With enhancements in technology, some businesses make videoconferencing part of their recruiting process. Companies such as AT&T, Dell Computer, Shell Oil, and Nike use videoconferencing to initially interview candidates. A dozen firms provide videoconferencing facilities, including Radison and Hilton Hotels, Kinkos, and Search Linc. Some recruiters stream video interviews to their clients via the Internet. A number of managers can watch the video interview. Videoconferencing represents another step in the hiring process and can reduce the time and cost of interviewing.

Most sales managers interview too many unqualified candidates because they don't do enough prescreening. Time and knowledge are your most valuable resources. I suggest limiting yourself to five candidates for face-to-face interviews. If those five don't produce a finalist, then expand the field.

Creating a Simulation

Now you begin the art and black magic of in-person interviewing. The interview is an opportunity for the candidate to persuade the sales manager that he or she should be hired. The sales manager's strategy is to create an interview situation which simulates an actual sales call in that particular industry.

For example, pharmaceutical salespeople have two or three minutes of face time with physicians to present their firm's medications. Persistent follow-up with physicians proves very important. To reflect these requirements, a regional sales manager for a large pharmaceutical company uses the five-minute interview. After a candidate arrives for an interview, she informs him or her that she has been called into a meeting at the last moment. She apologizes, lets the candidate know the meeting will only be an hour, but asks the candidate in the five minutes before the "meeting" to explain why he or she should be hired for the job. Some candidates do very well in this environment and some do not. Then she explains why she has done this and the interview continues. At the end of the interview, if she is interested in hiring a candidate, she asks him or her to call back at a precise time on a specific day. She is never available, but she tracks how persistent the candidate is in follow-up calls and what techniques are used to reach her.

If your salespeople make presentations to groups of customers, have group interviews to see how the candidate reacts. If new product sales and high customer rejection represent important parts of the sales process, have the candidate sell you their present product or service and throw some rejection at them.

For example, a sales manager for an advertising agency tells all candidates she interviews that although their backgrounds are interesting, they are not appropriate for this sales job. Then she listens to their response. Some candidates agree with her statement, others get mad, but those she hires try to persuade her she is wrong. On the second interview she takes telephone calls to see how a candidate deals with this. Can he refocus? Does he get angry? This simulates actual sales calls in the advertising industry.

The sales manager for an innovative software firm asks all candidates who are invited back for a second interview to be prepared to sell him a product or service they are familiar with. Then the sales manager evaluates the candidate's ability to establish rapport; ask probing questions establishing needs; present features, benefits, and proof; overcome objections; and close the sale. The sales manager for a fund-raising telesales organization asks candidates to sell her their previous product or service over the phone.

The sales manager for a money center bank finds her present salespeople lack closing skills. She ends each candidate interview by crossing her arms, remaining silent, and looking the candidate in the eye. Some candidates get anxious and reveal information heretofore not mentioned. Some candidates ask probing questions or remain silent themselves. She looks for a candidate who seizes the moment by saying, "I assume by your silence that you agree I am the best candidate. What is the next step toward my being hired?"

These provide examples of sales managers tailoring the interview to their firm's particular sales process. This proves a powerful screening technique.

If applicants live nearby, you should conduct interviews in your office. If the available territory is out of town, initial interviews should take place at a hotel in that area.

INTERVIEWING

Interviews prove more productive if the sales manager knows exactly what type of candidate he or she seeks, and if the sales manager prepares a written list of questions based on matching the candidate's résumé and personal history to the candidate profile and job description. You should also use information obtained in the telephone interview to formulate questions for the face-to-face interview. Again, you may seek people similar to your current best performers. Don't waste time asking questions that have already been answered on the résumé or personal history application, such as where the candidate went to high school.

The most reliable guide to a salesperson's future performance is his or her past record; therefore, obtaining a reliable picture of the past record represents an important aspect of screening. In the telephone and face-to-face interview, ask the candidate to comment on specific past achievements with each employer.

Compensation history becomes an extremely important indicator of past performance. Has compensation increased each year? Was compensation primarily fixed or based on performance, and what does that tell you about the candidate? Do you want people who have succeeded with a high portion of performance pay because that indicates motivation, or with a high portion of fixed pay because that indicates a team player?

Unfortunately, people seldom change their bad working habits. The mediocre sales performer continues to perform at mediocre levels. The job hopper continues to hop. The person with financial problems usually finds new ones. The salesperson who works four days a week seldom switches to five and in fact often regresses to three.

Start the interview by introducing the candidate to other people in your office, such as an administrative assistant or an associate. See how he or she relates to them. This indicates how they might react to a new customer.

To make applicants comfortable and more willing to talk, immediately establish a rapport by discussing some common interests you discovered on the résumé. Don't dive into the interview. Take a few minutes to establish a bond and dissipate nervousness.

Next, state the purpose of the interview and how long it will last. Sixty to ninety minutes should be the maximum, especially with multiple interviews. The interview purpose is to first learn more about the candidate, then explain the position and answer any questions. To relax the candidate, let him or her know a hiring decision will not be made today. To put a little fear in their heart, let them know you have many applicants.

Just because you happen to be the interviewer, don't assume that you are cleverer than the applicant. Some salespeople have had many more interviews than you have given, and some have read books on interviewing techniques. Some salespeople prove more professional at interviewing than at closing a customer sale. Probing questions, reference checking, and scrutinizing of résumés usually identifies this person.

Don't show the candidate the job description, candidate profile, or discuss specifics of the position until you have asked all your probing questions. Then, realistically describe the position and truthfully answer all his or her questions. As mentioned, don't oversell the position; it only leads to disappointment. A good candidate will ask to see the job description and ask probing questions about the position. Acknowledge the questions, but defer them until later. If a sales manager tells a candidate the job specifics at the start of an interview, the candidate will just feed back what the sales manager wants to hear. However, handing a qualified candidate the job description toward the end of the initial interview and asking how he or she would prioritize the tasks can be an insightful method. Use the job description as a tool to learn more about the candidate. In today's tight labor markets, waiting to describe the position requires courage, but it produces better hiring results.

According to the March 2000 issue of *Sales & Marketing Management* magazine:

A recent study by Development Dimensions International, a human resource consulting firm in Pittsburgh, shows that job candidates are seeking companies that offer in order of importance: a solid reputation, generous benefits, a positive corporate culture, and potential for advancements. Companies with the best recruiting strategies were nearly 20 percent more likely to offer these advantages, as well as stock options, learning opportunities, and competitive pay.

Although many sales managers feel they are more interesting than the candidate, the interview's purpose is to learn more about the candidate. That requires the sales manager to listen 80 percent of the time. Display empathy and understanding, but don't talk about yourself. We have two ears and one mouth for good reason. Selling and interviewing require probing questions and good listening skills. What do the answers tell you about the candidate? The more the applicant talks, the more you will learn. Tailor questions to the candidate. Don't use canned questions unless you want canned answers.

If, on the first interview, a sales manager creates a nonthreatening atmosphere in which candidates feel free to talk, they will volunteer all the information you desire. In the first interview, a sales manager can best put the candidate at ease by being punctual, not accepting phone calls, not rushing through the interview, not putting a desk between the two of you, and sitting in chairs of equal status. Don't criticize the candidate or you will find future responses guarded. When you want more information on a subject, agree with the applicant. When the conversation veers from the subject at hand, subtly steer it back in the desired direction. Once you have established a rapport, keep the candidate talking about himself or herself, and don't let the conversation lapse into sports, global politics, or the stock market.

If you nod your head or say "uh huh," the candidate senses you are listening and will talk more. By occasionally stopping to summarize a prospect's point or answer, you give feedback to confirm understanding and interest. Don't feel compelled to fill voids caused by silence. Instead, use silence to put pressure on the prospect. You want to know how he or she would react to this in a selling situation. Often applicants bridge a silence with significant information.

Open-ended probing questions, that cannot be answered with yes or no are the key to good interviewing. Such questions tell the sales manager a great deal about what is important to the salesperson. A candidate will return to the same subjects in answering these questions—for instance, the importance of family, customer satisfaction, an unfair boss, superior competition, and weak support services. The amount of time a candidate devotes to each subject reveals a great deal about his or her personal characteristics and what is important to them. Questions about the family or customers receive long, detailed answers, while questions about the boss or the competition are dealt with quickly. Some candidates quantify the answers to probing questions; some are analytical, critical, logical, and/or linear thinkers.

Exhibit 2.4 lists scores of probing questions and interview probes to choose from when interviewing highly experienced salespeople or recent college graduates. A sales manager must determine what the answers tell him or her about the candidate. You can discover a great deal about an applicants' skills, motivation, personal characteristics, and experience by asking how they organize their day, what they think of their current employer, and what they like most and least about past positions, as well as through self-analysis questions that elicit their own opinion of personal strengths and weaknesses and areas to change or further develop.

Some sales managers like to ask why a candidate chose sales as a career. Many answer for the money; others say they like people. Some talk about a mother who was a salesperson, and still others reply they like to persuade people. Most managers like the last two answers much better than the first two. A candidate who chooses a sales career for the money might be very disappointed in certain industries.

Some sales managers ask candidates for their long- and short-term career goals. The candidate might reply, "My short-term goal is to be the number one salesperson; my long-term goal is to move into sales management." This candidate might not be a good fit for a firm with a limited career ladder.

Some sales managers like to ask candidates for examples of their best and worst boss. If a candidate replies that the best boss was there when he or she needed him but otherwise stayed out of my way and you are a micromanager, it might be a bad fit.

Other managers ask candidates "How was your performance evaluated and was it fair?" Many salespeople can't answer this question or just refer to results. A good salesperson knows the metrics on which he or she was evaluated.

Most managers say, "I plan to ask your previous supervisors for a reference. What do you think they will say about you?" This puts a reality check on the interview and encourages the candidate to speak candidly.

The answers to situational questions are also revealing—for example, "Tell me about your best customer, your worst customer, your most difficult customer, and a customer you lost." Often the best customer is a friend or a captive account. The worst customer frequently is a person the candidate could not get along with. Did the candidate sell the most difficult account? Did the candidate try to win the lost customer back?

Probing Questions.

Sample Questions

The following are questions that can be asked during an interview. However, whenever possible, your questions should be contingent on the previous response of the interviewee.

A. SCREENING QUESTIONS

- Tell me about yourself.
- What are your long- and short-term goals?
- What are you doing now?
- Why did you choose selling as a career?
- How do you feel about it?
- Why are you looking for a new position?
- What are you looking for?
- What type of person would you like to work for?
- Would your previous employer hire you back? Why?
- What would your boss say about you if I called?

B. WORK HISTORY

- Could you tell me about your work history? How would you compare the companies you worked for?
- How did you select the first company you worked for?
- What was the company like? What are you looking for in a company?
- What type of individual was the person you reported to?
- What were your responsibilities?
- What do you feel were some of your major accomplishments? Why?
- What are areas in which you feel you could have been more productive? In what way?
- What type of person do you like to work for?
- What was your best boss like? What was your worst boss like?
- How would you compare them?
- What do you consider to be some of your greatest accomplishments?

- What do you consider to be some of your most disappointing work experiences?
- What type of individuals do you like to have working with you?
- Have you ever had any fellow workers or a boss who did not function at the level you expected? Tell me about it.
- If they did not live up to your expectations, what was your approach?
- What do you think determines a person's progress in a good company?
- What are the advantages and disadvantages of working for a small as compared to a large organization?
- How do you feel your career progress has been to this point?
- What are some examples of important types of decisions you have been called upon to make or problems you had to solve?
- What do you feel contributed to your effectiveness as a salesperson?
- What do you feel may have interfered with your effectiveness as a salesperson?
- In what respects do you feel you have improved most as a salesperson during the past few years?
- How many hours do you feel a person should spend on his or her job?
- What do you see for yourself in the future?
- How do you spend your spare time?
- How do you see yourself in relationships with others?
- What do you feel are some of the greatest motivating forces for your fellow workers?

E x h i b i t 2.4 (continued)

C. EDUCATIONAL BACKGROUND

- Could you tell me about your education-al background?
- Why did you select that particular school?
- What were you looking for in the institu-tion in which you attended?
- What was your major field of study?
- How did you select your major?
- Where did you live on campus?
- What would you consider to be the advantages and disadvantages of living in a fraternity or sorority as compared to private or university housing?
- Were you involved in extracurricular activities?
- If you held an elective office, how did you campaign for such a position?
- Did you make any changes while you were in office?
- How would you compare the individuals who lived in your housing unit to those in other units?
- How would you compare your college experience to your high school experi-ence?
- Select the professor that you liked best. What type of individual was he?
- What courses did you like best? Why?
- What courses did you like least? Why?

(If one is asked, the other should always be included as a follow-up question.)

- If you changed majors, why?

- How did you determine what new cur-riculum to pursue?
- Describe your university. What type of place was it?
- How was the school spirit?
- Where there any changes that could have been made on the campus so as to make it more beneficial?
- How do you feel such changes could have been initiated?
- How were the college administrators?
- Did you have a roommate?
- What type of individual was he?
- What are his or her future plans?
- How did you spend your vacation peri-ods?
- Overall, how did you do from an acade-mic perspective?
- Are there any things that you wish you could have changed about your acade-mic background?
- How effective was your academic back-ground in preparing you for the future?
- Considering your accomplishments, what are some of the reasons for your successes?
- What are the advantages and disad-vantages of sales as a chosen field of endeavor?
- What personal characteristics do you feel are necessary in order to succeed in sales?
- What do you find to be unique about yourself?

Don't ask leading questions that signal the response you hope to hear, such as, "Do you like to work with people?" Questions that ask "why," "how," "what," or "tell me" elicit more complete answers.

Behavioral questions can also tell you a great deal about the candidate. A sales manager might ask the candidate, "Who do you most admire and why?" The candidate can choose a family member, a business person, an athlete, a movie star, a politician, or any other category. Which category the "most admired person" is chosen from says something about the candidate's interests. Why this person is most admired tells the interviewer about the candidate's own values and goals. A grandmother is chosen because she was honest, raised a family, and made great personal sacrifices. An athlete is chosen because of skills and achievements.

A sales manager might ask the candidate to describe his or her greatest disappointment, problem, or setback and what he or she did about it. The candidate must choose between a professional or personal disappointment. What he or she did about it indicates the candidate's ability to deal with rejection and adversity, a very important trait for salespeople. The disappointments range from divorce or sudden death of a loved one to a bad grade or loss of a job. One candidate told me his greatest disappointment was being terminated last year from a great job. He also admitted he has been unable to overcome this rejection and still finds job interviews difficult. A sales manager will learn more about the candidate from these two questions than he or she would after years of association.

Occasionally a candidate will give fuzzy replies or no replies to such questions as "Why did you leave your last job?" or "What was your compensation?" To elicit a more forthright response, drop the questions for a while and go on to something else. Then return later to the subject and probe further by phrasing the questions differently—for example, by asking, "What sort of a person was your boss?" If related questions continue to produce indistinct or weak replies, you have found a problem area, which after the interview will require independent investigation through reference checking.

When possible, record in writing your impressions and key information immediately after the interview. After six interviews, as after six sales calls, information and impressions merge, unless you have made notes. If you wish to take notes during an interview, ask the salesperson's permission, and make your notes at regular intervals, not after revealing statements. Candidates attach importance to what you record, so don't tip your hand.

As you record information, it is a good idea to mark each item with a plus, minus, or zero, depending on its bearing on the candidate's desirability. Try to look for information that helps you reject or accept the applicant. After the interview, organize this information in two columns with pluses on one side and minuses on the other. Human resource professionals tell us not to keep notes on a candidate's résumé. Should there be litigation based on the interview, the placement of these notes is often misunderstood.

I know of one instance where a sales manager hired the wrong candidate from two finalists because he relied on his memory for the requisite information. When the candidate, now an employee, reported for his first day of work, the sales manager realized his mistake but decided not to admit it. The story has a happy ending, however, because that salesman proved highly successful. When the sales manager retired, he told the story at his farewell dinner, while his successor, the wrongly hired salesman, listened in astonishment.

In interviewing candidates, salespeople who criticize past employers and bosses signal a problem that requires further investigation. The fault often does lie with the previous employer, but you need more information. Ask whether their previous boss would rehire them or what that boss would say about them.

The rigors of some sales positions require a great deal of energy, which not all people possess. In such a situation, look for active people who channel their energy into work and don't just talk about working hard. A person who works long hours or Saturdays generally meets this requirement. Salespeople at a bakery supply distributor make their calls on independent bakeries from 6:00 a.m. to 3:00 p.m., and end their long day by calling on ice cream and yogurt shops from 3:00 p.m. to 6:00 p.m.

During the interview, watch for verbal slips or for stories and anecdotes that reveal personal weaknesses. A candidate once told me about a "funny" incident that involved missing an important selling date because he had accidentally walked under a sprinkler and gotten his suit wet. Another candidate told me that every Friday he "got gassed," then corrected himself to say that every Friday he "bought gas."

Watch for body language when a candidate answers sensitive questions concerning compensation, advancement, the boss, or company politics. Do they look you in the eye, wet their lips, wring their hands, sit erect, play with their pen, grimace? Most people can't hide anxiety, and anxiety points to problem areas. The salesperson who claims to be sincere but does not look you in the eye, or claims to be confident but whose voice shakes raises doubts.

To end the interview, ask the candidate to summarize why he or she feels qualified for the position and if he or she has any more questions for you. Tell the candidate what your next step is and when it will occur, such as "I will arrange for you to meet my boss in two weeks," or "Your skills and background are great, but we need someone who has traveled the territory." Don't make false excuses for not hiring someone.

Although candidate profiles are essential, don't stereotype the ideal candidate. As mentioned, we have a tendency to hire people we like, who don't threaten us, and who fit the company mold. I recently attended a sales meeting where no one was taller than the sales manager, who was 5 feet, 1 inch.

Many of us make judgments early in an interview and then look for information to support that decision. Public relations professionals claim that lasting personal impressions, often based on appearance, are made in the first ten seconds of an interview—for instance, "I sized him up as a phony the minute he walked in," or "I liked her style and confidence the moment I saw her." Use the interview to obtain a complete, well-rounded profile of the candidate. Save your decision until the end. Again, set standards, be critical, and sit in judgment.

Often a single unfavorable or favorable item will warp your judgment—for example, "He is friendly with the purchasing agent at our largest account," or "She drives an old car." Look at the whole picture before making a decision.

Often a glib, egocentric, evasive, talky, or argumentative candidate forces us to lose control of the interview. Be direct. Tell the applicant the questions you want answered. Don't hesitate to end the interview if this disruptive behavior continues. Remember, the interview allows a sales manager to view the candidate on a personal sales call.

Continuing Interviews for Finalists

After the initial face-to-face interviews, a few candidates will be selected for the next round. These candidates should be interviewed for a second time by the sales manager, his or her supervisor, at least one salesperson, and the manager of a related department (e.g., engineering, operations, customer support). Before these interviews, a sales manager should meet with those doing the interviewing to review the job description and candidate profile and to coordinate each person's questions. After the interview, each interviewer independently recommends in writing to the sales manager whether or not to hire the candidate and why. Once these recommendations are received, the group meets to discuss the candidate. The sales manager is the decision maker; other members of the group are advisors. If hiring a salesperson becomes a group consensus decision, the dominant personality or highest-ranking member prevails.

Including top salespeople in this decision makes them feel useful, important, and worthwhile. Their involvement has motivational value, and their job knowledge makes them an important filter. As an example, a Fortune 1000 global manufacturer of long-haul trailer trucks insists that all finalists spend a day calling on customers with a key salesperson. The candidate receives a firsthand look at the job, and the key salesperson can evaluate the candidate at the moment of truth. At this point, some candidates decide the job is not of interest, because dealing with small family-owned dealerships proves too frustrating. This self-selection proves less expensive than hiring the wrong person.

Based on reference checking and a reexamination of résumés, along with personal history forms and notes from the previous interview, the sales manager prepares a written list of questions to ask on the second interview. Differing from the first interview, the questions are specific, not general. If one former boss has reported employment dates and a reason for leaving that differ from what the candidate told you, what explains the inconsistency? Or, although the candidate has a marvelous past record selling established products for large companies, how will he or she adapt to selling a relatively unknown product for a small company? In the second interview, take some phone calls, create some anxiety, challenge the candidate, and see how he or she reacts. Again, simulate a sales call.

Make sure that you have honestly answered all the finalist's questions about the company and the position. Allow the applicant several opportunities to ask questions. When inviting finalists to a second interview, send them product or service literature and general company information. End the interview by telling the applicant that you will call within a certain time frame.

REFERENCE CHECKING AND BACKGROUND INVESTIGATIONS

If you don't check references, you might as well throw darts or flip a coin. Don't delegate reference checking to human resources or an outside service. A sales manager needs to reach the right people, ask probing questions, and listen to the words and the music. Most sales managers don't check references because it challenges their infallible judgment, it is time-consuming, burdensome, difficult, and awkward, and they mistrust what the references say. In fact, however, most sales managers misunderstand how to correctly check references.

During the interviews, you asked for professional references, and for permission to contact past supervisors, customers, and competitors. If the applicant currently holds a job, you usually cannot contact the employer. If the applicant asks you not to contact past supervisors, customers, or competitors, ask why. This could be a red flag. What is the applicant hiding? The candidate must give you written permission to call customers, competitors, and previous supervisors for references.

Disregard written references provided by the candidate, because obviously these represent a form of advertising. Telephone interviews with past supervisors, customers, and competitors, however, will provide useful information.

Customers represent a reliable source of information about a candidate. Few legal restrictions apply here. Often a sales manager knows key decision makers at customers' firms who will speak freely about the candidate. Sales managers must ask customers, competitors, and previous supervisors appropriate questions which fill in information gaps. After looking at notes from the previous interviews, the job description, candidate profile, résumé, and personal history, the sales manager might be concerned about a candidate's ability to open new competitive accounts, sell new highly technical services, travel extensively, or provide in-depth service. A sales manager might ask a candidate's customer, "Did Alex follow up on and solve service problems?" "Did he increase his share of your purchases or sell you new products?" "Was he enthusiastic and confident when faced with rejection?" "Could you suggest other customers I could call who worked with Alex?" "Would you recommend Alex as a salesperson to represent your firm?" Some sales managers ask candidates for permission to call their "worst" customer or a customer they lost. A candidate's reaction to this question makes it worth asking.

If the candidate sold a product or service noncompetitive to yours, and you know competitors in that industry, their input could be useful. They can provide information on the applicant's employer and possibly on the applicant as well.

Previous supervisors represent a critical source of information about candidates. As discussed previously, decide specifically what you want to know and formulate questions around this. General questions produce unreliable general answers. Ask the candidate for his or her previous supervisor's work and home phone numbers. Again, in many cases, you cannot call the candidate's present employer.

Some previous supervisors remain with the same firm, but most have moved on to another sales management position, which makes them more agreeable to candidly discussing the candidate and vastly reduces any legal liabilities. I suggest calling these references at home, because they are more relaxed.

Quickly introduce yourself as the sales manager of your firm, and quickly establish a rapport so the previous supervisor does not feel you are a telephone solicitor. Refer to a common acquaintance, trade show, or customer. After several minutes of warm-up, state the purpose of your call: "We have a common acquaintance who worked for your firm, and I am considering hiring him. Sales manager to sales manager, I have a few questions which will take fifteen minutes to discuss."

If the sales manager has changed employers since he or she supervised the candidate, you will generally receive a positive reception. If the sales manager is still employed by the same firm, you may encounter difficulties. If the sales manager is receptive, have your five questions ready. Besides the five specific questions, you might try a few of these: "What type customer did the candidate have trouble selling?" "Did you try to convince the candidate to stay?" "How does the candidate compare to his or her replacement?" "Have you seen the candidate's résumé?" If so, discuss it; if not, fax one and then discuss it. One sales manager at a financial services firm said she faxed a candidate's résumé to a reference and when he read it, there was laughter. If possible, verify dates of employment, salary range, and reason for leaving.

Find out the reference's exact title and past relationship to the applicant. I once discovered the reference was the applicant's ex-brother-in-law. You also may wish to contact the reference's immediate supervisor if he or she knew the candidate. Some sales managers will ask fellow salespeople who were employed with the candidate for a reference.

If the sales manager is still employed by the same firm, he or she may refer you to human resources and refuse to answer questions, stating perhaps, "Our company policy is not to discuss previous employees." The previous employer has some legal liability for references, which varies by state. There is little if any legal liability in asking for references.

In these situations, be ready with another set of questions related to the company, not the candidate. You might say to the referee, "I understand the problem. Our firm has similar rules. May I ask you a few questions about your company?" Generally, the answer is yes. You might then ask, "Do you require salespeople to prospect for new accounts or provide technical services to existing accounts? Is overnight travel required? Do you provide sales skills training? Who are your target account?" The answers to these company-related questions will help you better understand the candidate's skills, knowledge, experience, and personal characteristics and may contradict answers received directly from the candidate.

Last and most importantly, ask, "Would you rehire the candidate?" Company policy often prohibits rehiring. In this situation ask, "If company policy allowed rehiring, would you rehire this individual?" This is the moment of truth, when previously withheld information comes tumbling forth. I have encountered reactions such as "Never," "Only if his father-in-law made me," and "I would, but my boss would not."

As with the candidate interview, listen carefully to the previous employer's responses and tone of voice. Phrases such as "unfortunate circumstances," "personality clashes," or "chose to resign" usually indicate problems.

Be aware that if the previous employer is your competitor, you may receive a false recommendation. The competitor may wish to burden you with one of its previous problems.

Background investigations on the finalists are a useful precaution. Contact the secretary of state for a driver's license check. Equifax Inc. of Atlanta, Trans Union Credit Information Co. of Chicago, and TRW of Orange, California, all offer a service that investigates appropriate court and financial records and, if necessary, verifies places of residence and past employers. These reports cost $50 each, and large credit agencies offer online computer access to their databases. Through such an investigation, one sales manager discovered that the finalist had just lost his driver's license. The job required extensive use of a car. Knowing how applicants handle bills, loans, and other financial obligations helps predict their responsibility on the job. A salesperson who remains preoccupied with lawsuits or overdue loan payments will be distracted from selling customers. One company was won over to background checks after a new hire was apprehended for stealing from a customer.

Under the Federal Fair Credit Reporting Act of 1971, you must advise candidates that credit reports will be used. Should the report provide information leading to rejection, you must supply the candidate with the source's name and address, and you might ask the candidate to comment on this information.

TESTING

Intelligence, personality, and interest tests for salespeople can be administered and scored either by yourself or by outside services. Such tests provide insight into the subject's learning and reasoning ability, emotional stability, confidence, and occupational interests. The problem lies in interpreting the results. Which test results can accurately predict positive or negative job results? Have your current sales force take the test, then correlate their individual test results with their individual sales performance. You can then use your best performers' test results as a standard by which to evaluate candidates. If the best performers don't test any differently than the not-so-good, then testing may not prove useful.

A sales manager obtains from testing what he or she puts into it. If you are willing to devote time and energy to this area, you can obtain useful information. These tests are available from distributors for a number of companies, including Strong Vocational Interest, Minnesota Vocational Interest, Martin Bruce Test of Sales Aptitude, Thematic Apperception Test, California Personality Test, Guildford-Zimmerman Temperament Survey, John G. Geir Personal Profile System, Otis Quick-Scoring Mental Ability Tests, Wesmon Personnel Classification Test, Adaptability Test, Concept Mastery Test, Wonderlic Personnel Test, Caliper Human Strategies, Inc., Personality Dynamics, Inc., and Gallop and Kolby Conative Index.

Testing is a tool to help you hire outstanding candidates, not a crutch to make the decision for you. Don't substitute test results for your judgment. Narrow the field to the three best candidates, test each, and compare results. Use tests to eliminate certain candidates or to better understand strengths and weaknesses. However, don't use the results to choose one over another. Also use tests to customize a training program for the person hired.

Tests cost between $100 and $200 per applicant. Turnaround times vary from a day (using fax, email, online testing, or overnight delivery) to a week (using regular mail).

MAKING THE FINAL CHOICE

To assist in making your final choice, classify each item listed on the job description and candidate profile as a "must" or a "want" with a numeric value weighting its importance. For each duty, skill, level of knowledge, or area of experience and for each of several personal characteristics, decide which are the "musts," which are the "wants," and how each ranks in importance in selecting a salesperson. Any finalist possesses all the "musts," so in making your choice, review which finalists have the most important "wants." Never be rushed into a dubious decision by the need to put a warm body on the street.

One last word of caution: Before hiring the final choice, many companies require drug, AIDS, and/or liver testing. In some states this may raise legal issues, so consult your human resources department and attorney. After hiring, most firms ask salespeople to take physical exams.

EQUAL EMPLOYMENT OPPORTUNITY (EEO)

During the entire recruiting process, including writing the job description, candidate profile, and interview questions, and while sourcing, reference checking and testing, keep in mind that the 1964 Civil Rights Act and extensive city, state, and federal legislation since then require that minorities, older people, women, and the disabled receive a fair and equal opportunity for employment. All aspects of the hiring process must be justifiable in terms of job performance. Federal legislation prohibits withholding employment on the basis of race or color, gender, religious affiliation, national origin, age, disability, or veteran's status.

Your objective is to identify people who can do the job. EEO legislation does not restrict you from any bona fide job-related questions, but when in doubt, consult a knowledgeable attorney. Human resource departments can mislead you with too much caution. However, questions seeking the following information (as well as job descriptions, candidate profiles, and candidate evaluations based on this type of information) are illegal:

- Date of birth
- Maiden name
- Previous married name
- Marital status
- Name of spouse
- Spouse's occupation and length of time on job
- Spouse's place of employment
- Number of children and their ages
- Arrest record
- Ancestry
- Age
- Gender
- Religion
- National origin (race)
- If child care has been arranged for
- Whether wages are garnished

Exhibit 2.5 lists specific questions you can and cannot ask. Again, when in doubt, contact a knowledgeable human resources attorney.

As North America becomes more globalized in the twenty-first century, equal employment laws will assume greater importance. As good corporate citizens, good global citizens, and good human beings, we should not only obey the letter of the law, which we must, but the spirit of the law, which will create a stronger social fabric for business.

In the twenty-first century, qualified salespeople will be more difficult to find. In this century, our customer base, whether business-to-business or business-to-consumer, will include many more women, people of color, and people with disabilities. To satisfy our employment needs and the needs of our customers, we must hire a more diverse sales force, which proves equally rewarding for the salespeople.

HIRING THE BEST

Hiring competent salespeople is a process with a beginning (the job description/candidate profile), an end (the offer), and steps along the way, such as sourcing, interviews, and reference checking. If you view recruiting as a process and consider all appropriate steps, even if you decide against using all of them, the probability of success increases, and the risk of failure decreases. Viewed as a process, you realize that hiring requires thirty to ninety days to recruit the right person. Hiring requires planning and anticipating needs.

QUESTIONS AND EXERCISES

- Create a job description and a candidate profile for your most recent job, a salesperson in your company, or a full-time salesperson at a company you are familiar with. On the candidate profile, note which items are wants and which are musts. On the job description, state the job title and which anticipated duties relate to strategy versus tactics.
- How would you determine if a candidate has the necessary skills and personal characteristics for the job?
- Where would you look for candidates? What sources would you use? Rank those sources by importance.
- List ten probing, open-ended questions you would ask the candidate and what the answers will tell you about the candidate.

Exhibit 2.5

Sample guideline for interviewing job applicants.

UNLAWFUL INQUIRIES

- Do not ask the applicant's age.
- Do not ask an applicant over 40 years old whether he or she can work under or with younger supervisors.
- Do not inquire as to age and relate how it affects health and pension benefits.
- Do not ask if an applicant has children or the age of an applicant's children.
- Do not ask who will care for the children if an applicant is hired.
- Do not ask applicant's race or question directly or indirectly indicating race or color of an applicant or an applicant's spouse.
- Do not ask about height or weight where it is not relevant to the job.
- Do not ask about U.S. citizenship or if an applicant intends to become a U.S. citizen.
- Do not ask an applicant if he or she has ever had his or her wages garnished. A credit check is a better method to learn this and other pertinent information. If an applicant is rejected because of the applicant's poor credit rating, you must inform the applicant the reason for the rejection and the credit service used.
- Do not ask an applicant if he or she was ever arrested.
- Do not ask an applicant whether he or she is married, divorced, separated, widowed, or single. (But you may ask how an applicant prefers to be addressed: "Mr., Mrs., Miss, or Ms.").
- Do not ask a female applicant for her maiden name or for her father's surname.
- Do not ask an applicant what church he or she attends or the names of his or her priest, rabbi, or minister.
- If an applicant is divorced, do not ask the reasons why.
- Do not ask for the name or address of any relative of an adult applicant.
- Do not ask about any organizations, clubs, societies, or lodges that the applicant belongs to, if this information would indicate through character or name the race, religion, color, or ancestry of the members.
- Do not ask an applicant if anyone resides with the applicant or the identity of any roommate.
- Do not ask a female applicant if she would be comfortable supervising men (or a male applicant if he would be comfortable supervising women).
- Do not ask an applicant if he or she owns or rents his or her home.
- Do not ask an applicant what his or her spouse does.
- Do not ask a female applicant if she would be willing to take turns making coffee unless it is part of the job description or men are also required to make coffee.
- Do not ask about an applicant's union sentiments or membership.
- Do not express any anti-union sentiments.
- Do not inquire about a name change or ask what the original name was unless it is necessary to enable you to check an applicant's work record.
- Do not ask about the nationality or birthplace of an applicant or an applicant's parents.
- Do not ask for photographs with the employment application or before hiring an applicant.
- Do not ask for the specific years of school attendance or graduation.
- Do not ask an applicant to identify his or her mother tongue or the language used in the applicant's home.
- Do not ask about an applicant's military experience other than in the U.S. Armed Forces, National Guard or reserve unit.
- Do not ask abut any physical characteristics such as scars, burns or missing limbs.
- Do not ask about the health of an applicant.
- Do not ask if an applicant has ever received counseling or seen a psychiatrist.
- Do not ask if the applicant has ever had a drug or alcohol problem.

E x h i b i t 2.5 (continued)

- Do not ask about an applicant's workers' compensation history.
- Do not ask how a disability occurred or if the disability is indicative of an underlying impairment.
- Do not ask the applicant if he or she has any potentially disabling impairments.
- Do not ask an applicant whether the applicant will need a leave for treatment.
- If an applicant volunteers information about a medical condition such as cancer or HIV, do not ask about the progress of the illness or whether it is in remission.
- Do not ask if family members have had a history of illness.
- Do not ask if the applicant has any disability or medical condition that will prevent the applicant from performing the job.

LAWFUL INQUIRIES

- What language do you speak fluently? (Only if job-related)
- (To a homemaker, former stay-at-home spouse, or retired person) Why do you want to return to work?
- How many years experience do you have and what functions have you performed?
- What do you like to do or what do you do best?
- Can you do extensive traveling? (Only if job-related)
- Who recommended you to us?
- Whom can we notify in case of an emergency?
- What academic, vocational, or professional education as well as schools have you attended? (If job-related.)
- What specific skills, such as reading, writing, word processing, computer, and public speaking do you have? (If job-related)
- Where do you reside, how long, and where are you presently located?
- How long have you been a resident of this city or state?
- If we offer you a job, will you be able to furnish us with proof of U.S. citizenship or the granting of a visa which permits you to work in the United States?
- Have you had any felony convictions? If so, give us the dates, the nature of the offense, and other relevant details.

Following are additional guidelines for lawful inquiries:

- If the applicant appears to be underage, do not ask, just state that proof of age will be required if the applicant is offered a job.
- You can ask about an applicant's military experience in the U.S. Armed Forces. You can inquire about the dates of military service, military occupation, and date and type of discharge.
- You can ask whether the applicant has received any notice to report for duty in the Armed Forces.
- You can ask an applicant about his or her membership in any professional, trade, or service organization.
- You can ask the names of persons who can supply professional and character references.
- You can ask for the name of the person who suggested that the applicant apply for a position.
- You can state the attendance requirement and ask whether the applicant can meet them.
- You can ask the applicant if he or she knows of any reason that he or she cannot perform the essential functions of the job.
- You can ask questions relating to an applicant's ability to perform job-related functions and tasks.
- You can describe or demonstrate a job function and ask whether the applicant can perform the function with or without a reasonable accommodation.
- You can ask an applicant to describe or demonstrate how, with or without reasonable accommodation, the applicant will be able to perform job-related functions.

SALES MANAGERS' MAJOR MISTAKES/WEAKNESSES IN HIRING/RECRUITING

- Hiring the best of a bad bunch
- Hiring under pressure and making snap judgments
- Hiring people we like, including comfortable and nonthreatening people
- Not networking, not keeping files, no continuous process
- Not continually upgrading the sales force through continuous improvement
- Not using a variety of sources
- Not checking references
- Not asking probing questions at interviews
- Talking too much at interviews
- Not preparing a job description or candidate profile
- Not matching candidate to buyer behavior, type of selling, or type of sales process; relationship selling, consultive selling, closer, order taker, partnership selling, application sales
- Not terminating weak performers; not "weeding the garden"

CHAPTER 3

Training for Results

THE MODEL

You should first pay salespeople more than they are worth, then make them worth more than what you pay them. That is what training is all about. In the new millennium's changing landscape, sales force training creates a competitive advantage in an otherwise commoditized marketplace.

Sales force management is a process, where one step logically follows another. Control the pieces and you control the whole. Chapter 2 examined the model and methodology for hiring salespeople; this chapter discusses the model and methodology for training these people. Hire the right people, train them well, and you are two-thirds of the way toward a more productive sales force.

A sales manager's job is to get work done through other people. Your success depends on their success. For salespeople to be successful, they need training in product, competitor, and customer knowledge, as well as sales skills. You provide this training through the continuous process of initial programs, followed by field coaching and sales meetings.

Training makes direct and indirect salespeople and support personnel more productive. If you sell through distributors, brokers, or independent sales representatives, they are no better than your ability to select the proper organization and train them. A good training program forces channel partners to devote more time and resources to your company's products/services, making them more productive partners, not adversaries. Channel partners spend time where they are comfortable, have a commitment in human and financial resources, and obtain the best return on invested dollars.

Similarly, a well-conceived training program with proper resources proves equally important to telesales and customer service people as it does to a field sales force. A weak sales force reflects weak management.

TIME LOG

Most sales managers do not devote enough time to training. Make a list of your duties/activities and prioritize them by importance in driving revenues. Include hiring, training, organizing, and evaluating salespeople, along with personal selling, management meetings, conflict resolution, motivation, and administrative duties. What percent of your time is devoted to initial training, field coaching, and sales meetings? For sales managers supervising five to seven salespeople, 40 percent of their time should be devoted to training. Keep a time log of your activities for a typical month each year. Often an inverse relationship exists between hours spent on each activity and the activity's importance in driving revenues. What action can you take to correct this?

STRATEGIC ISSUES

Like form follows function, structure follows strategy. Therefore, a sales manager must understand the strategic issues and objectives of training. Key strategic objectives for training include reducing the time it takes to make a salesperson fully productive, teaching salespeople how to reduce the sales cycle from customer search to purchase, and reflecting buyer behavior in the training program. Strategic training topics include pricing, targeting, change management, group decisions, complex decision-making processes, negotiations, and differentiation.

Depending on your industry and the skill/experience level of salespeople hired, it may take one year for a salesperson to generate revenues/gross margins equal to his or her compensation, benefits, and expenses. It may take two years for the salesperson to reach full productivity and become a profit center. We will look at some specific numbers in Chapter 5.

Do you know the break-even point for a salesperson in your firm? For example, a business selling premium tires to trucking firms compared the cost of putting a salesperson on the road to the revenues/income necessary to break even and become fully productive. It required one year for a salesperson to break even and two years to become fully productive. By using the techniques described in this chapter and the previous one, the time was cut in half. Reducing their training cycle changed the paradigm for deployment and staffing. A more effective training program allowed the tire company to hire more salespeople, reduce territory sizes, and increase market share.

A distance learning company which provided MBA courses to top executives at Fortune 500 firms was experiencing a year between initial customer contact and a buying decision. The closing ratios and costs were prohibitive. The sales manager remedied this by training salespeople to track and measure their progress through the many steps in the buying process and to identify each manager's role in the group decision. The sales cycle was reduced to six months, closing ratios increased, and market share doubled.

Training is an area where marketing and sales management must work together. Buyer behavior, discussed in the previous chapter and illustrated in Exhibit 2.1, influences the training process. A firm dealing primarily with new systems buyers, first-time buyers, or one-time buyers (telephone or security systems) must emphasize training in consultive sales and product knowledge. But a firm dealing with existing systems buyers and, modified rebuys (e.g., semiconductors, frozen doughnut batter, or truck tires) must emphasize training in relationship sales, negotiations, pricing, and customer knowledge. A firm calling on new product buyers (e.g., toys, apparel, consumer electronics) must emphasize training in selling skills. Finally, a firm calling on commodity buyers (e.g., die castings, plastic injection molding), who often delegate this task, must emphasize time management and IT training.

If your firm expects salespeople to negotiate price, delivery, and product/service customization, you must train them in negotiating skills and pricing theory. If you don't, your customers will have an unfair advantage. Salespeople will sell at the lowest price unless they are trained to maximize dollars of margin/revenue over time based on competitive advantage, type of customer, and type of product.

Many of these strategic training topics were mentioned in the previous chapter as strategic hiring issues appearing on the job description and candidate profile. This includes training salespeople in how to identify target customers, markets, and products. A sales manager can increase sales force productivity by teaching salespeople proper call frequency on target customers and prospects with the greatest present and potential revenues and income, lowest cost to sell and service, and highest probability of success. Specifics of this will be dealt with in Chapter 5.

In the twenty-first century, marketing and sales management must work together in training salespeople on strategic differentiation. Who are your direct and indirect competitors, what are the competitive issues, which are expected/demanded, and how does the customer make a choice? The tactical application of this strategic concept, known as the competitive grid, is discussed later in the chapter.

In Chapter 1, we discussed shorter product/service life cycles, longer, more complex sales cycles, group decisions, reduced customer loyalty, and global competition. These changes in the landscape require new training. To deal with reduced customer loyalty, salespeople require training in quantifying benefits. For example, a dozen business-to-business (B2B) ecommerce firms service the paper, pulp, corrugated, and folding box industry. The provider which charges a 3 percent transaction fee has a 50 percent market share. The other 50 percent is divided among the remaining eleven B2B firms, all of which charge a 1 percent transaction fee. The company charging a 3 percent transaction fee with 50 percent of the market trains its salespeople to quantify for each step in the supply chain how its Web site lowers customer costs, increases customer revenues, or reduces inventory and capital expenditures. This quantification justifies in dollars the higher price.

BENEFITS OF A WELL-TRAINED SALES FORCE

Training a sales force well not only increases their productivity and capacity but also improves sales force confidence and enthusiasm, reduces turnover, and makes salespeople feel useful, important, and worthwhile. A poorly trained sales force creates another excuse for nonperformance.

Confidence and enthusiasm represent important personal characteristics for a successful salesperson. They are included on the candidate profile. Well-trained salespeople certainly feel more confident and enthusiastic.

As you know from Chapter 2, sales force turnover proves very costly. Properly trained salespeople earn more compensation and are less likely to change jobs.

A major benefit of a well-trained sales force is motivation. When a sales manager rides with salespeople or salespeople attend a sales meeting, they feel useful, important, and worthwhile. Salespeople who do not receive proper training feel just the opposite.

ARE SALESPEOPLE MADE OR BORN?

Which proves more important: training or hiring? As this chapter demonstrates, we can train salespeople in product, customer, competitive knowledge, and selling skills. However, we can't train salespeople in personal characteristics such as confidence, enthusiasm, the ability to accept rejection, self-motivation, persistence, passion, or eagerness. We can reinforce these traits. When hiring, probing, open-ended interview questions help you discover these important personal characteristics. By the end of this book you should know whether salespeople are made or born and whether hiring or training represent a more important part of the sales management process.

CURRENT TRENDS IN TRAINING

Mentoring can help train salespeople and more efficiently use a sales manager's time. The sales manager asks more experienced salespeople to mentor less experienced salespeople. The mentor does field coaching and answers questions on product, competition, customer knowledge, and selling skills. One example of a successful mentoring program is provided by a deli products distributor in Cleveland which expanded geographically by buying a similar firm in Toledo. The Cleveland distributor sent its more experienced salespeople to Toledo once a week to work with the less experienced people. The Cleveland salespeople were motivated by being chosen as mentors and improved their own knowledge and skills in order to train the Toledo salespeople. The Cleveland salespeople started opening more new accounts and selling more new products than in the past. This worked so well that members from both the Cleveland and Toledo teams received a bonus based on joint results.

To enhance the success of a mentoring program, establish clear goals so each person knows what to expect from the relationship, and track effectiveness of the program to ensure the mentee is learning. Use quarterly performance evaluations, discussed in Chapter 8, and testing to measure results. Some mentoring programs last a month and just involve field coaching. Others last a year and involve continuous training. Some programs only involve new hires; others involve all junior salespeople. Some mentoring programs team one mentor to one mentee; others team groups of mentors to groups of mentees. The group approach prevents the spreading of bad habits and encourages a multitude of best practices. Make sure mentors are knowledgeable, skilled in training, and interested in helping. At some firms mentoring represents a stepping stone into management.

Keep in mind, however, that as sales manager you must maintain control over the training process. Don't abdicate the ultimate responsibility to other salespeople or human resources. If a salesperson succeeds or fails, so does the sales manager.

Training salespeople involves daily objectives and testing. At the start of each day of initial training, at the start of each ride-with and sales meeting, salespeople need to know the training goals. Goals will range from learning about pricing or closing skills to product knowledge and competitive information. At the end of each day of initial training and at the end of each ride-with and sales meeting, conduct a test related to these goals. Have the salesperson calculate prices for a particular project, perform a role-play on closing, answer narrative questions on product knowledge, or create a competitive grid. Knowing there will be a test to measure understanding creates more attention during training. Salespeople can then grade themselves using answer sheets. The answer sheets become lasting training tools and sometimes even sales aids.

Salespeople object to testing the first few times, but then they become very competitive and start comparing scores. Some sales managers offer a small prize for the best score or scores above a certain level.

Many companies are testing all their salespeople every six months on product, competitor, customer knowledge, and selling skills. The results are compared to their scores on previous tests and benchmarked against peers. This represents a reality check for both the salesperson and sales manager and identifies areas where each salesperson needs more training. Don't assume your salespeople are well trained just because they heard the material. Many companies use these tests as the basis for salesperson advancement in responsibilities, compensation, and title.

At the end of each training session, ask salespeople to evaluate the trainer, determining what was good, what was not so good, and how future sessions can be improved. The evaluations apply to field coaching, sales meetings, and initial training. Based on the evaluation, take corrective action.

Finally, in an effort to reduce the training cycle, companies place newly hired salespeople in front of customers as soon as possible. The days of spending months at the corporate or regional offices before selling have ended. After a week of orientation, newly hired salespeople make customer calls with another salesperson, a trainer, or their sales manager. This allows them to understand the application of training material. Many firms alternate weeks of inside training on product, customer, and competitor knowledge with weeks of outside training traveling with a salesperson calling on customers.

Newly hired and tenured salespeople each need customized training programs reflecting their knowledge and skills. Training programs also differ from company to company depending on customers' and salespeople's needs. The training program for a belt salesperson calling on department store buyers differs from the training program for a software salesperson calling on hospitals. A belt salesperson or a software salesperson with strong product knowledge hired from a competitor needs different training than the person hired from another industry or out of college. You cannot mass-produce training.

Your most successful salespeople need customized, continuous training, since they produce the majority of your firm's revenues. Many companies have separate training programs for top producers. These interactive, experiential programs allow top producers to share best practices, are considered a reward for excellence, and seldom occur in a classroom setting. Topics differ from more basic training and might include major account or multilevel sales.

TRAINING CHECKLIST

The training checklist is a universe of topics which a salesperson must understand to be successful at your company. The job description and candidate profile provide sources for these topics. The training checklist represents a key control point for sales management. Out of it flows a quarterly development plan for each salesperson, which represents yet another key control point.

The training checklist should contain the following general headings down the side:

- Product knowledge
- Competition
- Competitive issues and advantages
- Customer knowledge
- Market and industry knowledge
- Selling skills
- Company policy
- Time and territory management
- Administrative tasks
- Company organization and history
- Conflict resolution

Under each heading, the sales manager fills in topics appropriate for his or her company. Across the top of each page a heading for the subjects/topics should appear, including the date completed, who completed it, and comments. Comments would indicate whether training was accomplished by field coaching, sales meetings or initial training. Exhibit 3.1 illustrates a training checklist used by a home health-care provider.

Salespeople often complain about wasting time in training, which casts a bad image on your firm. Therefore, the training agenda presents a daily schedule for initially teaching these topics/subjects to salespeople, who has responsibility for each session, and the session's objectives. The training checklist and agenda provide structure to a training program and force sales managers to organize the process. Exhibit 3.2 illustrates a training agenda used by a consumer goods heath and beauty care firm.

You should also ask new salespeople to track their progress on the training checklist and agenda. What did they learn from whom and when did they learn it? What topics still need to be covered or revisited? Ask more experienced, longer-term salespeople to review the checklist and note areas where they need additional training. From this process flows each salesperson's quarterly development plan, a key control point. For example, this quarter, one salesperson needs to work with technical support on product knowledge; last quarter, her development plan involved attending a seminar on computer skills. Another salesperson needs field coaching on closing skills; last quarter, his development plan involved presenting a competitive analysis at the sales meeting.

Job descriptions, training checklists, agendas, and training records also can prove important from a legal standpoint. Say, for example, you terminate a salesperson for not performing the duties on the job description or

Exhibit 3.1

Training checklist for a home health-care provider.

SUBJECTS	DATE COMPLETED	BY WHOM	COMMENTS

ACCOUNT REPRESENTATIVE _____ DATE HIRED _____

1. REFERRAL SOURCES
Physicians
- GP/FP/Internist
- Hem/Onc
- Neurologist
- Cardiologist
- Infectious Disease
- Gastroenterology
- Orthopedist
- Pulmonologist
- Endocrinologist
- Gerontologist
- HIV/AIDS
- Pediatrician
- Neonatolgist
- OB/GYN
- Other:
Payors
- HMO/PPO
- Physician Practice
- Self-Insured
- State/County
- Other:
Facilities
- Hospitals
- Extended Care
- Subacute
- Surgery Centers
- Rehabilitation
- Infusion Suites
- Other:
2. PRODUCT KNOWLEDGE
General Nursing
Traditional IV
Diabetes
- Type I
- Type II
Asthma
- Pediatric
- Adult
Hip & Knee
Pressure Ulcer
Cardiac
Hemophilia
Pediatrics
Rehabilitation

E x h i b i t   3.1 (continued)

SUBJECTS	DATE COMPLETED	BY WHOM	COMMENTS
3. COMPETITION			
Apna			
Corum			
Columbia			
Local Hospitals			
Local Home Health Care Firms			
Nurse Finders			
Chartwell			
Staff Builders			
Interim			
4. COMPETITIVE ISSUES AND ADVANTAGES			
Pricing			
Availability			
Comprehensive Care			
Holistic Approach			
Number of Caregivers			
Disease State Management			
Rare Chronic Care Management			
Partnership With Drug Company			
Cost Control with Quality Outcomes			
Efficient Organization Model			
Training/Screening of Caregivers			
Nursing at Core			
Continuity of Caregiver			
Reliable			
Large Pool of Caregivers			
Name Recognition			
Market Share			
Image Reputation			
Breadth/Variety of Services			
Specialty Programs			
Key Customers			
Strategic Partners			
Size, Years In Business			
Market Share #1 In 4 Categories			
Financial Strength, Reliability			
600 Locations in United States			
Strengths and Weaknesses			
Market Philosophy			
5. CUSTOMERS/REFERRAL SOURCES PROFILES			
Competition and Competitive Issues			
Decision Maker			
Expectations			
History			
Personnel, including Habits, Interests, Tastes, Concerns, Needs, Problems, Opportunities			

E x h i b i t   3.1 (continued)

SUBJECTS	DATE COMPLETED	BY WHOM	COMMENTS
Customer and Decision Makers Priorities			
Strategy			
Objectives			
Demographics and Key Drivers of Referral Source			
Profile			
6. PAPERWORK/ ADMINISTRATIVE			
Contracts			
Territory Manual			
Monthly and Weekly Planner			
Writing Skills			
Daily Call Report			
Expense Reports			
Quarterly Sales Plans			
Customer/Prospect Profiles			
Customer Files			
Phone/Fax/Voice Mail			
Collateral Review Ordering			
Presentation Binder Review			
ACT			
Weekly Activity Report			
7. TIME AND TERRITORY MANAGEMENT			
Number and Type of Calls per Week			
Clustering Accounts, Quadrants, Cloverleaf			
Daily Planner			
Weekly Call Schedule			
Daily Goals			
Managing Time with Customers			
Managing Time Between Calls			
Time Wasters/Traps			
Car/Trunk Organization System			
8. COMPANY POLICIES			
Pricing			
Entertainment			
Automobiles			
Expenses			
Code of Conduct			
Operations			
Human Resources			
Evaluations			
9. SELLING SKILLS			
Prospecting			
Making Appointments			
Precall Planning			
Research on Each Account			
Objective for Each Call and Account			

E x h i b i t   3.1 (continued)

SUBJECTS	DATE COMPLETED	BY WHOM	COMMENTS
Using Customer/Prospect Profiles			
Building Rapport			
Finding Problems to Solve			
Showing Empathy			
Questions that Uncover Needs/ Problems			
Competition and Competitive Advantage			
Long, Complex Sales Cycles			
Decision-Making Process			
Budget			
Time Frame			
Value-Added Proposition			
Strategic Sales			
Using Benefit Statements			
Building Interest			
Asking Questions to Obtain Agreement			
Using Referrals and the Reference Sell			
Overcoming Objections			
Closing Commitment			
Negotiating Skills			
Listening			
Self-Analysis			
Postcall Analysis			
10. CUSTOMER COMPLAINTS, SERVICE PROBLEMS, CONFLICT RESOLUTION			
11. COMPANY ORGANIZATION AND HISTORY			
Names of Key People			

INDICATE BY EACH ITEM HOW TRAINING WAS GIVEN:
(IT)   Initial Training
(FT)   Field Training
(SM)   Sales Meeting

for marginal results. However, the salesperson claims he did not receive the appropriate training. The training checklist, agenda, and records document what training took place, along with when and how. The job description, candidate profile, training checklist, and agenda specify the topics included in each salesperson's performance evaluation, which we discuss in Chapter 8.

E x h i b i t   3.2

Training agenda for a health and beauty aids firm.

Sales Representative _____ Date Hired _____
Territory _____

Activity and Date	Objective	Where	Responsible Person
Week One			
Day One: Call on customers with trainer.	Sales process	Field	Trainer
Day Two: Review competitive grid and competitive catalogues.	Competitive knowledge	Office	Sales Manager
Day Three: Work on assembly line.	Product knowledge	Factory	Foreman
Day Four: Work in new product laboratory.	Research and development	Lab	Chemist
Day Five: Work in order processing.	Accurate orders . and pricing	Office	Customer Service Manager
Week Two			
Day One: Call on customers with senior salesperson.	Selling skills	Field	Senior Salesperson
Day Two: Review customer profiles.	Customer knowledge	Office	Sales Manager
Day Three: Ride on delivery truck.	Learn distribution	Field	Transportation Manager
Day Four: Complete online activity reports.	Computer software	Office	Information Systems Manager
Day Five: Call on customers with junior salesperson.	Sales skills	Field	Junior Salesperson

PRODUCT KNOWLEDGE

Most companies do an acceptable job of training salespeople in product knowledge. After all, most sales managers were salespeople in the same industry/market, sometimes at the same firm, and because of their strong product knowledge, they feel comfortable in training salespeople on this subject. In fact, often salespeople receive too much product knowledge at the expense of competitive/customer knowledge or sales skills. Product knowledge helps salespeople's confidence, but technology and operationally based firms often overemphasize this area. Too much product knowledge confuses customers and deceives salespeople.

Keep in mind that product knowledge is more than specifications. For instance, one leasing firm that specialized in financing the purchase of used computers taught its salespeople a great deal about the equipment but little about figuring monthly payments. Customers and prospects were impressed by their knowledge until the discussion turned to finance.

Let's return to Exhibit 2.1 on buyer behavior. If your salespeople call on new systems buyers, making one-time or first-time purchases, product knowledge has more importance than if these salespeople call on managers making modified rebuys or commodity purchases.

Essentially, you must teach salespeople whatever product/service knowledge the customer requires to make the buying decision. In some situations (such as a modified rebuy) the salesperson's product knowledge will not exceed the customers, or the customer may have questions the salesperson is not prepared to answer. When required, a salesperson should know where to obtain additional information.

In the twenty-first century, product knowledge can be more effectively taught through hands-on experience. Yes, salespeople need to study the catalog, product manuals, videos, audio tapes, and Web sites, but product knowledge requires application, hands-on, and experiential training. Many firms accomplish this by having salespeople work at or tour a customer's location. What better way to understand how a product/service is used, the needs satisfied, and the problems solved? Other firms teach salespeople product knowledge by having them work in or tour their factory or other departments/functions, such as dispatch, installation, maintenance, design, the lab, or engineering. Riding on the delivery truck, filling orders in the warehouse, or answering customer service phones also can provide product training. Some firms rotate salespeople through key company functions to provide product knowledge and appreciation for other departments, a salesperson's internal customers. At the least, you should take a salesperson with you to see the product or service in use. If you sell a hospital cleaning service, visit the hospital and watch the service being performed. If you sell refuge removal, have the trainee ride the garbage truck for a day and visit the landfill. If you sell sweaters, visit some stores that offer your merchandise. If you sell industrial robots, visit some factories that use them. Every day of product training should start with objectives and end with a test.

If possible, salespeople should also use the product. Apparel salespeople should wear their product, software salespeople should use their product, and food service salespeople should taste their product. Where possible, have salespeople take the product apart and reassemble it, and work with models, prototypes, samples, charts, and graphs.

COMPETITIVE KNOWLEDGE AND ADVANTAGE

Salespeople require knowledge, both of their own products or services and of their competitors'. To sell effectively, a salesperson must know the competitive advantages or disadvantages of each style, model, or service in the marketplace. Do your company's automatic welding robots cost more than your competitors'? Do they work faster, last longer, or move up and down as well as sideways? Do your company's wool/nylon sweaters require handwashing when competitors' sweaters can be laundered in a machine? Does your service clean hospitals two shifts a day as opposed to your competitor's one shift only? Does your refuse removal company pick up twice a week, while the competition picks up only once? Does your firm's life insurance policy offer dividends or dividend reinvestment, while other do not?

As mentioned, most firms do an acceptable job of product knowledge. However, they do a weak job of training salespeople in competitor knowledge. Salespeople's understanding of the competition not only allows them to sell more effectively, but to understand strategic issues such as market segments, differentiation, and targeting. As the saying goes, the best defense is a good offense. Attack the competition where you are strong and competition is weak.

Competitive grids for each product or product line or market help train salespeople. Marketing can assist you in organizing and obtaining information for the competitive grid. Across the top, list your competitors. Down the left-hand side list the competitive issues, such as how the customer makes a choice. List price last, since you want to train salespeople in selling value. For each competitive issue, show how your product/service compares to competition in features, benefits, and image. Is it better, worse, or the same and why?

While compiling the grid, be specific. For instance, don't list "quality" as an issue. Instead, list how the customer defines quality, such as mean time to failure, natural yarn or fruit content, handmade quality, capacity, value-added services, design, materials, speed, freeze-to-thaw time, efficacy, and billing accuracy. Exhibit 3.3 shows a competitive grid for a tire firm selling to trucking fleets. Exhibit 3.4 shows a competitive grid for a waste removal service.

It is essential to be honest in appraising your competition. All companies' products and services have strengths and weaknesses. Accurate knowledge allows the salesperson to target customers with the greatest

Competitive grid for fleet/commercial tire manufacturer.

COMPETITIVE ISSUES	BFCA	GENERAL	GOODYEAR	TOYO	MICHELIN	YOKOHOMA
Cost per mile						
Retreadability						
Availability/delivery						
Warranties						
Relationship						
Accessibility						
Expert advice on choice and use						
Training						
Tire tracking: Use; miles						
Casing resale value						
Road service: National Fleet Program						
Transaction price						
Terms						

need for the particular strengths your product or service offers. Accurate competitive knowledge allows the salesperson to feel more confident; to present features, benefits, and proof more effectively and forcefully; to make price less of an issue; and to sell the risk that a competitor's product/service may not work or perform as desired. Knowledge increases the probability of success; ignorance increases the probability of failure.

The competitive grid provides a great topic for sales meetings. Ask your sales force to arrive prepared to discuss it. At the meeting ask for a product, product line, or markets' competitors and the competitive issues on which customers make a choice. For each competitive issue have salespeople discuss whether your firm is better, worse, or the same as the competition and why. Quantify the differences and place the results at the appropriate spot in the grid—for example, "Our frozen batter has 40 percent more fruit," or "Our Internet site has 20 percent more functionality." Salespeople may not agree, but through a meaningful discussion, they will exchange valuable competitive information. Once you complete the grid, codify it, reproduce it, and make it available to present and future salespeople as a sales aid.

E x h i b i t 3.4

Competitor comparison waste disposal.

Competitive Issues	Competitor A	Competitor B	Competitor C	Competitor D
Length of Contract				
Condition of Containers				
Type of Equipment				
Number of Trucks and Containers				
Number of Salespeople and Drivers				
CSR, Dispatch, Telemarketing Staff				
Years in Business				
Variety of Services				
Landfill Access and Ownership				
Disposal Costs				
Markets Serviced				
Policy Concerning Ethics				
Safety				
Credit and Collection				
Financial Stability				
Reliability				
Image and Reputation				
Specialization				
Number of Customers				
Key Accounts				
Strengths and Weaknesses				
Thinks and Acts				
Price				

Salespeople must understand that some competitive issues are expected and demanded. For instance, you cannot sell digital cable unless it is ISO 9000. You cannot sell tier-two automotive manufacturers unless you offer next-day, just-in-time deliveries. But you recognize that the ability to deliver ISO 9000 products on time in China and Russia would be a real competitive advantage to global customers.

Some sales managers and marketing departments keep a library or database of material, catalogs, and articles on each competitor. Salespeople can then access it online or by visiting the file. Some sales managers assign one or several salespeople to collect or present information on a particular competitor. A sales meeting might include disassembling a competitor's product and comparing it to yours or having a recently hired salesperson who worked for a competitor present the competitive product/service.

Sources for collecting competitive information include customers, competitive salespeople interviews, trade shows, vendors, trade publications, catalogs, consultants, and the Internet. Remember: Knowledge is power. Know the competitor as you do your own firm. In collecting competitive information, emphasize ethics, the "spirit," and letter of the law.

CUSTOMER KNOWLEDGE AND PROFILES

Customers represent the most important asset of any organization. Salespeople need training in how to collect, organize, and use customer information. Often the vendor with the best product or service does not get the order; instead, the salesperson who knows the most about the customer does. Do your salespeople know more about their customers/prospects than the competition?

Your salespeople will have better customer knowledge if they maintain appropriate customer profiles. The sales manager should meet with the salespeople to design a customer profile. Determine what customer/profile information provides your salespeople with a competitive advantage. A well-designed customer profile forces salespeople to ask the right probing questions which identify customer needs, budgets, time frames, opportunities, decision makers, and the decision-making process. Obtaining personal information on the decision maker allows the salesperson to establish a rapport and build the relationship.

Contact-management software allows salespeople to record this information digitally and allows the sales manager to access and aggregate it easily. Companies that offer contact management programs include Act, Sales Logics, Saratoga Systems, GoldMine, Clarify, and Siebel. Generally, contact management is imbedded in more comprehensive customer relationship software. However, many companies continue to record customer profiles with pen and paper.

The important customer profile issues are what information to include, how to collect it, and how to motivate salespeople to use it. The required customer information can be divided into company information and personal information. Companies write the checks, but people make the decisions. Customer profile formats will differ from one market segment to another. A company selling surgical instruments to hospitals, outpatient surgical centers, and physicians will need three different formats.

Most customer profile formats contain business information on the following:

- The decision maker
- The decision-making process
- Budgets
- Time frame
- The relationship of purchasing to other departments
- Needs
- Opportunities
- Problems
- Competitors
- History with your firm
- Credit
- Past usage

- Potential dollars of purchases
- Whether to sell at corporate or division levels
- Type of product or service used
- Key drivers of customer's business
- Sales history
- The customer's competitors and customers
- Key metrics (number of)
- Locations
- Attitude toward your company

Most customer profile formats contain personal information on the decision makers, including education, past positions, hot buttons, issues not to talk about, hobbies, interests, families, important dates (e.g., birthday), decision-making styles, relationships with other employees, best time and way to reach them, and phone, email, and fax number. When a new or different salesperson is assigned to the customer, this information proves critical. Customers appreciate the continuity. We buy from experts (business information) and friends (personal information). Exhibit 3.5 is an example of a physician profile used by a pharmaceutical firm. Exhibit 3.6 is an example of a company profile used by a B2B Internet firm.

How customers use and filter information and make decisions represents an important training area for salespeople. Customers are not a homogeneous group. Some customers require a great deal of facts and data to make concrete, logical decisions. They spend a lot of time analyzing data, get bogged down in detail, and have difficulty making a final decision. Other customers prefer concepts to data and make fast decisions. A third group requires assurances concerning the negative impact of any buying decisions on other people in their organization. This group resists change. The final group not only prefers concepts to data, but thinks globally and makes quick gut decisions. Most salespeople attempt to persuade customers based on the salesperson's decision-making mode, not the customer's. When selling to group decision makers, this becomes more complicated. Exhibit 3.7 illustrates the four quadrants of decision making.

E x h i b i t   3.5

Physician profile.

- Name:
- Nickname:
- Primary and secondary office address; home address:
  - Phone:
  - Fax:
- Office manager or nurse:
- Receptionist:
- Primary decision maker:
- Schedule:
- Best time to call and/or see:
- Directions to office:
- Hospital affiliations
  - Title/responsibilities:
  - Privileges:
  - Location of hospital:
  - When is he/she there?
- HMO affiliation:
- Nursing home affiliation
- What other physicians refer to him/her?
- What physicians does he/she refer to?
- Our primary competitors:
- Patient demographies
  - Age:
  - Income level:
  - Type problems:
- Background and special interests
  - Previous locations and employment:
  - Status symbols in office:
  - Professional associations:
  - Honors:
  - Mentors:
  - Research interests:
  - Articles published:
- Education
  - College:
  - Medical school:
  - Residency:
  - Honors:
  - Extracurricular activities:
  - Internship:
  - Fellowship:
  - Board certification:
  - Military service:

- Rank:
- Attitude:
- Communication style:
- How he or she makes decisions:
- Prescribing habits:
- Products used and how:
- Knowledge of our products:
- Appropriate to ask out for a meal
  - Breakfast:
  - Lunch:
  - Dinner:
  - Cocktails:
  - Restaurant preference:
  - Food preference:
- Professional goals:
- Business goals:
- Physician's competitors:
- What are the physician's professional and personal priorities?
- What are the physician's professional and personal problems/needs?
- Family
  - Home address:
  - Phone:
  - Appropriate time to call:
  - Birth date and place:
  - Hometown:
  - Marital status:
  - Wedding anniversary:
  - Spouse's name:
  - Spouse's birthday:
  - Spouse's interests, activities, affiliations:
  - Spouse's education:
  - Children's names, birth dates, education, hobbies:
- Hobbies, interests, lifestyles
  - Clubs:
  - Community activities:
  - Leisure time recreational activities:
  - Vacations:
  - Sports:
  - Personal goals:
  - Product achievement:
- What not to talk about:

E x h i b i t   3.6

Customer profile for packaging industry; business-to-business Internet exchange.

Business name:	Our competitors:
Headquarters location:	Our competitive advantage:
Decision maker:	Critical risks:
Influencers:	Barriers:
Gatekeepers:	
Users:	**FOR EACH IMPORTANT**
Decision-making process:	**COMPANY CONTACT:**
Time frame:	Name:
Budget:	Title:
Technical proficiency:	Role:
Systems staff:	Phone:
Platform:	E-mail:
Operating system:	Location:
Hardware:	How to reach:
Software:	Professional experience:
Products manufactured:	Decision-making style:
Products purchased:	Likes to talk about:
Products sold:	Don't talk about:
Plant locations:	Education:
Their competitors:	Family:
Their customers:	Hobbies:
Their suppliers:	Interests:
Ownership:	Important dates:
Needs and problems:	Important corporate relationships:
Opportunities:	Professional and personal goals:

The best salespeople obtain customer information on every call. After each visit, salespeople should write at least two new things they learned about the business and the decision maker. Salespeople and marketing can find important customer information from Web sites, catalogs, trade publications, trade shows, annual reports, and vendors.

We motivate salespeople with love and fear, rewards, and punishments. Maintaining profiles represents an important competitive advantage for your firm. Yet many salespeople resist keeping customer profiles because easy access to this information makes them less valuable to their employer. Instead many salespeople insist they have perfect memories. Often sales managers include accuracy of customer profiles on the salesperson's performance evaluations and as an element in his or her bonus.

How we make decisions, use, and filter information.

	CONCRETE	ABSTRACT
LOGIC	Logical, organized, action-oriented. Sell the facts. Thinker and sensor, wants a lot of data, practical, Reality-based, likes information, and research (AIM, AIM, AIM). Make appointment, be on time, wants proof, gets bogged down in detail.	Likes ideas, concepts, theory, intuitive thinker. Sell the options. A Little preparation, test it, then see if it works. Bold, takes action (READY, FIRE, AIM). Innovation, enjoys change and risk. Provide direct, brief answers.
PEOPLE-ORIENTED	Concerned with impact on people, feeling, sensing, emotional, sincere. Sell the service. Wants to please and serve people. Harmonizer (READY, READY, READY). Likes status quo, resists change. Emphasize benefits that reduce risk.	Dreamer, concerned with big picture. Global, concerned with impact on people. Intuition, feeling. Sell idea. Innovator, action, no preparation, quick start, makes gut decisions (FIRE, FIRE, FIRE). Likes brainstorming, acts impulsively. Offer expert testimonial.

When customer profiles are kept digitally, a sales manager can easily access and even aggregate certain information from the company database. If kept in hard copy form, a sales manager should examine the customer profile and file during field coaching ride-withs.

Here are a few examples of what might occur if the customer profile is ignored. A newly hired software salesperson from Chicago calls on a business prospect in North Carolina. To establish a rapport, since it is October, he asks whether the decision maker hunts or fishes, only to find out he is a vegetarian and president of the Animal Rights Association. A refuse removal salesperson calls on a large Asian automaker in Ohio to sell recycling equipment. The salesperson refers to "associates" as "employees" and is reprimanded. The plant manager puts a twelve-minute sand clock on his desk and announces the call will end when the sand runs out. All of this information was on the customer profile, but neither salesperson reviewed it before the call. The lesson is this: Customer profiles create a competitive advantage; not using profiles creates a competitive disadvantage.

SELLING SKILLS

Now that the salespeople understand product, competitor, and customer knowledge, we must reinforce their selling skills. Many sales managers assume their salespeople can sell. After riding with and coaching hundreds of salespeople, my experience indicates most need improvement in sales skills. A sales force which understands strategic and tactical sales skills provides a strong competitive advantage in a commoditized world.

Outside trainers, seminars, videocassettes and audiocassettes, and books on sales skills are the place to start. Tom Hopkins, Brian Tracy, Miller Hyman, Xerox, and Wilson Learning are just a few resources. Ask your peers for references, read trade publications, visit trade shows, and search the Web.

The sales manager's job involves reinforcing and customizing these basic strategic and tactical sales skills. Knowledge is only power if we use it. Every industry, product, or service involves the individual use of certain broad-selling techniques. Training salespeople in selling skills involves de-aggregating these skills and then prioritizing the pieces most important for success in your industry. Long, complex sales cycles involving group decisions require different training than a shorter, less complicated sales cycles with an individual decision maker. Selling to one-time or first-time new systems buyers requires different skills than selling to a modified rebuy, existing systems buyer, a new product buyer, or commodity buyers. Some salespeople call on multiple types of buyers and need to understand both strategic and tactical sales skills.

Strategic sales skills primarily used in longer more complex sales cycles involve the following:

- Understanding the decision-making process
- Organizational issues
- The value-added proposition
- Quantifying benefits
- The decision-maker's motives

More basic tactical sales skills include the following:

- Qualifying customers
- Precall planning
- Obtaining an appointment
- Using probing questions to find needs and problems
- Presenting features, benefits, and proof
- Overcoming objections
- Obtaining a commitment

Exhibits 3.8 and 3.9 outline training topics for complex, longer sales cycles involving groups and the more basic tactical topics are included in the selling pyramid.

E x h i b i t   3.8

Training topics: Complex sales process, long sales cycles, group decisions.

UNDERSTANDING THE DECISION-MAKING PROCESS	VALUE-ADDED PROPOSITION
• Time frame. Sales cycle.	• Understand customers' problems, needs, and opportunities.
• Budget.	• Ask probing questions.
• Influencers. Decision makers. Committees.	• Study customers' competitors, competitive advantage, markets, customers, key drivers.
• New systems buyer, established systems buyer, new product buyer, commodity buyer.	• Quantify in dollars how you will increase sales, reduce costs, lower working capital and capital investment, increase dollars of margins. Benefit realization.
• Steps in decision-making process. Definition of a successful call.	
• Measuring the process.	• Offer features, benefits, proof.
	• Overcoming fragmentation.
STRATEGIC ISSUES	**UNDERSTAND THE PEOPLE/ PLAYERS, PROFILES**
• Relationships of customer personnel.	• How they use and filter information, make decisions.
• Organizational issues. Sell at what level.	• Hobbies/interests.
• Fox.	• Decision-making motives.
• Champion.	• Comfortable level of risk.
• Consultive versus relationship sell.	
• Competitor's history and relationship with customer.	

LONGER, MORE COMPLEX SALES CYCLES INVOLVING GROUP DECISIONS

Big-ticket items, one-time or first-time purchases, and new systems buys, such as a security or telephone system, enterprisewide software, consulting or legal services, navigational equipment for aircraft, and B2B Internet services, require salespeople to be trained in strategic sales skills as well as the basics. In such industries with long sales cycles, salespeople must understand the decision-making process, including time frame, budget, decision makers, and steps from search to purchase. A salesperson selling enterprisewide software who obtains this knowledge has a competitive advantage over a salesperson who does not have this knowledge.

But how does a salesperson obtain information about the customer/prospect's time frame for purchase, budget, decision makers, and

Exhibit 3.9

Tactical sales skills: Training topics

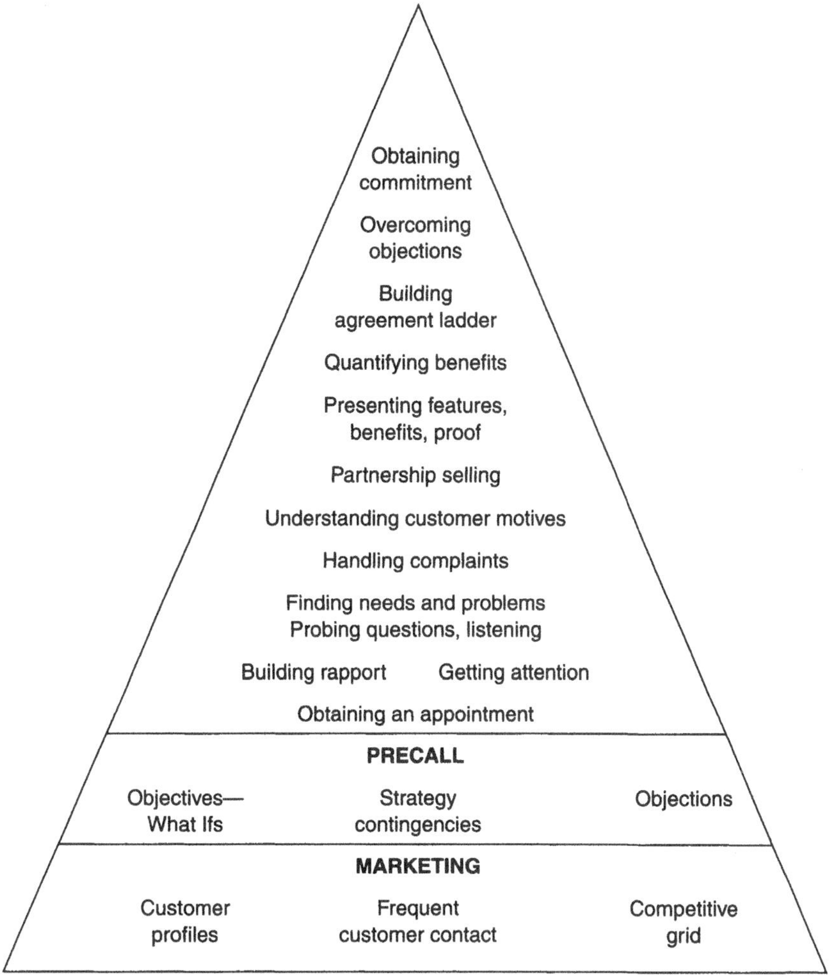

Obtaining
commitment

Overcoming
objections

Building
agreement ladder

Quantifying benefits

Presenting features,
benefits, proof

Partnership selling

Understanding customer motives

Handling complaints

Finding needs and problems
Probing questions, listening

Building rapport   Getting attention

Obtaining an appointment

PRECALL		
Objectives— What Ifs	Strategy contingencies	Objections

MARKETING		
Customer profiles	Frequent customer contact	Competitive grid

decision-making process? The salesperson needs a fox and a champion. The fox is not a decision maker but a knowledgeable influencer. The fox prefers your enterprisewide software program over competitors'. Because of this, he or she reliably and accurately answers a salesperson's probing questions on time frame, budget, decision makers, and process.

The salesperson also needs a champion. The champion is a decision maker who prefers your enterprisewide software and will support a decision to buy it. Your salesperson needs to supply the champion with information to help persuade colleagues and make the champion a hero. Some salespeople supply their champion with a list of possible objections which colleagues might raise and how to overcome them. Sales managers train salespeople on how to identify the fox and the champion and make clear that without their support the probability of failure is high.

The enterprisewide software salesperson must be trained to identify the key players in the decision-making process. Many people can say no; only one can say yes. Is this key decision maker the CEO, CFO, COO, CIO, or VP of purchasing? Who influences the decision and how? The CIO can say no, because the software does not integrate well with the company operating system. A plant manager, who might be a software user, can say no because features and functions don't meet his or her needs.

The salesperson must be trained to identify, track, and monitor the steps from search to purchase in the sales cycle. Steps for the enterprisewide software might include a needs analysis, a referral, a plant visit to a satisfied user, a demo, a presentation to the decision makers, an alpha test, a beta trial, analysis of results, a final presentation to decision makers, and a written proposal. The salesperson assigns a time frame, cost, and probability to each step. Success is defined by moving from one step to another within the time frame and cost budget. Each month the salesperson and sales manager discuss the status. Failure to move to the next step requires analysis and corrective action. Training salespeople in this process prevents unexpected disappointments.

Such a salesperson must understand buyer behavior and when to use consultive selling versus relationship selling, at what level to enter a prospect's organization, the relationship between various people in the prospect's organization, and the competitor's history there. For example, a high-tech miniature transformer sales manager teaches her salespeople to qualify prospects by first calling a design engineer at the plant level and not working with corporate purchasing until designs are submitted. She has found that starting at corporate purchasing wastes months of a salesperson's time.

In approaching large organizations, salespeople are taught to look for conflicts or alliances between key decision-making personnel. Who wants whose job? Understanding this prevents costly mistakes and builds relationships.

During long, complex sales cycles, the competitive grid provides basic knowledge. However, as mentioned, salespeople must understand as much about competition as they do about their own firm. Salespeople partner with customers/prospects in solving problems.

In the long, complex sales cycle, you must train salespeople on how to quantify benefits. For example, an enterprisewide software salesperson presents her customer a program with a price of $2 million—twice that of the competitor. However, the salesperson has spreadsheets proving that this program can increase the customer's sales by 3 percent, or $9 million, reduce material and labor costs by $1.4 million, and reduce inventory by $500,000. The competition does not have such a spreadsheet. The higher-priced, higher-value software vendor wins the job. Marketing and sales management cooperate in producing these spreadsheets.

BASIC TACTICAL SALES SKILLS

Salesperson training in long, complex group decisions reduces the sales cycle and separates winners from losers. All salespeople, whether their product has a short or long sales cycle, need training in the basic tactical sales skills outlined in the selling pyramid, shown in Exhibit 3.9. Constant reinforcement of this training is the sales manager's job.

Deaggregate the items listed on the selling pyramid in Exhibit 3.9. Pick those pieces in the sales process most important to the success of a salesperson in your firm. Concentrate your training on those areas.

Previously, we discussed the marketing issues, customer profiles, and competitive grid. Chapter 5 discusses call frequency. Also, salespeople must understand that if they do not have an objective and a strategy for the call, they should not make the call. Leave coffee calls for Sundays.

When moving from qualifying customers and obtaining an appointment to obtaining a commitment or closing, in general, the most common areas for reinforcement include probing questions to find needs and opportunities, presenting features, benefits, and proof, and overcoming objections

To drive growth in some businesses, the salesperson must know how to efficiently find additional prospects with greater-than-average needs for the product or service. In such situations, the sales manager must teach the proven unique techniques that have produced qualified leads for more successful salespeople or develop and test new techniques. Ask your more successful salespeople to share such information with their peers at a sales meeting. Test these skills and techniques with role-play.

Prospecting creates growth, but the time required and risks involved are not worth the reward unless leads are qualified. The sales manager must teach salespeople efficient ways to prospect for new customers. Track the closing ratio from prospecting. How can you train salespeople to improve it?

For instance, the sales manager for a distributor of ice-making machines instructed salespeople to prospect by following an ice delivery truck. The sales manager for a distributor of solar heat-reflecting shades and glass instructed salespeople to prospect by calling on offices with large windows and southern exposures. Remind salespeople that referrals from satisfied customers represent an excellent introduction to qualified prospects.

New-product salespeople, new-systems salespeople calling on first-time or one-time customers, and salespeople who depend on a constant stream of new customers must be taught proven techniques for selling the appointment. For example, in the giftware industry, a modified rebuy, having an appointment can double the size of your order. On the other hand, salespeople with delivery routes selling commodities don't require appointments, and salespeople calling on repeat customers for reorders, modified rebuy, have little difficulty arranging them.

In this century, salespeople need training on how to use email and faxes to help set appointments or create interest in appointments. Salespeople also need training on how to deal with voice mail. Pressing 0 to reach a gatekeeper who will find the person you are trying to reach represents one way to penetrate voice mail.

Calling early or late in the day, when you know the decision maker picks up his or her phone is another idea for contacting hard-to-reach people and avoiding voice mail. Salespeople must be trained to sell the appointment, not the product/service over the phone. People who make buying decisions lure salespeople into selling the product by phone so they can say no to an appointment. Instead, sell the benefits of an appointment. Offering alternative times to meet with a customer, especially at a quarter to and after an hour, works well.

You must continually remind the salespeople on your team that selling primarily involves listening, not talking. Salespeople should not present features, benefits, and proof until the customer and salesperson have agreed on the need, problem, or opportunity. In longer sales cycles, salespeople must continually reconfirm the customer's need, problem, or opportunity. Probing questions, customized to your industry, identify needs, problems, and opportunities. In the corrugated box industry, questions would center on yields and equipment utilization. In the semiconductor industry, a salesperson is trained to ask about failure rates and quality control. Empathetic listening and a knowledge of potential problems and opportunities helps identify customer needs.

The answers to probing questions also identify customers' needs. Many sales managers ask salespeople to submit their favorite probing questions and what the answers reveal. These often are listed on a board at the sales meeting and discussed. After the meeting, this list of probing questions and what the answers tell a salesperson concerning customer problems, needs, and opportunities is reproduced as a training aid and placed in the training manual.

In addition to identifying the best probing questions, presentation skills need continual refinement. Generally, salespeople know the product or service features and sometimes mention benefits, but they seldom offer proof. In surveys of people who make buying decisions, results show salespeople who know how the product/service features benefit the customer and can offer proof of this obtain the orders. The features of a B2B Internet site are the ability to transact purchases and sales efficiently, the benefit is an increase in revenues or a decrease in cost and inventory for the participants, and the proof can be actual trades done by other customers.

Sales managers test salespeople at sales meetings by going around the room asking each person to give a feature, benefit, and proof for a particular product or service. No one can repeat what already has been said. This forces salespeople to think on their feet in front of their peers, which, hopefully, will be repeated in front of their customers. When doing this exercise, salespeople quickly run out of complete features, benefits, and proof, indicating a need for more training.

To help the sales force close or move to the next step in the sales cycle, sales managers must continually reinforce salespeople's training in overcoming objections. Salespeople must understand that objections show interest: No objections, no interest—and probably a credit problem. Salespeople should smile when customers raise objections. The objection needs to be restated in a positive manner and then overcome.

Many sales managers ask salespeople to submit the most common customer objections. Then, at a sales meeting, the objections are prioritized and listed. Salespeople are asked to share how they overcome the objection. A meaningful dialog ensues, great ideas evolve, everyone learns, and the objections and ideas on how to overcome them are recorded and used as a sales aid.

Objections range from price or why a change should be made, to sizing, features, delivery, or a bad past experience. A good means to test salespeople on this is the "objection game." At a sales meeting each salesperson throws out an objection at another salesperson. He or she must restate the objections and quickly overcome it. If someone fails to do this, they are out. The last person in is the winner. One salesperson may ask another, "Why make a change? I am happy with my present situation." The other salesperson might restate the objection by saying, "Oh, you feel there is no reason to change?" Then follow with, "Who did you deal with before your present vendor and why did you switch?" This might produce the rationale for the customer to consider a new vendor.

Another key part of the selling process which requires constant reinforcement is closing, obtaining a commitment, or moving to the next step. Salespeople who do great presentations and probing questions often forget to close. Often the fear of failure or rejection prevents salespeople from attempting to obtain a commitment.

Salespeople must be trained that "no" is only "no" today, and it takes a certain number of noes to get a yes. The salesperson can always go back next week with another idea or product. Closing ratios vary by product/service and industry. The sales manager should measure the closing ratio for each salesperson quarterly and discuss means of improving it, such as qualified customers or quicker identification of needs. For longer, more complex sales, the closing ratio may not be reflected in an order, but in moving to the next step in the sales cycle.

Many sales managers believe that the key to closing is for both the salesperson and the customer to feel more comfortable. To create this comfort, they suggest the salesperson review what was agreed on. For a temporary help service, the salesperson might say, "Well, we agreed you need more people in your shipping department at the holidays. We agreed we did a good job for you last year and that our fees are within your budget." The word *agree* makes all parties more comfortable.

Next, the salesperson requires a partnership statement, such as "I know this is an important decision. I will drop by the first day you use our people. Here is my beeper number if you have questions." A partnership statement helps alleviate concerns that the salesperson will disappear after receiving an order. Last, the salesperson must offer a choice, such as "Should we start Monday or Tuesday? Do you need ten or twelve people?" Videotaped role-play provides the best way to test closing skills.

A successful sales call is determined by meeting the objective and agreeing on the next step. The objective may be an order or meeting a key decision maker. The next step may be the date for a trial run. The key point is, as sales manager, you must reinforce sales skill training or it will quickly be lost.

FIELD COACHING

Clearly, salespeople require knowledge of products, competition, customers, and selling skills. The sales manager delivers this knowledge through initial training, field coaching (ride-withs, work-withs), and sales meetings.

Because of the many benefits, field coaching represents a regional sales manager's most important responsibility. Field coaching allows a sales manager to train, evaluate, and motivate salespeople, share best practices, and establish rapport with customers.

Field coaching allows sales managers to observe salespeople in planning and critiquing a customer visit, along with observing their knowledge of customers, competitors, products, and sales skills. You cannot accurately evaluate a salesperson's skills and knowledge unless you observe them with customers. Sales results tell you the outcomes; field coaching gives you insight into the causes of outcomes. In critiquing a salesperson's performance, the sales manager reinforces positive skills, knowledge, activities, and personal characteristics and trains salespeople in areas of weakness. Salespeople often complain that sales managers don't reinforce initial training and sales meetings with field visits, and because of this, they have no evidence for performance evaluations.

Sales manager field visits make salespeople feel useful, important, and worthwhile, and satisfy their need to belong. For this reason, plus establishing a rapport with customers, you must work with both weak and strong salespeople. Your best salespeople can develop bad habits, and only riding with the underperformers creates an image of remedial training. Often the best salespeople or their customers will teach you a best practice which can be passed on to the entire sales force. After all, our best performers produce most of our sales volume, so any suggestions for improvement, such as proper targeting, can have a major impact on revenues. Field training and supervision gives salespeople confidence in you as a sales manager.

Furthermore, field visits give you a firsthand chance to learn more about problems and opportunities with customers, with products or services, with salespeople, and with competitors. When a customer complains to you in person about late deliveries or weak product performance, it has more impact than when a salesperson complains over the phone. Customers appreciate your time and interest. Also, should a salesperson leave, you have the customer profile, and with field visits, you have a personal rapport. Some sales managers make it a point to meet and know the top customers and decision makers in each territory.

Occasionally ask your boss to travel with your salespeople. This reinforces all the benefits, allows your supervisor some insight to the moment of truth, and allows him or her to suggest how you can improve sales force performance. However, unless there is a compelling reason, only one management person should ride with a salesperson at any time. Customers and salespeople feel uncomfortable when more than three people are present.

If the sales force resides locally and you have up to seven reports, spend at least 2 days a week, 100 days a year, riding with salespeople. If the sales force is national or if you have more than seven reports, three to four days a week may be required.

If the sales force resides locally, shorter but more frequent ride-withs prove most productive. This gives you an opportunity to observe change and reinforce best practices. If the sales force is national, economies of scale usually dictate longer, less frequent ride-withs.

Look at your job description, make a list of all your activities, and then track the time spent on training in general and field training in particular. As a sales manager, field training requires 40 to 60 percent of your time. If you find that training does not receive enough of your time, ask yourself the following questions:

- Are there non-sales-related activities which require too much of your time?
- Can these be eliminated or delegated?
- Are the reasons you don't spend more time on training really excuses?

Field coaching proves more effective if you and the salesperson have an objective. Focused ride-withs that alternatively concentrate on new products, new accounts, a particular product line, or market segments prove most effective. The focus may involve training the salespeople on selling a major account. Ask the salesperson for his or her input on the work-with goal/objective and have a different focus for each ride-with.

Occasionally do an unannounced ride-with. Call a salesperson, announce that your schedule has changed unexpectedly, and say that you would like to ride with him or her tomorrow. If that is not practical in your longer sales cycle business or if salespeople work long distances from your office, make a date for early next week. You will experience a more typical salesperson's day: fewer calls, shorter hours, a trip to the bank or daycare center, as well as a customer mix which includes fewer friends and more cell phone time. Salespeople quickly communicate the unannounced ride-with to their peers, which results in more attention to planning highly productive days. A salesperson who tells you he or she can't do a ride-with on short notice raises a warning flag. We manage with fear and love.

Field coaching proves especially important for managing channel partners. If you use indirect sales representative organizations, distributors, or brokers, field coaching not only trains and motivates, it obtains a time commitment. An indirect sales force that you ride with will devote more time and resources to your products or services. The obstacle may be getting channel partners to accept field training. Training makes an indirect sales force more comfortable and competent with your products or services. Many firms have contracts which require their indirect sales force to spend a certain amount of time at sales meetings and in field coaching.

Generally, we divide field coaching, ride-withs, or work-withs into five parts:

- Your phone call to arrange time with the salesperson
- In-the-field precall planning

- The sales call itself
- The post-call critique
- The end-of-the-day summary

Many sales managers spend the necessary time in the field but don't implement the correct process and thus don't improve their salespeople's productivity.

In planning each field coaching day, whether with a channel partner or direct field person, agree with the salesperson on the objectives: management selling of major accounts, new product placement, learning customer or competitive knowledge, or refining selling skills. At the end of your work-with day, were those objectives met? Some managers ask their salespeople for lists of what they would like help with and, in turn, send the salesperson a list of customers or market segments to be called on.

Before each customer call, review with the salesperson precall planning, what he or she should do when you are not there. What is the call's objective and strategy for reaching that objective? Remember, no objective, no call. As mentioned previously, too many salespeople engage in coffee calls. "I always call on my friends at Imperial on Tuesday morning." With shorter sales cycles and modified rebuys, such as bakery products, tires, or hosiery, the objective may be a reorder. The strategy may be sampling or discussing delivery dates. With longer sales cycles of first-time or one-time purchases, such as telephone systems, consulting services, or software, the objective may be moving to the next step in the sales process—that is, meet a key decision maker, agree on a trial, or obtain information on budgets and timetables. The strategy may involve quantifying benefits and referring to industry leaders who use your services.

Before each call, discuss competition at this account with the salesperson. What items are bought from competition and why? Are competitors "ants" (start-ups) or "gorillas" (the phone company) or both? What percent of this customer's business does your firm have? What are this account's problems, needs, and opportunities? Has competition made a mistake? Does this account need better deliveries or customized products? How can your firm help solve the problems and satisfy the needs?

What probing questions do you or will you ask to determine needs? What customer objections will we hear on this call, and how will we overcome them? Will there be an objection on price, delivery, space, content, a bad past experience, no budget?

I ride with twenty-five salespeople a year from many different industries. I always ask, "Tell me about the personal interests of the people we are calling on." I always ask for last and first names of key contacts. We buy from experts and friends. Generally, however, too many salespeople cannot answer these questions.

As a sales manager, always look at the customer profile and file, whether hard copy, digital, or hybrid. Is the salesperson accumulating appropriate customer information on usage, history, needs, opportunities, long-term goals, weekly activities, decision makers, and decision-making process.

End your field training precall planning by discussing what happened on the last call, how long this visit should take (thirty minutes or all day), what role you as the sales manager will play, and how you will be introduced. For new salespeople, you may wish to make the sales presentation with a few customers, then allow the salesperson the opportunity to do it. The new salesperson will learn from watching you in action, from critiquing your approach, and from your analysis of his or her performance.

With seasoned salespeople, let them make the presentations unless otherwise agreed upon, but define your role. You may occasionally help or be a silent partner. An experienced salesperson may ask you for specialized assistance selling a particular product/service or type of account. In this case, you would make the call as an expert, but allow the salesperson to show what he or she has learned by making the presentation on a similar account.

Because your presence could make your salespeople uncomfortable, before the call express confidence in their ability. This sets them at ease. One sales manager found that her salespeople often locked keys in their cars when they traveled together because they were so nervous.

Sometimes major customers or prospects prefer to be sold by management. Similarly, when you call on management rather than on the buyer, purchasing agent, or design engineer, a presentation by sales management or a dual presentation by you and your salesperson may be preferred. Dual presentations allow you and the salesperson to share the responsibility so that no customer need or benefit is missed. Discuss with your salesperson before the call who will make the presentation and what your role will be. Again, discuss how you will be introduced—as an associate, as the sales manager, or in some other capacity. Customers are complimented by the sales manager's presence, but then sometimes the conversation is directed toward you rather than to the salesperson.

During the sales call, when the salesperson makes the presentation, try not to interfere; however, if you must inject something, be gentle. You accompany the salesperson on this call primarily for training purposes, not necessarily to write an order. Salespeople learn from failures as well as from successes. If you interfere, the buyer becomes confused and the salesperson embarrassed, which strains the relationships. You may gain an order but lose a customer and a salesperson. You may travel with a particular salesperson for 4 days annually, but remember that on the other 236 he or she travels alone. When the sales manager sells for the sales force, the sales force stops selling.

Often, salespeople prefer that you take over on a field trip. It takes them off the hook. However, keep in mind that while your instinct in front of a customer is to sell, the purpose of this trip is training.

When you must interrupt, use a question to make the point indirectly. For example, if the salesperson suggests the wrong model, ask if the customer might also be interested in the correct model. If the salesperson concentrates on price when another benefit should be emphasized, ask if the customer might wish to have the other benefit explained.

If the customer directs questions to you, turn them over to the salesperson. Sit farther away from the buyer than your salesperson does. Take yourself out of the conversation. Lean back rather than forward in your chair. During a joint sales call never speak to the customer/prospect as "executive-to-executive" or do anything else to make the salesperson feel less than equal in the customer's presence. Maintain the chain of command, or customers may start contacting you directly for concessions. Don't volunteer concessions to a prospect/customer simply because you have the authority. Avoid "piling on" when the salesperson is trying to close.

Many sales managers ride with salespeople for the purpose of field coaching, but don't know what to look for during the sales call. For example, the sales manager should note the following:

- Does the salesperson establish a rapport with the customer by discussing personal interests from the profile before asking probing questions about the business?
- Does he or she demonstrate knowledge of the decision makers, influencers, and the decision-making process?
- Does the salesperson demonstrate knowledge of the customer's business, operations, competitors, key drivers, and usage of his or her product or service?
- Does the salesperson ask probing questions to identify key problems, needs, and opportunities?
- Does the salesperson suggest solutions, products, and services?
- Does he or she properly present features, benefits, and proof?
- Does he or she quantify benefits in dollars?
- Does the salesperson actively listen?
- Does he or she overcome objections?
- Does he or she appear well organized by using sales aids?
- Does the salesperson use a reference sell?

- Does he or she act like a consultant, think like a customer?
- Does he or she properly ask for the desired action (possibly an order or a trial)?
- Does the salesperson establish the next action (another meeting or samples)?

As a sales manager, know what you are looking for, set standards, be critical, and sit in judgment. Exhibit 3.10 is an example of a field coaching salesperson evaluation. Use this list of topics and format or one like it to help set standards, be critical, and sit in judgment.

After each work-with sales call, do a post-call critique or analysis before driving to the next customer. A good salesperson will eventually employ self-analysis after each sales call, but to help develop this faculty, ask the salesperson how he or she felt about the call. What went well? What went poorly? Were the call objectives met? They will do most of the work for you in the assessment. Agree on follow-up actions and objectives for the next call on this customer.

After this self-analysis, share your thoughts on the strengths and weaknesses of the presentation. If you first tell the salesperson what was done right, it will be easier for him or her to accept criticism on what was done wrong. Reinforce skills used effectively. Review the extent to which call objectives were met. Give the salesperson credit for any positive accomplishments, including writing the order or agreeing to the next step. Your comments should be logically organized, easy to understand, and action-oriented so that corrective steps can be taken on the next call. You will obtain best results through analyzing major issues rather than by outright criticism or by trying to cover too many areas. The fewer the messages, the better they will be understood. Use questions to make points. "Do you think you emphasized their lease plan enough?" To emphasize points, do some role-playing before the next call. Salespeople are self-conscious and often not at their best when accompanied by their sales manager. You must factor this into your evaluation.

After the call, what information, if any, did the salesperson add to the customer's profile? Ask the salesperson, "What did you learn about the business and the person?" Generally, their response is less than adequate. Then add your own list of items, discuss the list, and ask for agreement. Hopefully, the salesperson will observe and note such information when you are not there.

At the end of each field coaching day, summarize key issues with the salesperson. Ask the salesperson how many hours and what percent of the time was spent in front of the customers. On a work-with, "eyeball time" versus "windshield time" drives results. Generally, salespeople overestimate the actual customer/selling hours. For each account/call, keep track of

E x h i b i t   3.10

Field coaching—Salesperson evaluation.

Name: _____

Date: _____

SUCCESS PROFILE

This report gives an overview of the major factors associated with good sales performance. Each factor is evaluated on the "Performance Scale" from poor to excellent on the graph below. Additional information and personal recommendations for improvement are provided in the paragraphs that follow.

	Poor	Fair/Avg.	Good	Excellent
Product Knowledge				
Account Knowledge				
Presentation				
Preparation for Calls				
Knowledge of Customers' Needs				
Visits have Purpose				
Proposal Was Made ❑ Yes ❑ No				
Personal Rapport with Customer				
Questioning Technique				
Reporting				
Records				
Call Frequency				
Appearance				
Closing Skills				
Comfort Level				
Attitude				
Working with Others				
Gross Sales				
Gross Margins				
Overall Performance				

◄——— PERFORMANCE SCALE ———►

EVALUATION AND PERSONAL RECOMMENDATIONS

Primary areas needing improvement are listed below. Refer to the following pages of this report for more specific information and recommendations for improving your job performance.

❑ _____

❑ _____

❑ _____

❑ _____

❑ _____

❑ _____

actual time spent toe-to-toe. Point out the actual hours versus the salesperson's perception. This creates self-awareness on how few hours and what a small percent of a salesperson's time is actually spent with customers. This allows you an opportunity to summarize the day's activities in terms of number of calls, markets, customers, and products focused on. This also gives you an opportunity to discuss which of the agreed-upon work-with objectives were met.

Next, ask the salesperson how far you drove today and for the odometer reading. You should casually note the odometer at the beginning of the day. Generally, salespeople grossly underestimate driving miles. You should point out the importance of customer face time versus car windshield time. For some sales jobs, this represents a key issue; for others, it is less appropriate.

Next, have salespeople evaluate themselves using the Field Coaching Salesperson Evaluation Profile shown in Exhibit 3.10. Then, using the same format, evaluate them and together agree on goals, objectives, and a development plan. Include this in your follow-up letter.

Last, ask, "What did you get out of our time together?" This question asks salespeople to evaluate the field training, plus it allows you another opportunity to summarize key issues. Most likely, the answer will be similar to "I learned about my need for more probing questions, better product knowledge, and more accurate customer profiles." To this you might answer, "Did you also get a better understanding of overcoming objections and competitor knowledge?" However, be prepared for candid answers such as "Not very much, but I enjoyed your company and the free lunch."

When you return to the home office and write to the salesperson, you can both acknowledge certain strengths and remind him or her of specific weaknesses. Make sure the memo includes agreed-on action, objectives, and a time frame for correcting these weaknesses.

The sales manager for a seed company uses a "Work-With Checklist" (Exhibit 3.11) to assist in properly performing field coaching.

SALES MEETINGS

Periodic, well-planned sales meetings provide a productive format for communication, motivation and training. The basic purposes of a sales meeting are as follows:

- To provide continuing training to sales personnel
- To offer a forum for sharing problems and successes by salespeople and management
- To make salespeople feel useful, important, and part of something larger

Exhibit 3.11

Seed company work-with checklist.

BEFORE EACH CALL—PRECALL PLANNING

- Establish objectives—for example, to write an order for a new variety of cuttings or seeds or sell a seasonal product such as poinsettias.
- Discuss what items competition sells to customer and why. What percentage of their business does our firm have?
- Agree on a strategy for reaching the objective—for example, sampling, discussing markups, merchandising, and techniques for closing.
- Discuss customer problems and needs.
- Discuss possible customer objections (for example, no production space) and how to overcome them (what is your slowest-selling variety?). Examine the "what ifs." What could go wrong?
- Agree on customer's personal interests to open conversation with and probing questions to discover needs.
- Review customer file, account history, usage sheet, and profile.
- Establish what role regional sales manager will play.
- Discuss what happened on the last visit and how long this call should take.
- Discuss long-term goals for this account.

DURING EACH CALL, DID THE SALES REPRESENTATIVE:

- Establish rapport with a few minutes of nonbusiness personal-interest conversation? Build relationship? Use information from profile?
- Know the names of decision makers and influencers?
- Review the usage sheet and what happened on last visit?
- Look at what is being grown (production space) and brought (competitors)?
- Suggest items?
- Properly show a new product, a new variety of a present product, a seasonal product, or an existing product not presently carried by the customer?
- Ask questions to get the customer talking and discover needs/problems/ opportunities? What percentage of the time did the salesperson talk versus listen?
- Make benefit statements about the product using power words (Can save you time, waste, money. Increase margins, customer satisfaction, shelf life, and so on)?
- Quantify benefits in dollars?
- Answer any technical questions?
- Answer objections?
- Appear well organized? Focus on strengths?
- Use a reference sell and sales aids?
- Act as a consultant? Think like the customer?
- Properly ask for new business? For instance:
  - Review what was agreed on

E x h i b i t   3.11 (continued)

- Make partnership statement
- Offer a choice
- Establish next action? (For example, "I will bring a sample or picture next week.")
- Work on growing our products with greenhouse supervisor?
- If appropriate, discuss overdue invoices or credit application?

AFTER EACH CALL — POST-CALL ANALYSIS

- Ask each sales representative what went well and what went poorly.
- Did he/she achieve their objective?
- What did he/she find out about the customer to add to the profile?
- Add your observations of what went well and poorly, and what to add to the profile.
- Ask for the salesperson's objectives and strategy for the next call on this customer. What are the long-range goals and future opportunities?
- What follow-up action is needed with customer? What corrective action is needed for sales representative?
- Estimate the actual amount of time spent with customer.

AT THE END OF EACH RIDE WITH DAY

- Estimate how many hours you and the sales representative spent in front of customers versus in the car versus on the phone. Discuss how time in front of customers might be increased and made more productive. Compare mileage out in morning to final mileage at end of day.
- Evaluate the sales representative 1, 2, 3, 4 (1 is best) on each area of this checklist. Have the sales representative evaluate him/herself. Discuss each area.
- Summarize the day. Number of calls, number of cold calls, markets, and products focused on.
- Review with the sales representative corrective action based on your discussion of this checklist and a timetable for implementation.
- Send a follow-up letter putting this in writing.
- Ask how you were helpful.

- To give salespeople recognition for their achievements or motivation through peer pressure to perform
- To allow salespeople personally to meet management
- To give management a chance to disseminate policy to the sales force
- To provide an opportunity for management to visit salespeople with minimum travel

Contrary to popular belief, being a field salesperson is a lonely job full of disappointments and rejections. The sales meeting helps assure salespeople that someone cares. They arrive dusty and tired from the commercial battlefield, and with luck and intelligent planning, they leave refreshed, enthusiastic, and ready for new challenges.

Sales meetings strongly influence salespeople's image of the company, which they pass on to customers. It is therefore very important that they leave feeling upbeat. Have you ever had an unsuccessful sales meeting? What effect did it have on your short-term sales?

To justify the cost, time, and energy involved, the specific objectives of your sales meeting must be well thought out. These objectives must reinforce your marketing plan. Holding a meeting because you had one last week, last month, or last year does not constitute a justifiable objective. You need a more concrete reason. Decide in advance what you specifically hope to achieve, and then carefully plan toward those goals. The objectives might include a combination of

- Introducing a new product or service
- Alleviating tensions between the sales force and management
- Explaining a sales contest, forecast form, appraisal form or new compensation plan
- Convincing the sales force that the company can stay in business
- Analyzing the competition
- Opening new accounts
- Retaining or expanding old accounts
- Discussing sales force automation
- Improving selling techniques
- Improving collections
- Obtaining leads
- Managing time better
- Defining new territory boundaries
- Discussing safety or legal issues

Open-ended sales meetings don't work. If you don't have an objective and an agenda, you shouldn't have a sales meeting. Many sales managers have weekly or even daily sales meetings to review each person's results. In my opinion, this is better done in individual meetings. Ask salespeople what they would like to discuss at their sales meetings. They know what is needed.

Sometimes, even with proper objectives, these functions become stale and monotonous. At that point everyone needs a rest. If you feel the meetings no longer achieve their goals, change the format or stop convening them for a while.

Time is limited and subject matter must be applicable to the entire group. Group training loses its effectiveness unless all participants share a similar level of proficiency. Training the most experienced salesperson with the least experienced and the strong performer with the weak often dilutes results. The material may be too challenging for the least experienced and weaker salespeople and not challenging enough for the most experienced and stronger salespeople. For certain training, you may remedy this problem by forming subgroups at the sales meeting.

Many sales managers strongly dislike sales meetings because there they can't control the salespeople, who outnumber them. Also, they must listen to salespeople's complaints and accept criticism in front of the entire group. A good sales manager, however, will be sensitive to complaints and criticisms and welcome them because they generally contain important messages.

Turn this potential problem into an opportunity by devoting limited time in the middle of your meeting to complaints and criticisms that concern the entire group. Salespeople need a forum in which to express their frustrations, and if they know their "day in court" will arrive, the rest of the meeting will be more productive. A salesperson who presents a problem must also present a possible solution. Criticisms and problems raised by salespeople require a management response now or in the future. Criticisms or problems that don't involve all the salespeople can be handled at individual meetings.

Sales meetings can be made more interesting by having salespeople present certain topics and even run the meeting. Salespeople learn best through proactive, interactive group discussion, and sharing best practices, successes, and problems—not through lecture-type presentations by management. They believe each other a lot more readily than they believe management. Encourage all salespeople to participate in the discussion by asking questions.

The sales manager for a dental equipment firm assigns one salesperson to manage each sales meeting, which represents the ultimate of salesperson participation. That salesperson suggests the agenda and presenters for the manager's review. Once approved, the salesperson is responsible for content and delivery. At this company, salespeople pay special attention to sales meetings because responsibility for the meeting rotates among salespeople and they may run the next one. Salespeople who present at or run sales meetings feel useful, important, and worthwhile. Rewarding high performers with responsibility for sales meetings motivates them to achieve even greater results.

Similarly, the sales manager for a financial services software firm runs the sales meetings but has salespeople present topics on selling skills, prospecting, or product, customer, and competitor knowledge. Often he chooses the salesperson with the best performance record to present a topic, but sometimes weaker salespeople are chosen in an effort to improve their skills.

To make their sales meetings more interesting, an aircraft navigational instrumentation firm invites a customer to each sales meeting. The customer speaks for twenty minutes on how he or she selects a vendor in that industry and the salesperson's role in influencing that selection. The next forty minutes consists of questions and answers from the sales force, which allows salespeople to have a candid, nonthreatening discussion about their job with a customer. This company invites customers from various market segments; invites a variety of decision makers, engineers, and controllers; invites firms not sold by them; and invites previous customers who no longer buy. Careful selection of customers proves important. Most customers are complimented by the opportunity. One year the sales meeting was held at their largest customer's facility. The agenda included a plant tour and presentations by many decision makers and influencers. Major customers may have interest in this type of partnering.

To begin on a positive note, the sales manager for an independent digital and voice telephone firm starts her sales meetings by asking salespeople to tell a success story or a problem-solving story. The stories might involve opening a difficult new account, saving a problem customer, resolving a conflict, adding an additional service to a major customer, or beating out a major competitor. Salespeople compete to tell their success stories in front of their peers, and meetings start on an upbeat note.

To create competition, the sales manager for a giftware firm uses sales meetings for scoreboarding. Each month she ranks the fifty salespeople from one to fifty based on attainment of their year-to-date revenue forecast. The salesperson most above forecast is number one, and the salesperson most below forecast is number fifty. The rankings are changed monthly and are posted on the firm's intranet. Number one runs faster to stay ahead of number two. Salespeople work hard to avoid remaining in the bottom ten. At each sales meeting, salespeople sit according to their ranking. At lunch all salespeople above forecast get fish or meat and those below forecast get franks and beans. Everyone has fun with the concept.

The regional sales managers for a semiconductor equipment firm organized their agendas so that they devote a portion of each quarterly sales meeting to product knowledge, selling skills, current customer issues, changes at competition, administration, and territory management. Each regional manager announces the dates and agendas for the next four quarterly meetings in January. This procedure forces the sales managers to plan in advance and have a balanced agenda.

The sales manager for a reform math textbook firm reinforces some aspect of selling skills at each meeting. For example, she devoted a portion of one meeting to discussing probing questions, another to best practices for obtaining an appointment, presentation skills, overcoming objections, and closing. She used the techniques discussed early in the chapter under "Selling Skills."

Having competitors' products, product lines, service brochures, or service agreements at a meeting generates a lively and informative discussion. You might assign each salesperson or a team one competitive product or service to analyze for the group. In such a discussion, be sure the sales force understands both the firm's competitive strengths and weaknesses. Just concentrating on strengths does not prepare a salesperson for the realities of the marketplace. Earlier in this chapter, we discussed how competitive grids could be used at a sales meeting to teach competitive knowledge. If you employ a salesperson who has worked for a competitor, he or she might volunteer to present that competitor's products/services.

To create a variety of presenters and control costs, a food service distributor asked a different supplier to present their line at each sales meeting. Your suppliers and vendors represent inexpensive trainers for sales meetings and field coaching. Be sure to limit their time at sales meetings and give them a list of topics to be covered. Suppliers and vendors emphasize product knowledge but often forget how this helps to make a sale. Topics should include target customers, competition, features, benefits, and proof. For example, are the frozen desserts targeted at country clubs or company cafeterias, who is the competition, and why should customers buy the product?

You might also take your salespeople to visit a vendor facility. For instance, a furniture retailer took her salespeople to visit a different company supplier each month. Often this included touring the manufacturing facility.

Skits and role-playing that enact customer–salesperson interchanges represent powerful, realistic, nonthreatening learning techniques at sales meetings. One salesperson takes the role of the customer, while the other plays himself or herself. Use a script to describe the particulars of the situation. For example, you have neglected to call on this account regularly or the purchasing agent has recently been approached by a particular competitor. Pick two people who will take the task seriously, and allow them to rehearse. Use a tape recorder or video camera and occasionally stop, critique, and replay the action. Then, after the role-play or during the playback, ask for analysis and comments from the group.

A variation of this role-play is to assign three people to each group. One person plays the customer, another the salesperson, and the third observes and comments. Roles are rotated. After each of three role-plays, each with a different scenario, the participants view the video and discuss what went well and poorly.

An electronic subcontract assembler of PC boards has their purchasing agent play the customer. Occasionally, this firm asks a customer design engineer to act as the customer. Videotapes of their role play are given to salespeople for review.

Salespeople often dislike role-play, but it represents the best non-threatening way to simulate an actual sales situation. Furthermore, when salespeople know role-play is part of the agenda, their attention level increases. The techniques described above make role-play fun, lower salesperson resistence to it, force them to take it seriously, and thus make it more valuable.

With a group of senior salespeople, brainstorming can produce creative ideas and motivate your high performers. For instance, say you see an unfilled need in the marketplace for a small business waste disposal service. You ask your waste disposal salespeople if they perceive the same need. If so, how could it be structured, presented, and priced?

A new trend in sales meetings involves the use of computer-software-generated games which simulate sales situations. The computer plays the customer, asking for, evaluating, and responding to different combinations of prices, product mix, delivery, and customization. Customized board games can also provide this experience. Salespeople can see the impact of their decisions on company revenues, costs, and margins.

A continuing trend at sales meetings involves salespeople solving problems in groups to promote team building. All these techniques make sales meetings more interesting for the participants.

Films, videotapes, or guest speakers discussing such topics as selling techniques, motivation, collections, good listening habits, time management, or prospecting can spice up your meetings. Video Arts, Xerox Learning Systems, American Medica Inc., Training Store, and Films Inc. all rent and sell films and videotapes. Most local telephone companies and utilities offer free guest speakers for sales meetings.

A salesperson's customers are both inside and outside the company. So, at each meeting, devote some time to a presentation and discussion of company functions outside of selling, such as quality, operations, manufacturing, human resources, credit, transportation, and deliveries. Use other members of your company's management team to present appropriate topics. For instance, invite the credit manager or controller to talk about collections, the manufacturing or operations manager to discuss quality, your boss to talk about pricing, a supplier to talk about features and benefits, and a channel partner to talk about target markets. These outside speakers often offer a fresh perspective.

Many sales managers invite inside sales and customer support personnel to attend all or some of the sales meeting. For companies with career ladders into sales, this is especially appropriate and inexpensive.

If your firm uses channel partners, either invite them to the direct sales force sales meeting or hold a separate meeting for them. As mentioned earlier, well-trained channel partners have many benefits.

An upbeat way to end a sales meeting is by recognizing certain salespeople for their outstanding performance and/or by presenting awards. You might present the salesperson-of-the-month award, announce contest results, present bonus checks, or thank a salesperson in front of the group for opening a major new account. Often at multiday national sales meetings, this is done at an awards dinner.

At the end of each sales meeting section or topic, hand salespeople a short test on the subject matter. After completing the test, hand them the answers and ask for their scores. The best score receives a small, fun prize. The answers codify what they have learned. The test reminds salespeople what the meeting's objectives are and rewards them for paying attention.

At the end of each sales meeting or each day of a multiday event, ask people to evaluate what went well and what went poorly, and to submit ideas for improvement. Ask salespeople to rate the subject, the presenter, and what they learned.

Sales meetings fail when administrative matters receive more time than selling matters, when one or more salespeople dominate the meeting, when trivial matters encroach on more important subjects, when management threatens and criticizes salespeople rather than training them, when the format consists of lectures rather than discussion, when participants do not share a similar level of proficiency, when there is no agenda, and when the meeting takes too long. Do not devote more than 25 percent of a meeting to administrative matters such as proper order writing, credit and collection, sales reports, expense reports, or putting enough postage on order envelopes.

Do not allow any salesperson, whether superstar or laggard, to turn the meeting into a personal speaking platform. Remind these people that you have scheduled individual meetings to discuss individual problems. Also, involve people who have not participated by asking them questions. You must run the meeting and not let the meeting run you.

Do not let the discussion digress into unimportant aspects of important matters. When a salesperson notes that the welding seam in your new ultrasonic cleaning tank rises 1/2 inch rather than 1/4 inch, remind this person that the new tank degreases customer components at half the cost in half the time of any competitive product.

Criticize in private; praise in public. Some sales managers feel obligated to start a sales meeting by telling their salespeople how bad they are. This creates a real turn-off and does not support the purpose of the meeting. You are blaming both the strong and the weak performers and at the same time limiting the meeting's training and motivational benefits. Instead, start the meeting by asking a salesperson to share a success story.

As mentioned earlier, group meetings can also lose their effectiveness when all participants do not share a similar level of proficiency. Mixing the most experienced salespeople with the least experienced and training the strong performers with the weak can dilute the results. For certain subjects, you can remedy this problem by forming subgroups at the sales meeting.

When the entire sales force resides locally and overnight accommodations are not necessary, meetings can be held frequently, but for short periods of time. For example, meetings could be held on the first Saturday of every other month or the last Friday afternoon of each month or every Monday morning. For local sales forces, sales meetings should be held no more frequently than once a week and no less frequently than once a month, and they should last two to six hours. If most customers can't be seen Friday afternoons, have your meetings then. If each week you offer new services, have a meeting on Monday mornings.

When the sales force lives a plane trip away, economics necessitate less frequent but longer meetings. In such instances, two- to three-day gatherings once or twice a year, or possibly every other year, generally provide the best use of time and money. In the twenty-first century, teleconferencing via phones and video will supplement in-person sales meetings for the national sales force. Many sales managers use weekly conference calls for discussing best practices, which, again, supplements formal sales meetings.

Annual, semiannual, or biennial sales meetings requiring several days should be scheduled during slack periods or at the start of a selling cycle. You don't want to remove a salesperson from his or her territory during a peak selling period. For example, many menswear manufacturers and book publishers schedule sales meetings in early December, because at this time retailers are too busy to see salespeople and January begins a new wholesale selling season.

Sales meetings can consist of formal group meetings, formal individual meetings, informal social gatherings, official social functions, or some combination of these. Participants should receive an agenda before they arrive, so that everyone will know where to be, when to be there, what material is going to be covered, the objectives of the meeting and what preparation is necessary. The agenda might state that once a formal group meeting has begun, you will lock the doors until break time. This eliminates a tendency for people to use the phones, straggle in, and thus interrupt the gathering. You'll find that once you initiate the locked door policy, no one arrives late.

Whether you conduct three-day sales meetings twice a year, one-day sales meetings six times a year, half-day sales meetings monthly, or two-hour meetings weekly, you should allocate from 60 to 80 percent of your time to all formal group matters. The company president and other top management should attend some of these formal group meetings.

In these sessions, management and senior salespeople introduce and everyone discusses subjects such as:

- New or problematic products, services or programs
- Opening new accounts or account retention
- Price increases
- Collections
- Company policies and organization
- Selling techniques
- Overcoming objections
- Time management
- Software, sales force automation, laptops, and customer relationship management
- Obtaining qualified leads and appointments
- Sales promotions
- Advertising
- Competition
- Sales contests and compensation plans
- Evaluation forms, forecast, and budget procedures

The subject matter must be applicable to the entire group and capable of being meaningfully presented in the time allotted. For example, a discussion of individual customers would not involve the entire group and would therefore be an inappropriate subject. The topic should be discussed at individual meetings. Likewise, selling in general represents too broad a topic, whereas selling benefits or opening new accounts or qualifying leads could be handled in ninety minutes.

If you manage a far-flung national or international sales force and meetings are held annually or semiannually, you may want to schedule individual meetings with each salesperson or at least some salespeople.

Here you share concerns that do not affect the entire group. Have a list of items you wish to discuss, and don't let the meeting digress into trivia or small talk.

At such an individual meeting, you may wish to discuss a change in personnel at a customer's or a prospect's company that requires a visit. You may have brought for discussion expense reports, call reports, or a customer analysis containing puzzling information. The salesperson may wish to discuss fears that a competitor has added more service people in the territory.

Do not use these individual conferences at sales meetings for formal compensation reviews or formal performance evaluations. Such procedures require more than an hour and considerable preparation, and they conflict with the learning and social atmosphere of a sales meeting. Compensation reviews and performance evaluations deserve separate handling in a different setting.

If your sales force resides locally and you have sales meetings weekly or monthly, you may wish to schedule one or two salesperson meetings around the group event. With a local sales force, individual meetings can be arranged anytime.

Salespeople probably learn more from casual conversations with each other than they do in formal gatherings. So, at annual or semiannual national sales force meetings, afternoons (between formal individual meetings) and evenings should allow opportunities for socializing. When salespeople get together, they do not discuss sports or politics; they discuss their jobs. "Who did you sell what, and how?" Although order sizes inflate by a third, the participants share valuable information. Maintaining a casual atmosphere even with tight scheduling promotes socializing.

Even at its most social moments, the gathering revolves around shoptalk, and for this reason, not to mention the additional costs involved, sales meetings work best without spouses. Also, some spouses resent and feel uncomfortable in the commercial atmosphere of a sales meeting.

After weekly or monthly local sales force meetings, occasionally invite the group to lunch, dinner, golf, bowling, or a social hour. Even local sales forces benefit from the opportunity to socialize.

Official social gatherings range from casual breakfasts or lunches to a more formal dinner at which speeches are made and awards presented. Generally, at a multiday national meeting, participants arrive in time for an opening dinner at which acquaintances are renewed, management delivers a welcoming address, and everyone unwinds. During dinner on the second evening, the president presents a state-of-the-company address, and this becomes another opportunity for management and the sales force to socialize. The state-of-the-company address gives some insight into the "big picture," enlightening the sale force as to overall corporate performance and plans for the future.

A sales force that knows management on a personal basis becomes more involved: "I had dinner with the president of my company. He knew who I was. He is a pleasant fellow, and certainly has his hands full." A management team that knows the sales organization on a personal basis has more empathy. The company president might comment, "After spending several evenings with the sales force, I more fully appreciate their problems in reopening accounts we have lost because of late shipments. The salespeople are a noisy bunch, but they work hard at a difficult job."

After dinner on the second evening, the company president presents awards for outstanding performance and prizes to winners of the sales contests. Outstanding performers should be officially recognized by management in front of their peers. If possible, have an employee take photographs of these events and mail copies to the participants.

Several times a year, after local sales force meetings, invite participants to a formal social gathering, usually lunch or dinner, with upper management. The benefits and format are the same as those for national sales meetings.

Hopefully, everyone returns home from the sales meeting with renewed vigor and pleasant feelings. The sales force has learned, participated, and enjoyed. The company has said, "Thank you for doing a fine job" by attending to their needs and showing them a good time. A successful sales meeting is a celebration that strongly influences the salespeople's image of their company, which they pass on to your customers.

QUESTIONS AND EXERCISES

- Prepare a training checklist and a training agenda for your sales force or a sales force you are familiar with.
- Prepare competitive grids for your various product lines and markets or for product lines and markets you are familiar with.
- Prepare the format for a customer profile.
- Prepare the agendas for your next four sales meetings.

SALES MANAGERS' MAJOR WEAKNESSES/MISTAKES

TRAINING

- No checklist or agenda
- Not devoting enough time; overdelegating
- Using ride-withs to do personal selling, not training
- Using sales meetings for results and administrative matters, not training
- Not customizing training to each salesperson's needs
- Not enough hands-on training and outside training
- Too much product training, and not enough customer, competitor, and sales skills training

CHAPTER 4

Sales Force Compensation

As mentioned in an earlier chapter, to attract, retrain, and motivate the best salespeople, you should pay them more than they are worth. Then using proper techniques for hiring, training, organization, deployment, planning, nonmonetary motivation, evaluations, and automation, you should make these well-paid salespeople worth more than what you pay them. However, remember that money is not a universal incentive. Salespeople reach complacency plateaus and comfort zones. In the twenty-first century, salespeople have two-income families and other income-producing assets such as real estate, stocks, and bonds. Also, career salespeople who have no interest in management or no opportunity for management require nonmonetary motivation.

Sales force compensation involves deciding how much your successful salespeople should earn in total dollars and then what portion of that total should be fixed versus performance pay. Total compensation depends on the complexity of the salesperson's selling tasks. The mix between performance and fixed pay depends on: (1) balancing salesperson and company needs, (2) the type of salesperson you wish to attract, (3) the salesperson's influence on the sale, (4) the type product/service sold, and (5) rewarding the salesperson's specific actions/results most important to the company's success. Sales force compensation involves not only salary, commission, and bonus, but fringe benefits and reimbursed expenses.

A company's sales force compensation plan communicates to salespeople where management wants them to focus, but this compensation plan may not change salespeople's behavior. For example, a nonresidential, commercial security service offered customers smoke and motion detectors plus window sensors. The firm paid salespeople a higher commission and bonus for leases rather than outright purchases, for renewal of central monitoring contracts, and for new accounts. However, salespeople did little prospecting for new accounts, contract renewals remained low, and leases were seldom offered. This firm did not properly hire and train salespeople for these tasks, and although the compensation program gave a strong message on where to concentrate, the salespeople did not alter their behavior. A good compensation plan loses its effectiveness when applied to a weak or badly trained sales force.

Some managers abdicate their sales management responsibility by rationalizing that the compensation system will direct all salespeople's behavior. The ultimate example of this are companies that compensate salespeople on 100 percent performance pay, which may be a commission based on revenue or margins. In such a situation, the manager often does not spend enough time and thought hiring, training, planning, motivating, or evaluating salespeople, claiming that 100 percent commission will self-select the right people and self-direct them to work hard/smart, train, and evaluate themselves. These are dangerous assumptions.

Each year successful sales managers reevaluate the sales force compensation program. As stressed throughout this book, business is a dynamic process; the future is a moving target. In this century the landscape changes quickly and often. As an agent of change, the sales manager must expect and manage change. If you were to totally reconstruct the compensation program, would it look the same? In the last year, how have your products, customers, competitors, technology, salespeople, strategy, the sales cycle, the customer decision-making process, and prices changed? Does the compensation program reflect these changes? Since a compensation system acts as a natural filter in attracting and retaining salespeople, annual changes should be modest rather than dramatic. Increasing compensation for a new product or revenue growth while decreasing it on matured products or previous revenue levels represents acceptable adjustments. Going from 100 percent salary to 100 percent commission will create confusion and salesperson turnover. Admitting the mistake by changing back to the original program proves difficult, like putting toothpaste back in the tube.

The compensation system is often a legacy issue that is inherited from a predecessor, is continued year after year, follows industry tradition, or is copied from a competitor. A follow-the-loser strategy does not work in the type of dynamic environment described in the previous paragraph.

TYPES OF SALES FORCE COMPENSATION

Salespeople receive direct compensation, fringe benefits, and reimbursed expenses as part of their total pay package. Direct compensation consists of fixed pay (salary), performance pay (commission), and deferred performance pay (bonus). Fringe benefits range from mandatory Social Security, Medicare, and unemployment insurance to required medical and health plans to optional profit sharing, stock options, and tuition reimbursement. Reimbursed expenses range from salespeople paying their own expenses to employers sharing of these costs to total salesperson reimbursement on all travel, entertainment, communication, and office expenses. The key is giving salespeople an economic incentive to spend wisely. This chapter deals with all these alternatives in some detail.

TOTAL COMPENSATION

In constructing a compensation program, you first decide the total dollars of compensation for a successful or top salesperson. Your next decision is dividing those dollars between fixed and performance pay. The total compensation appropriate for a successful salesperson is determined by the complexity of the sale and type of selling. You define a successful salesperson as someone who ranks in the top 25 percent of your sales force in terms of results (annual dollars of sales or margin and growth).

A successful or top salesperson involved in a long, complex, multistep, consultative, partnership sales process should receive over $100,000 annually in total direct compensation regardless of the mix between fixed and performance pay. As discussed in Chapter 2 under "Buyer Behavior," salespeople selling enterprisewide supply chain software and services, B2B ecommerce sites, or telephone systems, all of which involve long complex sales cycles, generally receive total annual direct compensation in excess of $100,000. Such a salesperson often sells a product/service to a one-time, first-time, new systems buyer.

A successful salesperson involved in multilevel relationship sales, which includes modified rebuys of existing systems, which may require some post-sale service generally receives $60,000 to $100,000 annually in total direct compensation regardless of the mix between fixed and performance pay. Salespeople selling equipment and supplies to dentists, tires to truck fleet managers, semiconductors to consumer electronic firms, contract programming to IT managers, home health care to hospitals, or pharmaceuticals to doctors generally receive annual direct compensation between $60,000 and $100,000.

A successful salesperson involved in route sales of a homogeneous product/service requiring a multitude of daily customer visits, feature selling, and order taking from a person delegated by the buyer's decision maker generally receives under $60,000 a year in total direct compensation, regardless of the mix between fixed and performance pay. Salespeople selling and servicing grocery stores with food products, drugstores with giftware, midsized businesses with temporary help services, and manufacturers with die-casting or injecting molding products generally receive annual direct compensation under $60,000.

Where does your firm fit, and does total direct compensation reflect these criteria? Is there a disconnect? If so, why? Can it be corrected?

Most firms have salespeople in at least two of these classifications. Should they be paid differently depending on the type of selling and complexity of the sale? Most firms also have salespeople whose duties include several levels of complexity, but one remains more dominant.

Some managers claim that the higher the dollars of direct compensation, the more control they exercise over their salespeople's behavior. Other managers claim that the higher fixed pay as a percent of total compensation, the more control they exercise over their salespeople. Many managers who should pay more performance compensation to reward specific results important to the success of their firms rationalize not doing this by claiming such actions would reduce their influence over the salesperson. Is salesperson loyalty and control a function of dollars of total compensation or fixed versus performance pay? My experience points to total dollars of compensation, allowing the manager to more easily direct a salesperson.

The ECS Report on Sales and Marketing Personnel Compensation, 1999/2000, published by Watson Wyatt Data Services, Rochelle Park, New Jersey, surveyed 2141 organizations and collected data on 100,944 job holders. The report is over 800 pages long. Exhibit 4.1 presents some highlights on total cash compensation and mix by buyer type.

In September 1999, *Sales & Marketing Management* magazine reported total cash compensation for different levels of salespeople involved in transactional sales, value-added sales, solution sales, and feature/benefit sales. Exhibit 4.2 presents the results, which do not support accepted compensation theory discussed in this chapter.

CHOOSING THE CORRECT MIX BETWEEN PERFORMANCE AND FIXED PAY

The mix between performance and fixed pay depends on: (1) balancing salesperson and company needs, (2) the type of salesperson you wish to attract, (3) the salesperson's influence on the sale, (4) the type product/service sold, and (5) rewarding the salesperson's specific actions/results most important to the company's success.

The correct mix between performance and fixed direct compensation must reflect the company's and salespeople's needs. Basically, the company needs to attract, retain, and motivate salespeople who produce a desired level of sales at a cost that generates profits and allows necessary percentage returns on sales and invested capital. Good salespeople need a compensation plan that relieves them of basic financial worries, gives them pride in what they earn, reflects their qualifications and experience, and equals or betters that of the competition. Compensating salespeople on the basis of the cost of replacing them—or just the cost of preventing them from leaving—

Exhibit 4.1

Total cash compensation and mix by buyer type.

Buyer Types

	All Buyer Types Combined			Consumer			Industry			Distributor			Retailer			Health Care			Government			Not-for-Profit		
	Base	TCC	Pay Mix	Base	TCC	Pay Mix	Base	TCC	Pay Mix	Base	TCC	Pay Mix	Base	TCC	Pay Mix	Base	TCC	Pay Mix	Base	TCC	Pay Mix	Base	TCC	Pay Mix
Sales Trainee	$35.2	$39.7	47/53	$31.7	$34.6	48/52	$37.5	$40.7	48/52	$39.9	$40.4	50/50	$32.1	$37.7	46/54									
Sales Representative	$39.0	$51.5	43/57	$35.9	$46.6	44/56	$43.8	$56.2	44/56	$39.4	$54.0	42/58	$35.8	$54.0	40/60	$46.9	$65.4	42/58	$40.9	$45.8	47/53			
Senior Sales Representative	$52.9	$70.0	43/57	$47.9	$63.3	43/57	$60.3	$74.1	45/55	$56.3	$74.6	43/57	$48.5	$94.4	34/66	$56.8	$77.9	42/58	$51.9	$61.4	46/54	$54.9	$59.9	48/52
National Accounts Manager	$76.5	$98.2	44/56	$70.8	$102.3	41/59	$83.2	$97.6	46/54	$73.3	$94.5	44/56	$82.0	$94.1	47/53	$72.0	$95.0	43/57						
National Sales Manager	$98.0	$109.9	47/63	$98.0	$104.2	48/52	$99.1	$112.5	47/53	$89.7	$100.0	47/53	$98.0	$105.4	48/52	$97.9	$121.2	45/55						

Total Cash Compensation (TCC) = Base salary plus annual incentive.

All $s are median numbers updated to January 1, 2001.

All $s in thousands.

ECS Report on Sales and Marketing Personnel Compensation

Watson Wyatt Data Services

April 1, 1999

E x h i b i t   4.2

Salespeople's annual total cash compensation.

	Transactional Sales	Value-Added Sales	Solution Sales	Feature/ Benefit Sales
Top Level	137,500	98,800	90,200	86,400
Mid-Level	45,000	66,500	60,100	59,300
Entry-Level	40,000	40,300	43,900	40,500

Sales & Marketing Management, September 1999

Top Level (stars of the sales team)

Mid Level (beginners to more experienced reps)

Entry Level (trainees)

Transactional: Sell on price; product is a commodity.

Value-Added Sales: Solution more important than price.

Solution Sales: Tailored product to client's needs; price is secondary.

Feature/Benefit Sales: Price and features equally important.

Top-level transactional salespeople received the highest dollars of annual cash compensation. However, in the mid-level category, salespeople at companies using a value-added approach earn 33% more than their counterparts at companies selling commodities. Entry-level salespeople earned approximately $40,000 regardless of the product/service sold.

does not satisfy these needs. Generally, you will obtain better results with fewer but more qualified and more highly paid salespeople than you will with a larger sales force that includes less qualified, lower-paid people.

A universal objective for all sales compensation plans ought to be simplicity. Often salespeople do not understand or remember complicated plans and companies have difficulty administering them. A good sales compensation plan must have fairness and equitableness built into it. For example, orders that a salesperson's customers phone, fax, or email directly to the office should be credited to the salespeople's account just as if they had been written in the field. Also, nothing dulls a salesperson's enthusiasm more than "house accounts." Taking lucrative accounts out of a territory for handling by management or family members hurts morale.

Channel conflicts challenge many firms' ability to provide fairness. In the twenty-first century most firms will reach their customers through multiple, hybrid sales channels, including a direct field sales force, telesales, ecommerce/Web sites, distributors, brokers, and independent sales representative organizations. Does the direct field salesperson receive credit and full performance pay for ecommerce, telesales, and distributor orders placed by his or her assigned customers? In such a situation, is performance pay split or reduced? The present trend is to make full performance pay to both parties but establish detailed guidelines on channel conflicts. Most firms accept but do not encourage channel conflict, because though inevitable, it hurts salespeople's morale. When Hewitt Associates LLC surveyed 120 Fortune 1000 firms, 61 percent reported using multiple channels.

A good compensation plan provides a certain level of stability so that salespeople have some downside protection for their incomes. The income of a salesperson who loses a large account might decline by 25 percent, but not by 50 percent or to a level that threatens his or her ability to meet mortgage payments. Such a salesperson requires time to obtain another major account. The income of salespeople selling to cyclical industries such as the auto, aircraft, steel, and farm equipment industries should be less in bad times than in good, but not so much less as to threaten their ability to put food on the table. Such salespeople must survive the bad times in order to write orders when business improves. Rewards must reflect results, but a certain minimum level must be assured.

The mix of performance versus fixed pay acts as a natural filter in attracting certain types of salespeople. Review the candidate profile you prepared for hiring the sales force (see Exhibit 2.3 in Chapter 2). Pay particular attention to the desired personal characteristics. Fixed-pay-oriented compensation plans generally attract salespeople who are team players, ambitious to climb the executive ladder, steady rather than top performers, more professional than commercial, and who prefer presold products. Once hired, salaried salespeople often develop rigid but comfortable routines and often expect considerable sales assistance from management.

Performance pay weighted compensation plans generally attract aggressive career salespeople with no ambition for promotion into management. These salespeople are lone wolves, and top producers, but they are erratic and more interested in the sale than the selling technique. Sometimes these characteristics strain customer and company relations or result in a salesperson who prefers to highlight a large territory rather than saturate a smaller one. Does your firm's compensation plan attract the type of salesperson described in the candidate profile?

The more influence the salesperson has on the sale, the more performance pay should represent as a percent of total direct compensation. Closed biding; requests for quotes (RFQs); branded, presold, heavily advertised goods/services; team selling; rigid product/service specifications; the importance of price—all these things lessen the salesperson's influence on the sale. Also, people selling to government agencies or other businesses that require bids operate in conditions with no adequate measure of performance. Was the salesperson or the bid responsible for the sale? Here again, salary must prove appropriate. How much influence do your salespeople have on the sale and does your compensation plan, fixed versus performance pay, reflect this? A branded men's shirt company with heavily advertised products which are presold by management and occupy a large share of each department store's shelf space pays its salespeople 80 percent salary. Its unbranded competitors, who fight for shelf space and orders, pay salespeople primarily on commission and bonus.

Certain types of products and selling lend themselves to a higher weighting of performance pay, while others lend themselves to more fixed pay. Presold, branded, heavily advertised products/services; cyclical, long, complex sales cycles; higher-ticket items; team selling; and post-sale service all lend themselves to more fixed pay. Nontechnical, unsophisticated products/services with lower unit prices and modified rebuys, which require constant customer revisits for reorders lend themselves to a higher weighting of performance pay. The type product also reflects the salesperson's influence on the sale. When Hewitt Associates LLC surveyed 120 Fortune 1000 firms in 2000, 60 percent reported using broad-based variable/performance pay programs, up from 47 percent in 1998.

For example, sales of durable goods, such as machine tools or equipment for utilities, which fluctuate dramatically with business cycles, require considerable time working with customer engineers, purchasing agents, and plant managers to make a sale, often require the salesperson to be accompanied by a sales engineer, and involve the salesperson's assistance with installation, lend themselves to fixed pay. Machine tools or equipment for public utilities, like many big-ticket technical products, and new systems that involve few orders but many dollars and have long, complex sales cycles lend themselves to salaried sales compensation. Items presold through national advertising, such as pharmaceuticals, soap, toothpaste, liquor, and petroleum, lend themselves to salaried sales compensation. In these situations the salesperson functions as order-taker, not an active seller, and has less influence on the sale. Does your compensation system reflect the type of product or service being sold?

Some new salespeople require salaries during their training period because they could not survive financially on the basis of their performance. Salespeople assigned to new territories with no established business require a salary until they can build up a volume.

REWARDING POSITIVE ACTION AND RESULTS

As mentioned, total dollars of direct compensation must reflect the complexity of the sales process. The mix between performance pay and fixed pay must reflect the general corporate objectives, the type of salesperson you wish to attract, the salesperson's influence on the sale, and the type of product sold. However, equally important, the sales force compensation plan must reward actions and results on the part of salespeople which are most important to the company's success. Salespeople with better results in these key areas must receive superior pay. Most companies' sales force compensation plans do not meet these criteria. Often a disconnect exists between strategic corporate objectives and the activities/results for which salespeople are rewarded. Once a year, review your firm's sales force compensation plan. Does it meet the criterion stated previously? If not, why? What can you change to better align it?

What positive action and results on the part of your salespeople are important to your firm's success? If you plan to reward people for these activities and results, you require metrics to measure them.

Pharmaceutical firms reward salespeople for market share gain in particular medications. Several market research services track prescriptions written by doctors and filled by pharmacists. A bonus is paid for reaching specified levels of market share.

In another example, a reform math K-6-grade textbook firm rewards salespeople for opening new school districts and for further penetrating existing customers. The company pays a bonus on the opening order and a progressive commission rate on revenues generated within a district. As revenues within each district increase, so does the commission rate.

A firm which sells emission control systems to diesel engine manufacturers rewards salespeople for account and territory profitability. For each customer and territory, all direct expenses are subtracted from revenue to arrive at dollars of margin. A commission is paid on these margin dollars.

A food distributor pays its salespeople a progressive commission rate to reward growth. The rate on this year's sales until they meet last year's total is 6 percent. Once a salesperson exceeds this threshold, the commission rate jumps to 8 percent. The food distributor also pays a bonus for collecting overdue accounts receivable. For salespeople with established business, commission often loses its motivational impact. The established business functions like an annuity, and so you require a progressive rate to reward growth.

Utilities, which have difficulty rewarding salespeople based on results, pay a bonus for customer satisfaction as measured by customer surveys. Firms selling to mass merchants often reward salespeople for in-service training of retailers, amount of shelf space, stock taking, or proper merchandising. All these activities lead to a sale.

If salespeople have a pricing window or the discretion to give discounts, allowances, and promotions, a portion of their compensation should be based on dollars of gross margin for their territory. Similarly, if you wish to reward the sale of higher margin items, you might want a compensation system which pays a commission on dollars of gross margin or pays a higher commission rate on revenues of one product line versus another. A semiconductor equipment manufacturer pays a different commission rate for equipment and spare parts sales. It pays a bonus for selling postsale service contracts. A women's apparel manufacturer pays a commission rate on gross margin dollars because salespeople have some discretion to negotiate price.

If your firm has a long, complex sales cycle with many steps from search to purchase, consider paying a bonus for activities that lead to a sale or for moving major customers/prospects from one step to the next. Salespeople selling big-ticket items involving long, complex sales cycles don't respond to rewards based on revenues, because it may take years to make a sale. A financial software firm, that sells real-time data bonuses salespeople based on the number of demos, trials, and presentations. A management consulting firm bonuses salespeople for identifying decision makers, making presentations to CEOs, CFOs, and CIOs, and obtaining requests for proposals.

A home health-care provider wanted its compensation system to reward teamwork. Major branches had a salesperson calling on physicians, another calling on third-party payers, and a third calling on hospitals. All three salespeople received 25 percent of their compensation based on the branch's results using metrics that included the number of patients, product mix, margins, and customer satisfaction.

Many firms reward new product placement through their compensation plan. A salesperson exerts the most influence on a customer's decision during a product/service introduction and the least during a product/service's decline. Some firms pay a higher level and rate of performance pay on new products and a lesser level and rate of performance pay on mature or declining products/markets. For new products/systems sales, a business-to-business software firm rewards salespeople with higher-than-normal commission rates. With growing or maturing software, salespeople receive a commission based on volume and also a bonus based on gross margin dollars. On declining, older software, a small bonus is paid for maintaining gross margin dollars. This compensation system reflects the life cycle of the product or service.

If new product placement represents an important corporate objective, consider rewarding superior results with special compensation. For example, one cruise line continually offers new destinations and tours. Salespeople call on travel agents and receive a commission based on revenue generated from their territory. On their new cruise offerings, the sales manager gives salespeople a "placement" quota based on past history with each travel agent. A certain number of agents must send a certain number of travelers on these new cruises to meet the quota. Once that threshold is met, commission rates increase dramatically on additional revenue over the threshold for these new cruises.

A major high-energy candy bar manufacturer pays salespeople no commission on the initial placement of new products. However, they pay a double commission on all repeat orders within the next ninety days. This compensation program recognizes the salesperson's impact on retail sell-through.

A sales manager must not only be concerned about proper compensation for direct salespeople but also for sales support personnel. If your firm supports direct salespeople with product specialists, sales engineers, or customer service representatives, consider performance pay for these support people. A miniature high-tech transformer firm pays sales support people 25 percent of their total compensation based on performance. Each product specialist, sales engineer, and customer service representative is assigned to specific direct salespeople and accounts. Of their total compensation, 25 percent is based on the total revenue, new accounts, and present account growth of the salesperson he or she supports. When Hewitt Associates LLC surveyed 120 Fortune 1000 firms in the year 2000, 71 percent reported having a variable/performance pay plan for sales support positions, up from 55 percent in 1999. The August 1999 issue of *Sales & Marketing Management* magazine reported on a survey conducted by the American Teleservices Association on Compensation for Technical Service Representatives and Customer Service Representatives. The results appear in Exhibit 4.3. The survey included 200 companies, with an average total sales volume of nearly $50 million. Respondents come from a variety of industries; most (63 percent) engaged in outbound telemarketing and 61 percent marketed to consumers.

Brokers, distributors, and outside sales representative organizations generally receive 100 percent performance pay. Channel partners need specific rewards for positive action and results important to the success of your firm. For your indirect sales force to become partners rather than adversaries, they require training and correct monetary incentives. Apply the same criteria to your indirect sales force that you did for the direct people. A storm window manufacturer pays their stocking distributors a year-end bonus based on maintaining certain levels of inventory in key items and exceeding their revenue goals. An electronic component manufacturer pays their indirect independent sales representatives a commission based on gross margin rather than revenue, along with a higher commission rate for growth.

Exhibit 4.3

Compensation for full-time telesales and customer service reps.

		Paid Annually		Paid Hourly	
		TSRs	CSRs	TSRs	CSRs
Base Pay	Minimum	$3,600	$15,000	$4.25	$6.00
	Median	23,256	22,656	8.52	9.13
	Maximum	48,000	52,932	21.00	16.10
Commissions	Minimum	600	420	0.10	0.50
	Median	12,000	2,784	2.00	1.00
	Maximum	36,000	31,992	12.00	2.00
Bonuses	Minimum	240	240	0.09	0.05
	Median	1,416	1,500	1.10	0.88
	Maximum	12,000	6,000	3.58	1.25
Total Pay	Minimum	13, 380	15,600	6.75	6.00
	Median	30,300	24,612	10.00	9.65
	Maximum	75,996	63,984	21.00	16.85

RUNNING THE NUMBERS AND OBTAINING SALES FORCE AGREEMENT

Before deciding on annual alterations to your compensation program, prepare spreadsheets of what each salesperson earned last year compared to various scenarios for this year. If this year's results mirror last year's, how much will the new, altered compensation plan cost in total dollars compared to last year? Run the same analysis for each salesperson. Then run a best- and worst-case revenue scenario for the firm and for each salesperson. Which salespeople earn more, which less, and what percent of revenue does total salesperson compensation represent? Which plan maximizes dollars of contribution margin over time? How will you handle the salespeople whose earnings decline? Will guarantees be necessary? Do the right salespeople receive more compensation? Does this plan meet company objectives? These spreadsheets represent a reality check. Share these spreadsheets with human resources and top management. Ask for their agreement on the changes to prevent surprises during the year.

One way to sell compensation changes to the sales force involves including them in the decision-making process. Select a representative group to participate in the analysis, suggest changes, and anticipate problems. The salespeople must understand their role is advisory but important. Management must understand that the salesperson committee does not guarantee acceptance of compensation changes by the salespeople. Most salespeople resist changes in compensation because they fear the unknown. As managers, we must be sensitive to these concerns.

Performance pay that rewards positive action and results can create windfall earnings for salespeople. Be aware that additional compensation usually upsets fellow employees, who feel entitled to more money. In some years, top salespeople earn more than top management. To prevent this, some firms cap earnings, raise future quotas, or create declining rewards as salespeople move into windfall levels. However, such action negates the positive communication and motivation of performance pay. Salespeople lose their trust of such firms, and top performers may leave. Estimate the probability of a windfall, and discuss this with top management to prevent surprises. Establish a plan for dealing with it. If necessary, use thresholds rather than regressive performance pay. A tier-two supplier of automotive electronics allows salespeople to earn windfalls but defers payments over a certain dollar amount to the next year and the year after. This often lowers the salesperson's income tax rate, lowers the firm's turnover of top performers, and prevents complacency and disappointment the following year.

Windfall salesperson earnings can produce unexpected outcomes. A commission salesperson from a small industrial gear company increased his income tenfold on one order from a conveyor concern. He used the six-figure commission check to buy out the family that owned the small gear company.

SALARY PLANS VERSUS COMMISSION PLANS

Salary provides salespeople with a fixed amount of pay per period regardless of their recent activities or results. Nonetheless, when results exceed or fall short of expectations, you can adjust the salary accordingly. However, the reward for good performance or penalty for weak results is not immediate or direct.

Straight salary provides the salesperson with a steady income and does not stress the immediate importance of writing orders. Salary emphasizes the importance of nonselling activities and encourages the salesperson to engage in these activities. Often a salesperson must perform services after the sale that will not necessarily result in a reorder. For example, the salesperson for a small concern renting expensive tropical plants to offices may be required under the rental agreement to check and treat the plants monthly.

Because payments are the same each period, salary is easy to administer and dollars of direct selling expenses remain fixed regardless of volume. Before each month begins, you know the exact amount required for your salespeople's compensation.

A commission provides an immediate reward for successful performance. If sales increase, your people make more money; if sales decrease, they make less. Commission emphasizes the importance of writing orders and encourages the salesperson to engage in activities that culminate in order writing. Increased sales often require the salesperson to perform many tasks besides writing orders, including prospecting for new accounts, setting up display fixtures, counting stock, calibrating equipment, training, programming, or solving a data entry problem. Commission provides the sales force with an incentive to work hard and earn a great deal of money. Only time, energy, and territory restraints limit the salesperson's compensation.

Generally, commission plans are easy to understand and to compute. You multiply a fixed percentage times dollars of sales, or a fixed dollar amount times units of sales. Each day your salespeople know their earnings. Each month the payroll department performs simple multiplication to arrive at each person's compensation.

Where commissions have to be split, because the sale involved channel conflicts, team selling, more than one person's efforts, or when different rates are used for different products, administration proves more difficult. To prevent arguments, details of commission splits must be decided before a sale, not afterwards.

With commission plans, sales compensation costs remain a fixed percentage of your revenues whether they rise or fall, thereby protecting profit margins and helping cash flow. When sales decline, the company is not saddled with a large fixed expenditure. For smaller companies and start-ups with limited capital, this feature is very important. New ventures especially benefit from commission plans, because initial sales costs are lower, reflecting the low sales volume. Sometimes new ventures use high-performance pay compensation plans which do not properly reflect the salesperson's influence on the sale, type of service/product sold, type of salesperson required, or specific action/results most important to reward. Sometimes these start-ups never mature because sales force compensation was poorly designed to start with. As the business matures, legacy issues can prevent changing to a more appropriate plan.

Because no career ladder exists in many organizations, the opportunity to earn large sums from commission takes on added importance. In some small and medium-size concerns, top salespeople regularly earn more than the sales manager or president. Commission also proves more appropriate for businesses where the sales forces are often smaller but the territories are larger and have unlimited potential.

The major disadvantages of commission plans are that they lack emphasis on nonselling activities and encourage highlighting, or calling on a small number of large accounts at the expense of a large number of smaller ones. They can also result in high sales force turnover during weak sales periods, in excessive income from large nonrecurring sales, and in salespeople overselling unneeded features in addition to overloading customers with inventory. Commission compensation stresses the benefits (immediate orders) of shorter-term customer relations rather than the longer-term benefits of a growing relationship. However, proper sales training and supervision can overcome many of these disadvantages.

It is difficult convincing commissioned salespeople to collect past-due accounts unless their commissions are penalized for bad debts. It requires more persuasion on the part of management to obtain weekly call reports from commissioned people than it does from salaried; the salespeople must believe that call reports help their performance. Commission attracts salespeople with a need for freedom and independence—people who feel they are in business for themselves.

Because large accounts generate more sales and commission dollars, a nonsalaried salesperson often concentrates his or her efforts on the majors and neglects small accounts. Through proper training and supervision, management must convince the sales force that smaller accounts also have virtues. For example, small accounts often take less time to sell, remain loyal, and require less service.

Some commission salespeople sell customers unneeded features and overload inventory. Proper sales training can prevent this. Commission people must understand that there will be less commission next year if they mistreat customers this year—because their sales will be lower. Over the long term, the salesperson must satisfy customer needs.

If a compensation plan allows commission people to earn a good living, then management can obtain their cooperation in correcting some of these disadvantages. A salesperson earning a good living does not wish to lose his or her job. A commission sales force that trusts and respects management will modify its behavior. On the other hand, if the commission plan merely results in a mediocre level of total compensation, it will be more difficult to take meaningful corrective action.

The rate of commission must allow a salesperson to earn a competitive and living wage from average results, but a superior wage from superior results. Also, the rate of commission must allow your company to maintain necessary profit margins and return on capital. Commission rates vary from 3 percect on sales of commodity food products and lumber to 20 percent on software, medical supplies, and scientific research equipment.

As prices rise for a product or service, so do commission dollars. A salesperson gets paid more dollars for selling the same units this year than last if the unit price increases. However, a decrease in unit volume because of the price increase can offset this gain. Commission rates require annual review to measure the effects of inflation and unit sales.

Commissions can cause frustration when territories do not contain equal potential. When small territories or realigned territories limit or decrease sales volume, you may have to consider guarantees. Commission compensation plans require territories of equal potential, which is discussed in Chapter 5.

BONUSES

Bonuses represent an excellent means of using performance pay to reward positive action and superior results. Many firms defer bonuses to year-end because the bonus is paid on cumulative results. Some firms defer bonuses to the next year to help with tax planning and lower turnover. Often a bonus provides an extra, deferred reward for some form of outstanding performance over and above the forecast or goal. Often bonuses increase as salespeople exceed goals. Hewitt Associates LLC surveyed 120 Fortune 1000 firms, of which two-thirds used quota-based bonuses. Of these, 80 percent felt their quota-setting process was effective, and two-thirds used a top-down quota-setting process relying on historical data and management projections.

Many salespeople feel quotas used for bonuses do not fairly reflect market potential or accurate forecasts. Often this results from a lack of reliable data. Better historical tracking systems and knowledge of buyer behavior is improving accuracy. To obtain salesperson buy-in, include them in the quota-setting process.

Some companies that pay bonuses based on quotas also have an announced policy of terminating salespeople who miss quota two years in a row. Companies in rapidly growing markets significantly increase quotas each year. Between 50 percent and 75 percent of salespeople who receive a bonus based on exceeding a goal do exceed that goal.

If possible, pay part or all of a bonus quarterly to bring the reward closer to the action/results. For example, a portion of the annual bonus can be paid quarterly if the previous quarter's performance exceeds a proration of the annual goal. If this is not possible, inform salespeople monthly about their performance progress toward the goal and remind them of the resulting bonus.

Bonuses can be used to reward salespeople for new accounts, new product placements, product mix, gross margin, revenue growth, team results, computer skills, product knowledge, call reports, or customer profiles. Decide what positive action and superior results can be best rewarded by commission and which by bonuses. Bonuses provide the manager with additional flexibility for compensating salespeople.

A pharmaceutical firm switched from a bonus based on exceeding quota to a bonus based on scoreboarding salespeople. A companywide bonus pool is based on company earnings. The bonus pool is divided among each salesperson depending on the absolute dollar sales and percentage growth of certain products. Salespeople who generate the most absolute dollars and the largest percentage growth receive more of the bonus pool than lesser performers.

COMBINATION PLANS

Some combination of salary, commission, and bonus represents the most widely used form of sales compensation. Because the objectives of a compensation plan usually involve quickly and effectively rewarding a combination of action, results, and behavior, rather than one simple action, combination plans prove most appropriate. Combination plans can be targeted to encourage the specific behavior, action, and results most beneficial to your sales effort and to eliminate the disadvantages of straight commission or straight salary.

Combination plans lack the simplicity of straight commission or straight salary plans, however, and this makes them more difficult for the company to administer and for the salespeople to understand. A common mistake of combination plans involves offering a specific compensation for too many activities, rather than emphasizing the most important ones—for example, paying a bonus for new accounts and new product placement, a commission on sales increases and gross margin, plus a base salary for retention. Because of their complexity, combination plans can require more frequent revision than either straight salary or straight commission.

EXPENSE REIMBURSEMENT

In addition to direct compensation, the sales force is also rewarded through reimbursed expenses and fringe benefits. Regardless of product or service, any expense reimbursement plan should be fair, controllable, fast, simple, easy to understand and administer, and flexible. Salespeople should have an economic incentive for controlling their expenses and for using expense money productively and efficiently. If no economic incentive exists because expenses are open-ended, salespeople use them as an additional form of compensation. Similarly, management cannot ask its salespeople to pay for expenses when this would lower their total compensation to an unacceptable level.

Salespeople should be paid and expenses reimbursed promptly. Many smaller companies finance themselves by remaining months behind in paying portions of their sales force's expenses and performance pay. Many larger companies with weak back-office administrative systems do the same. Such behavior increases turnover of salespeople and certainly hurts morale and productivity. Salespeople must thoroughly understand what is included in the expense plan so they can act accordingly. Make your expense plan as simple as possible to facilitate administration and understanding. Put the expense plan in writing, and have salespeople sign and return a copy to you each year.

A good expense plan requires a certain amount of flexibility for exceptions. Say, for instance, your Denver salesperson receives a call from a hot prospect asking him to be in her Salt Lake City office at ten o'clock the next morning. The salesperson flies both ways to save time, since he also has appointments in Denver the day following the Salt Lake City visit. Your company policy reimburses auto expenses but not airfare. You might consider making an exception in this case.

Salespeople can be asked to pay all their own expenses out of their basic compensation, the firm and the sales force can split expenses, or the company can reimburse the salespeople for all their expenses. Many variations exist within each of these possibilities. Expense policies, like salespeople compensation plans, require annual review and constant updating to reflect changing conditions.

Salespeople can be asked to pay all their own expenses if the level of compensation takes this into account. Commissioned salespeople in the apparel business, for example, receive a rate of commission high enough to pay all their own expenses. The rate of commission varies according to the level of anticipated expenses. The New York salesperson who travels between customers by subway might receive a lower commission rate than the Iowa/Nebraska salesperson who drives fifty miles between accounts.

If possible, making the salesperson responsible for all or most of his or her own expenses proves best for the smaller business. Under such a plan, the salesperson, who has the most to gain or lose and is the best judge, has total responsibility for expenses. Money will not be wasted on unnecessary trips or entertainment. If salespeople feel that money spent on travel or entertainment will result in orders, they will spend it. Certainly this arrangement is the easiest to administer and understand. Smaller businesses and start-ups often use channel partners to reach their target customers because compensation is variable and reimbursed expenses transparent.

A similar but more complicated arrangement involves the salesperson submitting reports and receipts for certain designated expenses, which the company reimburses until the total reaches a specified percentage of sales volume. Anything over that percentage becomes the salesperson's responsibility. At year's end the salesperson receives a portion of the amount saved should expenses total less than the agreed percentage. Here again, the salesperson has an economic incentive to spend wisely. The percentage rate varies accordingly to the territory, volume, and expense requirements. The sales volume figure against which you apply the percentage rate to arrive at a dollar expense limit may be last year's actual, this year's forecast, or this year's actual cumulative to date.

Some companies agree to pay a predetermined percentage of allowable expense items. For example, they may agree to pay 65 percent of all the salesperson's entertainment, travel, and telephone expenses. Salespeople submit invoices, receipts, and reports verifying their expenses, and the company then reimburses only 65 percent. Company and salesperson share the expense.

Some concerns merely give salespeople a flat monthly expense allowance to use as they see fit. Others allow a flat amount for certain expenses—for example, $60 a night for lodging and $40 a day for food. Both arrangements must vary dollar amounts to accommodate different expenses in different territories. A hotel room in Omaha will not cost as much as a hotel room in San Francisco. The flat monthly allowance allows you to accurately forecast this expense item. Both these plans are easy to understand and administer.

Some capital goods and financial services companies allow salespeople unlimited expense accounts but require a detailed annual budget for planning cash flow. The budget asks for expenses by type, customer, and month. Salespeople receive a bonus based on meeting the sales forecast and expense budget. A good expense plan gives the salesperson an incentive to spend wisely and limit expenses.

Some expense plans involve combinations of the above choices. For instance, airfare might be 100 percent reimbursable, but lodging and meals are paid for with a flat allowance.

Expense reports represent a mixed blessing for the salespeople and sales manager. Although laptops prove helpful, expense plans that require vouchers, receipts, invoices, and reports involve a great deal of administrative time on the part of salespeople and the sales manager. The salesperson must submit accurate information, and you must verify its correctness. This is necessary not only for internal controls but for reporting to the Internal Revenue Service as well. However, expense reports provide important information both on costs and on where the salesperson travels and who the salesperson calls on. Therefore, review all expense reports before turning them over to the payroll department. If submitted digitally, aggregate material and look for trends.

Unless salespeople pay their own expenses or you pay a flat monthly allowance, these costs are difficult to forecast. It is difficult to estimate in November what travel expenses might be incurred during the following year. For cash-constrained concerns, this can prove especially problematic.

Contact management and customized software programs for salespeople's laptop computers can reduce the time required for reporting and transmitting expenses. These same programs can aggregate expense data for the entire sales force by category and by salesperson, compare actual to forecast, and create budgets based on historical data.

Channel partners such as distributors, brokers, and independent sales representatives generally pay their own expenses out of their commission or margins. Occasionally, companies do provide channel partners with a travel, entertainment, sample, or trade show allowance.

For many firms, reimbursed expenses equal 25 percent of a salesperson's total direct compensation and require constant cost reduction analysis. Airfare, auto expenses, telecommunications, lodging, meals, and entertainment easily get out of control. Use part of a sales meeting to discuss the relationship between salespeople's time management and expense control. When possible, salespeople should use the telephone rather than a personal visit to qualify prospects, arrange appointments, handle service items, answer specific questions, or write small orders. Salespeople should plan the day ahead so as to see more customers and travel fewer miles. They should travel only economy class by air and, where possible, stay at budget-class lodgings. If the same city is frequently visited by air, consult a travel agent or use a Web site to purchase discount tickets. Some discount tickets can't be canceled, and others involve penalties. Finally, they should make fewer but longer trips. Also, management should negotiate special corporate lodging, auto lease/rental, airline, and telecommunication rates for the sales force.

FRINGE BENEFITS

As mentioned, in addition to direct compensation, sales force costs include reimbursed expenses, which often equal 25 percent of direct compensation, and fringe benefits, which often equal another 25 percent. Fringe benefits include mandatory items such as Social Security, Medicare, and unemployment insurance, plus expected items such as health, life, and disability insurance, vacations and retirement plans, and optional items such as profit sharing, stock options, education reimbursement, clubs, dental/vision insurance, and moving expenses. Fringe benefits vary from 15 percent to 40 percent of direct compensation, and this represents a significant expense item. In established firms, long-term incentives, such as stock options, are reserved for senior salespeople, national account managers, and sales managers. However, younger companies often offer stock options to lure salespeople away from established firms.

Channel partners such as distributors, brokers, and independent sales representatives pay their own fringe benefits. However, if a channel partner devotes over 50 percent of their time to selling your firm's products/services, your firm may be liable for their fringe benefits. Discuss this with the firm's legal counsel. Responsibility for travel expenses and fringe benefits should be clearly defined in the channel partner's contract.

Some employers offer salespeople a choice of fringe benefits and plans. They can choose reimbursed education expenses up to a certain dollar amount or dental/vision insurance. Deductibles can be chosen along with co-insurance amounts on health plans. Employees may be asked to share the cost of certain fringe benefits with their employer. For example, the employer pays 80 percent of health insurance and moving expenses. Because salespeople's needs are different, these "cafeteria" plans prove popular.

Retirement plans, profit sharing, and stock options are deferred fringe benefits which increase in value based on years of employment. Such plans help reduce sales force turnover.

INDIVIDUAL WRITTEN EXPENSE PLANS

Each salesperson should receive, sign, and return their annual compensation plan (see Exhibit 4.4). This prevents misunderstandings and allows the sales manager and salesperson to discuss the total annual cost of putting the salesperson on the road. The compensation plan includes specifics on

Exhibit 4.4

Sample Compensation Plan.

Name: Bill Locke   **Time Period:** Calendar 2002

Salary: $4000 a month payable every two weeks.

Commission: 2% of sales when shipped, less uncollectable accounts receivables, returns, samples, and advertising allowances. 4% of resulting gross margin. Commissions paid on the 20th of each month for the preceding month.

Bonus: Up to $3000 based on exceeding forecast.

Expense Reimbursement: up to $2000 a month cumulative for travel and communication expenses payable two weeks after expense reports are received. The difference between 12 months actual expenses and $24,000 to be split 50/50 if actual us under $24,000.

Fringe Benefits: Social Security, unemployment insurance, Medicare, health, life, and disability insurance; pension plan and stock options; reimbursed educational expenses. These fringe benefits would be spelled out in more detail.

dollars of salary, rates of commission, and dollars of bonus, as well as details of the expense reimbursements and fringe benefits. Because plans and fringe benefits change annually, can be individually customized, and involve combinations of salary, commission, and bonus, ask salespeople to show their understanding and agreement by signing their plan. Misunderstandings of direct compensation, reimbursed expenses, and fringe benefits waste time and demotivates a sales force.

These written individual expense plans allow a sales manager the opportunity to discuss with his or her salespeople their total cost. Most salespeople perceive their total cost as their take-home pay. Most sales managers never explain or fully understand how much more than direct compensation a salesperson costs the firm.

Once a year the sales manager should review and document with each salesperson the cost of putting him or her on the road (see Exhibit 4.5). Use both historic and forecasted numbers. Show past and projected earnings, salary, commission, and bonus, then total all reimbursed expenses and add the dollar cost of all appropriate fringe benefits. Compare this

E x h i b i t   4.5

The annual cost of putting a salesperson on the road.

Name: Bill Locke	**Time Period:** Calendar 2002
Direct Compensation:	
Salary:	$ 48,000
Commission: 2% of sales	$ 30,000
4% of gross margin	$ 20,000
Bonus:	$ 3,000
Total Direct Compensation:	$101,000
Medicare, Unemployment Insurance, Social Security:	$ 10,000
Health, Life, and Disability Insurance:	$ 10,000
Pension, Stock Options, Education:	$ 10,000
Total Fringe Benefits:	$ 30,000
Total Reimbursed Expenses:	$ 24,000
Total Direct Cost - Bill Locke:	$155,000
Percent of Sales:	10.3%
Cost per Day Using 240 Days a Year:	$ 646
Cost per Hour Using 8 Hours a Day:	$ 81
Cost per Customer Visit Using 2 a Day or 480 a Year:	$ 322
Percentage of time in Sales-Driving Activities:	33%
Cost per Hour of Sales-Driving Activities:	$ 243

total for various years. To make this total number even more meaningful, you may wish to show it as a percentage of the salesperson's territory's revenues. Then divide it by the number of days a salesperson works each year and the number of hours worked each day. If appropriate, divide it by the number of customer calls a salesperson makes each year or the number of prospecting calls or the number of new accounts. Have salespeople keep a time log of what percent of their time is spent in activities that drive sales—that is, in front of customers, on the phone with customers, preparing bids or proposals, or working with engineering on specifications. Most salespeople spend 20 percent to 40 percent of their time in these activities. Show the cost per hour of that customer sales-related time.

You and the salesperson will benefit from reviewing these numbers. Salespeople are an expensive, important human resource. Discuss with the salesperson how to increase his or her productivity. What additional inputs will increase outputs? Ask the salesperson how she or he can spend more time in sales-related activities, specifically with targeted customers. In the next chapter, we will discuss using these costs to determine a salesperson's break-even point and dollars of contribution margin.

QUESTIONS AND EXERCISES

- What positive action and superior result on the part of salespeople are important to the success of your firm? How does your compensation system reward salespeople for this?
- How much influence do your salespeople have on making the sale? Is this reflected in the amount of performance pay versus fixed pay?
- How complex is the sales process for your product/service? Does total salesperson compensation reflect this?
- Why does your product/service lend itself to performance pay versus fixed pay?
- What type salesperson is most successful at your firm? Review the candidate profile. How does your compensation program attract these people?
- When was the last time you revised your firm's sales force compensation program?

SALES MANAGERS' MAJOR WEAKNESSES/MISTAKES
SALES FORCE COMPENSATION

- Not rewarding specific action/results important to company's success. Strategic accounts and products
- Not rewarding superior results
- Not analyzing compensation each year
- Not reflecting the complexity of the sale in the level of compensation
- Not reflecting salesperson's influence on sale and type of salesperson you wish to attract in fixed versus performance pay

PART TWO

STRATEGY AND THE FIRM

CHAPTER 5

Sales Force Organization and Architecture

The sales manager must pay considerable attention to the structure of the sales force. The model for organizing a sales force progresses from the more general to the more specific, from the more strategic to the more tactical, from macros to micros. A firm's first decision is what channels are most efficient for reaching and serving the target customers. Are your own direct salespeople more effective or some combination of indirect sales organizations/channel partners? Will you use a combination of distributors, brokers, sales representative organizations, telesales/marketing, ecommerce, home shopping television channels, systems integrators, value-added distributors, or retailers?

Once you choose the appropriate combination of sales channels, the second decision is how to organize these channels: by product line, major customer or market segment, function, geography, or no restrictions. We refer to this as *sales force architecture*.

Moving from the more general to the more specific, next you should decide how many salespeople you need and the boundaries of each person's territory. We refer to this as *deployment and sizing*.

Last and most tactical, a sales manager must assist salespeople in time and territory management. How can a salesperson best allocate his or her time in the territory between prospecting for new customers and further penetration of existing accounts? How frequently should top accounts be visited versus less important customers? How can a salesperson most efficiently travel his or her territory?

Channel choice, architecture, deployment, and territory management can dramatically impact revenues and costs. As with compensation, the rapidly changing twenty-first century landscape dictates an annual evaluation of these issues. As products, customers, competitors, technology, markets, personnel, and strategy change, so must your channel choice, architecture, deployment, and territory management. As emphasized throughout this book, business is a dynamic process; the future is a moving target. Each year, wipe the slate clean. If you were starting again, what changes would you make?

Most sales managers inherited and continue their channel, organizational, and deployment structure or follow industry tradition. Be careful of legacy issues and following the losers. Proper staffing, deployment, channel choice, and territory management provide an opportunity to differentiate your firm in a commoditized marketplace. No matter how well you hire, train, and compensate salespeople, inefficient distribution channels, architecture, deployment, and territory management will prevent a sales force from reaching full productivity.

SALESPERSON BREAK-EVEN POINT AND CONTRIBUTION MARGIN

In previous chapters we discussed the strategic importance of reducing the sales cycle from search to purchase, reducing the training cycle, and more rapidly taking salespeople from "0" to full productivity or at least to a break-even point. Accomplishing these strategic objectives requires metrics and models to measure a salesperson's marginal cost versus marginal revenues.

In the previous chapter, we discussed the annual cost of putting a salesperson on the road. This represents a salesperson's marginal costs which now must be compared to marginal revenues to establish a break-even point. Subtract these annual costs from annual revenues to determine a territory's dollars of contribution margin.

A salesperson's break-even point varies depending on whether he or she works in a new territory or an existing territory. For example, a B2B ecommerce firm for specialty chemicals hires a new salesperson for an undeveloped territory in Louisiana, Texas, and Oklahoma. Using the format discussed in the previous chapter, you add the salesperson's salary, commission, bonus, fringe benefits, reimbursed expenses, and any variable costs directly related to that salesperson/territory. Let's also assume these total $150,000. Let's also assume the gross margin after manufacturing costs, or after costs of providing a service, or in this case cost of goods sold is 50 percent. The break-even point for this new salesperson in a new territory is $300,000 of new revenue, which will result in $150,000 of contribution margin after the 50 percent cost of goods sold. Existing selling, marketing, general, and administrative expenses are fixed and will not vary because of this new salesperson.

On the other hand, the break-even point for a salesperson in an established territory will be much higher. Let's assume our new salesperson, who costs $150,000 to put on the road, takes over an existing territory. The cost of goods sold remains 50 percent, but this existing territory must absorb a portion of existing fixed selling, marketing, general, and administrative costs which are allocated at 30 percent of revenues. After allocating selling, general, and administrative expenses, the company requires a minimum 20 percent operating profit from each matured territory. The break-even point for this same salesperson in an existing territory is $750,000 of revenue, which will result in an operating profit of $150,000.

We manage what we monitor. Knowing a salesperson's break-even point will assist you in staffing and deployment decisions. Knowing each salesperson's territory's contribution margin will assist you in evaluating territory boundaries, product mix, pricing, the salesperson's compensation, and reimbursed expenses. For example, the regional manager of a pharmaceutical firm has seven salespeople reporting to her. For each salesperson/territory the company provides the following quarterly and cummulative year-to-date data.

Net revenues after discounts and returns
Less:

- Salesperson's total direct compensation (salary, commission, bonus)
- Fringe benefits (Social Security, insurance, pension plan, etc.)
- Reimbursed travel, entertainment, communication, and office expenses
- Cost of samples dispersed to physicians
- Cost of in-service training sessions
- Local advertising, promotion, marketing expenses, trade shows

Resulting in a salesperson's contribution margin in dollars
Less:

- Manufacturing costs for product shipments to the territory.

Resulting in a salesperson's gross contribution margin in dollars.

The pharmaceutical company regional sales manager compares revenues, each line-item expense, and dollars of margin for each salesperson/territory. She also notes for each salesperson/territory what percentage of revenue each expense or margin item represents. Once a year, she shares the results for each territory with the appropriate salesperson. Once a quarter, she compares the results for each territory to each other. She has noted large dollar and percentage of revenue variations from one territory to another. Based on these variations, she has realigned territory boundaries, increased the number of salespeople, changed compensation and expense reimbursement plans, and reduced spending on samples and marketing. The difference between the salesperson's contribution margin and the salesperson's gross contribution margin is the territory's cost of goods sold/manufacturing costs for the products delivered to the territory. Salespeople impact this latter margin through their pricing decisions and product mix sales. Weak results in this area might require a sales manager to use targeted field coaching and sales meetings to reinforce product, competitive, and customer knowledge and selling and pricing skills.

As noted in the previous chapter, compensation may be partially based on these dollars of margin and expense control. You might pay a commission on margins or a bonus for expense control. Most firms capture the data necessary to construct a territory gross margin analysis. The sales manager must know what format he or she wants and work with the controller to obtain reliable figures. There are many variations of these formats. Effective sales managers use one of them.

CHANNEL CHOICE

Choosing the proper distribution channels depends on the type of selling performed by the sales force, the type of customers called on, operating issues, type of product or service sold, areas requiring control, and capital/costs. Review these each year to see what has changed and if these changes require an adjustment in your choice of distribution channels. Many of these issues are interrelated and repetitive.

Certain types of selling lend themselves to company direct sales people, others to an indirect sales organization or a channel partner. Long sales cycles with a great deal of consultative selling to first-time or one-time systems buyers lend themselves to a direct sales organization. The more influence a salesperson has on the sale, the more important a company direct sales force. Team selling and partnership selling lend themselves to the company direct model. On the other hand, relationship selling to repeat customers, modified rebuyers, display, commodity, and order taking lends itself to using channel partners.

Most sales managers choose hybrid sales organizations by deaggregating the demand generation tasks. For example, lead generation might be most efficiently performed by an outside direct-mail house or a Web site, and qualifying these leads might lend itself to an independent telesales organization. However, once you identify qualified leads, those with major potential require a visit from a direct company salesperson, while those with less potential can be seen by an indirect channel partner salesperson.

In both cases, the salesperson will do a needs analysis, quantify benefits, demonstrate the product/service, offer a free trial, overcome objections, and attempt to close. Postsale service, installation, and ongoing account management might be best performed by a distributor. Look at the demand generation tasks from search to purchase. What type of selling and sales channels will be most efficient?

Certain customer characteristics lend themselves more to company direct salespeople, others to an independent sales organization. A large number of widely dispersed customers, frequently ordering small quantities, may be more efficiently reached by several outside indirect sales organizations than by your own company-employed direct sales force. If your firm's target customers are leaders (Wal-Mart, Cisco) or innovators, rather than followers, they may insist on a company direct sales force. To enter new market segments, where you do not have customer contacts or knowledge, you may need a channel partner which does have these contacts.

Credit and hazardous material (for example, toxic chemicals) issues may sway you toward a channel partner who can more efficiently handle these risks. Consider how competition handles all these factors. Can you create a competitive advantage by doing it differently?

Customer needs and channel function requirements must be analyzed to determine the proper channel choice. This could vary by market segment, which means you may use a company direct sales force for original equipment manufacturers and stocking distributors for the replacement market. A situation where customers require one-stop shopping for a basket of products/services when you only provide a few products/services, or small lot sizes when you only provide large lot sizes calls for choosing a channel partner who better meets the customers' requirements. Similarly, customers may insist on certain after-sale services, such as engineering, warranty, logistics or transportation, which can be more efficiently provided by a channel partner.

As in hiring and training salespeople, it is imperative for proper channel choice, architecture, deployment, sizing, and time management that your firm has correctly targeted customers based on dollars of present and potential revenue and margin, cost to sell and service, and probability of success. You need proper metrics for determining each of these. Based on these metrics, present and potential accounts become designated A, B, or C. An A account requires more frequent calls than a C account and may require a different channel choice. You may use telesales people or ecommerce for C accounts, independent account representatives for B accounts, and your own direct salespeople for A accounts.

Operating issues such as inventory, spare parts, service, maintenance, repair, customization, engineering, design, installation, programming, customer training, just-in-time delivery, safety, and credit services influence channel choice and may be related to previously mentioned items. Who can more efficiently provide each of these services, your firm or a channel partner? Which of these services does the customer value and which can be deleted? You must do value engineering on each service offered by your firm and your channel partners. For instance, a sales automation software firm used value-added distributors to sell and provide post-sale service. Half of the product's cost involved training customers on proper use and installation. As the software/market matured, these services were no longer necessary because customers developed internal resources to provide them. The software company and their value-added distributors offered customers a choice between full or partial service with significant price differences. Most customers chose the less service-oriented package, and the software firm's unit sales and dollars of margin improved significantly.

Certain types of products/services lend themselves to company direct salespeople, others to indirect channel partners. Heterogeneous products which can be more easily differentiated, such as biotech or consulting services or semiconductor fabricating equipment, lend themselves to a direct company sales force. Homogeneous products/services which are more difficult to differentiate, like die castings or injection molding, lend themselves to channel partners.

In reaching customers, higher gross margin products or services generally use a direct company sales force, while lower gross margin products or services generally use channel partners. New products or services, where the salesperson has a strong influence on the sale, do best with a company direct sales force, while products or services toward the end of their life cycle are more efficiently handled by channel partners, telesales, ecommerce or customer service people. If you require tight control over pricing and limited customer selection, or you need feedback and good communication from the field, a company direct sales force will better satisfy these needs.

Because most sales organizations require more than one type of selling, have multiple types of products, customers, and markets, and have various operating issues and control needs, most sales organizations require hybrid channels of distribution. Often these hybrid channels of distribution conflict and compete with each other in certain market segments. For example, say that your own salespeople call on major supermarkets with a line of deli products. You use distributors for smaller grocery stores and brokers for hotels and restaurants One of the distributor's salespeople opens a large supermarket where she has excellent contacts and your salespeople have had no success. Your salesperson is furious. Do you refuse the new business or try and arrange a compromise? As discussed in Chapter

4, many firms will share or split performance pay in such situations. Be prepared for channel conflicts, and have a plan for dealing with them. In the twenty-first century, ecommerce will become a more important distribution channel creating a new set of channel conflicts. Use ecommerce to enable your sales force and channel partners not to compete with them.

Channel partners require performance pay that rewards positive action and superior results important for the success of your firm. To prevent channel partners from skimming the best accounts and low-hanging fruit, but not pursuing the middle market and smaller accounts, create performance pay which rewards the proper actions and results. You can pay a higher commission rate for one type of sale, customer, or product than another. You can give bonuses and rebates for product mix, number of new accounts, post-sale services, and inventory levels.

The last item in determining channel choice is to run the numbers for various alternatives. If you use a 100 percent direct company sales force, what will it cost, how much revenue and gross margin will it generate, and what operating income, EBIT (earnings before income taxes), or EBITDA (earnings before income tax, depreciation, and amortization) will result? Do the same analysis using channel partners or a hybrid channel choice. Run spreadsheets using various assumptions at different revenue levels for different channel choices. What combination produces the most dollars of contribution margin over time? For each alternative, what percent of sales do selling costs and salesperson compensation represent? What is your market share and number of customers? Is the channel or combination of channels supported by the other previously discussed criteria?

Generally, channel partners create variable expenses which remain constant as a percentage of revenues. You pay for performance. A company direct sales force has a higher fixed portion of cost. Many start-ups use channel partners when their own salespeople would prove more appropriate, because the salesperson compensation is variable and there are no fringe benefits or reimbursed expenses. But then as the start-up moves into a growth stage or maturity, it proves difficult to change to a hybrid or company direct channel.

SALES FORCE ARCHITECTURE

Once you have decided on what channel or combination of channels you will use to most efficiently reach the targeted marketplace, you must decide whether to organize these channels by major products/services, product/service lines, market segments, key accounts/customers, geography, functions (two tier), no restrictions, or some combination of the preceding. The choice depends on your particular products/services, size and type of customers, target accounts, markets, market segments, type of selling, core competencies, channel choice, and objectives. Choose whatever type of organization best meets customer needs and best uses your sales force's human resources, one that maximizes dollars of contribution margin over time by properly balancing expenses with revenues.

If your company offers a wide variety of dissimilar or unrelated products or services—especially if they are complex—or if your company's products or services are sold to totally different markets, you should consider a sales force organized by product line. A product line sales organization allows each of the various markets and each of the diverse or complex product lines to receive a high degree of specialized attention. It is difficult for one salesperson to effectively sell cost and activity tracking software to hospitals, human resource software to airlines, and supply chain consulting to tier three auto firms.

However, sometimes two or three salespeople from one company call on the same buyer which can cause confusion and frustration on both ends, result in greater travel expense, and sometimes require you to add more salespeople. Within a sales force organized by product line, each salesperson is assigned a specific geographic area or customer list to call on.

If your company sells large quantities of products or services to a limited number of major customers, especially customers with many branches, you should consider a sales force organized by account. A sales force organized by account allows each major customer to receive a higher degree of specialization. It allows the salespeople to partner with major accounts, obtain specialized account specific information, and better understand the decision makers, decision-making process, and culture.

One example of a sales force organized by major accounts is a local refuse-removal company in eastern Michigan, which specializes in recycling waste and has three sales/service representatives: one for General Motors plants, one for Ford plants, and one for DaimlerChrysler plants. Each representative knows the specific needs of each company.

A sales force organized by customer proves best for businesses where a few key accounts or national accounts represent a large percentage of sales. However, as with a sales force organized by product, this often results in greater travel expenses than in one organized by geographic area.

If your company sells similar or closely related products or services to a large number of widely dispersed customers in the same industry, then you should consider a sales force organized by geographic territory. This means that salespeople sell all your products or services to any appropriate customers within their assigned territories. Most smaller businesses use this format because of its simplicity and low cost. Unfortunately, most smaller-business people don't even think about the alternatives.

The geographic organization of territories allows salespeople to cultivate local markets more intensely by becoming more familiar with local problems, people, and conditions. Also, a person living in the territory often finds a more receptive ear than an outsider would. Texans know how to handle Texans, and New Yorkers know how to handle New Yorkers. Similarly, salespeople living in a territory can provide better service at less cost because, generally, less travel is required.

For example, a bakery supply distributor offers 4000 items to independent bakeries, restaurants, hotels, hospitals, yogurt shops, and grocery stores. The potential account base is immense. Salespeople often walk from one account to another. They are organized by geographic territory, but management is considering having market specialists.

If you offer a product that requires considerable service after the sale and different skills for selling than for servicing, consider a two-tier sales organization with separate functions. For example, nationally advertised underwear company with a large sales force stopped growing when annual sales reached $100 million. The sales manager asked a representative sampling of salespeople why his or her sales had stopped increasing. All replied that because they were so busy servicing current accounts, they had no time to open new ones. The sales manager hired part-time salespeople to count stock and fill display fixtures for existing accounts. This left the full-time salespeople with enough time both to write reorders at existing customers and to open new accounts. Eventually this grew into a two-tiered sales force with different functions, one concentrating on new account development and the other on account maintenance. The new account salespeople continued receiving a partial commission on customers turned over to the account maintenance sales force.

In a functional sales organization, customers sometimes dislike the change of salespeople and salespeople sometimes dislike the change of customers. However, if your salespeople show superior account development skills but a lack of interest in retaining or maintaining accounts, try the two-tier approach. You can test it in one territory at a time.

Related to several of the preceding models are sales forces organized by market segments. Based on dollars of present and potential revenue and income, cost to sell and service, and probability of success, the sales manager has chosen target accounts and target markets. A miniature transformer manufacturer targets the communication, consumer electronics, and auto markets. An avionics navigational instrumentation firm sells to the Department of Defense, plus to domestic and overseas airlines. In both cases, products are similar but the diversity of markets requires a specialist.

Salespeople who sell consumer services often operate without restrictions to products or services, accounts, or geographic territories.

Independent insurance agencies allow their agents to write any type of policies without territorial limitations. Security brokers may sell their services to anyone who cares to buy, and real estate salespeople generally do not have territories or customer limitations. A telesales firm selling gospel music to religious bookstores allows the telesales people to prospect and sell any account which is not presently an active customer.

The most effective use of a sales force often involves combining elements of product, account, geographic territory, function, and no restrictions. Because of varying market structures, you may wish to use a different type of organization in different geographic areas or a different type of organization for different product lines. Remember, simple but flexible structures work best. Generally, smaller companies are more flexible than larger ones, allowing them more readily to use combinations or hybrids.

A nationally advertised athletic shoe company organizes salespeople by geographic territory in the Midwest, where it primarily sells specialty stores. However, on the East and West Coast, where it primarily sells regional chains, the sales force uses a key account organization.

A branded tire manufacturer has one sales force for retail tire stores that is organized geographically, another sales force for auto manufacturers that is organized by key accounts, a third for fleet trucking firms that is organized geographically, a fourth for mass merchants organized by key account, and a fifth for off-road tires that is organized by product line and market (racing, farm, forestry, construction).

A reform math textbook firm has one sales force calling on local school districts in states where annual decision making is decentralized and another sales force calling on state adoption boards, where decision making is centralized and only done every three years. Should you choose a combination or hybrid, analyze potential conflicts and clearly state the ground rules.

In a smaller company, your most important resource is the human resource and your decisions concerning sales force organization must recognize this factor. If one of your salespeople has excellent contacts with certain major accounts, you may wish to assign him or her to these customers while organizing the rest of the sales force by geographic territory. If one of your salespeople has a very close relationship with a major customer, you may wish to have him or her sell all your products to that account while organizing the rest of the sales force by product line. If one of your better salespeople does well with smaller accounts but poorly with large, you may wish to place two salespeople in this territory rather than the usual one. Assuming available potential, the second person would call on large accounts, allowing the original salesperson to continue concentrating on the smaller ones. If one of your better salespeople cannot travel overnight, but your sales force is organized by widely dispersed key accounts, you may wish to build a geographic territory of nonkey accounts within a day's drive of this person's home. The flexibility of a smaller business allows you to fully utilize the human resource by combining various types of sales force organizations.

Recently, pharmaceutical and telecommunication firms have created hybrid organizations by hiring part-time, flex-time salespeople. Better company salespeople who left to raise a family or care for a parent can return on a part-time, flex-time basis. They must work at least twenty hours a week, receive excellent comparable compensation, and no fringe benefits, and have smaller territories. These territories are often built around their contacts and are close to home. A tight labor market for qualified salespeople has necessitated this.

SIZING AND DEPLOYMENT

How many salespeople do you need, how large should a salesperson's territory be, and how do you determine the territory boundaries? A sales manager's goal is to increase sales force productivity and capacity, reengineer the sales organization as he or she would a factory, be an agent of change, and manage change. He or she must hire the best, terminate the rest, train salespeople, and compensate them properly. However, without proper sizing and deployment, a sales organization will not operate at its full potential.

To maximize the sales organization's productivity, each salesperson's territory must have equal potential based on present and potential revenues and income, and present and potential number and type of accounts (call frequency) versus the salesperson's call rate/workload/capacity. The goal is for salespeople to economically make the optimum number of quality calls on the right customers and prospects. This will maximize dollars of contribution margin over time. Mapping software offered by Siebel, Saratoga, and Oracle, among others, can assist you in these tasks.

Sizing and deployment involves both strategic and tactical issues. The sales manager must properly identify target accounts and market segments. He or she must determine whether new customers or a larger share of existing customers' business represents the best opportunities. He or she must understand the cost of putting a salesperson on the road, a salesperson's break-even point, a territory's dollars of contribution margin, and how quickly a salesperson can be trained.

The benefits of proper sizing and deployment can give your firm a competitive advantage in a commoditized marketplace. Proper sizing and deployment prevents 70 percent of a firm's revenues coming from 30 percent of the sales force. It levels the playing field, allowing total sales to increase. Salespeople who do not have the call capacity to obtain the full potential of a territory allocate some accounts to qualified salespeople who are underutilized. Rather than trading dollars each year between new and existing business, one territory or product line and another; proper sizing and deployment allows net dollars of revenue and margin, net number of active accounts to increase. Proper sizing and deployment will increase the percent of a salesperson's time spent in front of customers and other sales-related efforts, increase the number of customer calls, reduce the cost per call, and match customer needs with your organizational structure.

As we have discussed, salespeople represent an important and expensive human resource. In the September 1999 issue of *Sales & Marketing Management* magazine, Hay Group's Sales Force Effectiveness practice estimated the average 1999 cost per in-person sales call at $164.70. Cost per call includes compensation, benefits, and reimbursed travel and entertainment, but no indirect allocated expenses. It represents the cost of putting a salesperson on the road, as discussed in Chapter 4.

The cost per call varies depending on sales approach, industry, size of sales force, and geographic region. The cost per call averages $83 for transactional sales, $156 for feature/benefit selling, $164 for solution sales, and $189 for value-added selling. Transactional sales rely on price to sell commodities. Feature/benefit sales rely on features and benefits to justify price. Solution selling involves helping customers to solve problems and customizing products/services to customers' needs; existing system sales, involve modified rebuy. Value-added selling involves first-time, one-time purchases of new systems, long complex sales cycles, and team selling, where solutions prove more important than price. These sales approach categories equate to buyer behavior (Exhibit 2.1) and the complexity of the sales process.

The cost per call averages $242 for service industries, $202 for industrial manufacturing, $113 for wholesale/distribution, $95 for manufacturing, and $80 for retail. Industrial manufacturers have long sales cycles and large travel and entertainment expenses. Service industry firms make fewer calls per week than firms selling to retailers.

The cost per call for a sales force with one to five salespeople averages $214, for six to nine salespeople it averages $163, for ten to nineteen salespeople it averages $154, for twenty to forty-nine salespeople it averages $107, and for fifty or more salespeople it averages $134. The cost per call in the Northeast averages $198, in the Central region $152, in the South $144, and in the West $119.

In Chapter 4, we analyzed the annual cost of putting each of your salespeople on the road. We divided those annual costs by the number of each salesperson's annual in-person customer visits to arrive at a cost per call. How do those figures compare to the averages stated in the preceding paragraph for your sales approach, industry, size of sales force, and region?

A major branded manufacturer selling household appliances to retailers analyzed each salesperson's territory relative to present and potential sales, and present and potential number of accounts versus the salesperson's call rate/workload/capacity. Fifteen out of the twenty regional sales managers found salesperson territories with major issues of over or under capacity. The required workload, number of calls, type of accounts, and frequency of visits did not match the salesperson's capacity. Each regional manager had ten salespeople reporting to him or her. Eight of the fifteen regional managers with workload issues reallocated some accounts; seven did not. For the next two years those regional managers which had adjusted territories to equalize workloads and potential had regional sales increases five percentage points above those that made no adjustments. Proper territory alignment can significantly increase revenues with little increases in expenses.

Smaller territories maximize market share and minimize travel expenses, but they often cannot produce significant enough revenues to support a salesperson, whether on performance or fixed pay. Larger territories can produce significant enough revenues to support a salesperson but can be expensive to travel and may not maximize market share. A key issue is the amount of potential necessary to support one of your salesperson and the appropriate metrics needed to measure that potential.

As with channel choice and architecture, each year you must reanalyze the sizing and deployment of your sales force and make appropriate changes. Each year changes in salespeople, customers, products, technology, markets, and strategy impact deployment and sizing issues. Don't let legacy issues create chronic inertia. Many sales managers inherit and keep their territory structure or just follow competition.

Often territories contain equal physical size or have been structured around each major city in the region or contain equal past sales and number of accounts. Instead, let's explore how to create territories of equal potential, based on present and potential sales and number and type of accounts (call frequency) versus the salesperson's call rate or capacity/workload.

CREATING TERRITORIES OF EQUAL POTENTIAL

The sales manager's first task in creating territory boundaries and deciding on staffing needs involves finding proper metrics to measure each territory's potential revenues for the company's various product lines. Many industry publications and associations, along with appropriate federal, state, and city government agencies (SIC codes), have this information. The pharmaceutical industry has private market research firms that track prescriptions written for various medications by physician, pharmacy, and zip code. The American Cancer Association has data on new cases of various types of cancer reported annually by state. Firms selling equipment, devices, and medication related to cancer use this data. Semiconductor equipment manufacturers use geographic data on the annual unit production of semiconductors by type to measure potential. The number of hospital beds, admissions, discharges, and Medicare cases by city provide metrics for hospital supplies and health-care providers. The National Restaurant Association has data on number of restaurants by size and type by zip code, which suppliers use to measure potential.

New home construction and sales in various price ranges by zip code provide metrics for the furniture and mortgage financing industries. Often the local Chamber of Commerce or newspaper has this data. The Commerce Department and an industry association have data on the number of mattresses sold by zip code. Consumer or industrial buying power indexes are used to measure potential for various products. *Sales & Marketing Management* magazine publishes an annual Survey of Buying Power which contains data on population, households, retail sales, and effective buying income (EBI) by region, state, county, and metro markets. The number of children in grades K through 6 by district determines the potential for reform math textbooks. Market potential for tires is measured by the numbers of truck and auto licenses by city and state. Obtaining statistical data is simply a matter of identifying the associations, government agencies, and publications in a specific field and getting the information directly from the source. There are a number of reference books that identify these sources: *Encyclopedia of Associations, National Trade and Professional Associations of the United States, Statistical Abstracts of the United States, The United States Government Manual, Guide to Special Issues and Indexes of Periodicals,* and *Standard Periodical Directory.* You can also use the Internet to search for and obtain this data.

Using the proper metrics for your industry, decide on how much market potential is needed to support a salesperson. If a firm has a 1 percent share of their market segment and the break-even point for a salesperson, including all fixed overhead expenses, is $2 million of revenue, a territory must contain at least $200 million of market potential to justify this salesperson. If this firm enters a new territory and does not include fixed overhead expenses in the salesperson's break-even point, considerably less market potential is required. Market potential and territory performance can also be measured in units rather than dollars. If the salesperson sells diverse products/services into many market segments, this calculation becomes more complex.

Assuming an existing sales force, using appropriate metrics, measure the market potential for each salesperson/territory. How can you equalize them? Do you need to hire another salesperson, switch accounts from one territory to another, or change territory boundaries? Assuming your compensation plan contains some performance pay, possibly a commission based on revenues, or a bonus based on meeting sales goals, salespeople require territories of equal or similar potential to earn equitable compensation.

Looking at current and previous years' actual sales by territory, what market share does each represent? Which salespeople have the highest and lowest market share and why? If the top 30 percent of your territories produce 70 percent of the results, ask why.

Next, for each territory, examine the current and potential number of and type of accounts, required call frequencies, and the salesperson's call capacity or workload. Refer to the format in Exhibit 5.1, Salesperson's Time Allocation Planner.

Using each salespersons' call reports, calculate his or her annual call capacity. A salesperson selling apparel to specialty stores averages five in-person calls a day, but a salesperson at the same firm calling on department

E x h i b i t   5.1

Salesperson's time allocation planner.

Sales Representative's Name _____

Territory _____

TOTAL NUMBER OF CUSTOMERS IN THIS CATEGORY	NUMBER OF ANNUAL SALES CALLS ON EACH TYPE CUSTOMER	TOTAL CALLS PER YEAR REQUIRED IN THIS CATEGORY
A _____	X _____	= _____
B _____	X _____	= _____
C _____	X _____	= _____
TOTAL _____		_____

Plus number of prospecting calls: _____

Plus service nonselling calls (e.g., training):   _____

Actual number of required annual calls: _____

Actual daily or weekly calls of sales representative call rate: _____

Projected annual calls of sales representatives, his or her universe: _____

Comparison to required annual calls: _____

stores makes two calls a day. The New York City salesperson can make four department store visits a day; the Los Angeles salesperson can only reach three specialty stores a day. Each salesperson's in-person call rate varies depending on type of selling, type of customer, industry, and density of accounts. For long, complex sales cycles with many steps from search to purchase, a salesperson may only call on one major account a day but visit five decision makers and influences within the group. If a pharmaceutical salesperson calling on pediatricians can make six in-person calls a day and works in the field 200 days a year, his or her annual call capacity is 1200.

The salesperson's call capacity is like a factory's production capacity; physical and time restraints prevent it from varying more than 10 percent from year to year. However, by changing the sales force organization or channels or with automation, the call capacity can improve. A salesperson's call capacity could increase by having a customer service or telesales person qualify leads or occasionally handle smaller accounts. A salesperson's call capacity could increase with laptops, contact management software, and cell phones. Ecommerce and Web sites increase sales force productivity and call capacity. Technology will not replace salespeople, but it will increase call capacity and lower the cost per call.

Next, compare a salesperson's call capacity to the number of calls required to sell and service present and new accounts (i.e., the salesperson's workload) in his or her territory. Classify prospects and accounts A, B, and C by present and potential revenues and income, cost to sell and serve, and probability of success. Based on this metric, A accounts need to be called on most frequently and C accounts least frequently.

A salesperson selling real-time database software to petroleum traders calls on brokerage houses, commodity traders, banks, pension plans, and international energy companies. The more users each customer has, the greater the revenue potential. At commodity traders, the cost to sell and serve is less and the probability of success is higher. They also eventually need the most copies. Commodity traders represent the A accounts, the target customers and prospects. Banks represent the other extreme and have a C classification.

Salespeople at this firm call on A accounts and A prospects twice a month (twenty-four times a year), B accounts and B prospects once a month (twelve times a year), and C accounts and prospect once every other month (six times a year). The Texas salesperson can make three calls a day and has an annual call capacity of 600. The Texas salesperson has fifteen A accounts and prospects, thirty B accounts and prospects, and thirty C accounts and prospects. Multiplying the number of accounts and prospects by classification times the required call frequency produces a workload for the Texas salesperson of 900 calls a year versus a call capacity of 600 calls. The salesperson cannot properly service and sell present and potential accounts.

Possibly another salesperson is needed, or C accounts should not be called on or frequency of calls should be reexamined.

Here's another example, a seed company sells plugs (small bedding plants), seeds, and supplies to greenhouses, nurseries, and growers for ornamental flowers. The three Illinois salespeople can each make four customer or prospect calls a day. Each salesperson has an annual capacity of 880 calls. In addition to selling, servicing, and expanding present customers, each salesperson is expected to make two to three prospecting calls a week, or 100 a year. The sales manager uses the Salesperson's Time Allocation Planner, shown in Exhibit 5.1, to construct each salesperson's workload. A, B, and C accounts are determined by square feet under cultivation, which correlates to dollars of potential sales. One salesperson has fifteen A accounts, thirty B accounts, and forty-five C accounts. Another salesperson has twenty A accounts, forty B accounts, and sixty C accounts. The third salesperson has twenty-five A accounts, fifty B accounts, and seventy C accounts. Salespeople are expected to see A accounts monthly, or twelve times a year, B accounts every other month, or six times a year, and C accounts quarterly, or four times a year.

Including 100 prospecting calls a year, the first salesperson is expected to make 640 calls a year, the second 820 calls a year, and the third 980. Based on each salesperson's capacity, the first salesperson with 640 required calls has excess capacity, and the third salesperson with 980 required calls is not able to service all existing accounts and do prospecting. If the close ratio is ten prospecting calls to obtain one new account, then each salesperson adds ten new customers annually that need to be serviced as A, B, or Cs. However, this might be balanced by lost customers. The first salesperson is at 73 percent of capacity, the second at 93 percent of capacity, and the third is over capacity at 111 percent. Possibly accounts can be switched from the third salesperson to the first, assuming each territory has equal potential sales and number of accounts. Various software packages can assist you in balancing workloads by preparing and analyzing this data.

The number and type of present and potential accounts in a territory can be obtained from your customer lists, along with industry trade association, trade publications, telephone directories, federal, state, and city government (SIC) data, and the Chamber of Commerce. Use the Internet to search for data and possibly download it. Much of this data is available online or on CD ROMs. The Commerce Department's *Survey of U.S. Industrial and Commercial Buying Power* lists by state and county the number of establishments by major SIC code, their shipments and receipts, and their percent of the U.S. total for their SIC code. *Sales & Marketing Management* magazine aggregates some of this data in their "Annual Survey of Buying Power." Territories may have equal potential revenues, but one may have a large number of small accounts, another a small number of large accounts. In balancing territory workloads, the sales manager must take this into account. Territories become defined then by classifying accounts as to importance, sales potential, and necessary call frequency, then by comparing current and potential accounts with desired market share and the physical call limits of a salesperson.

When the sales manager changes the boundaries of a salesperson's territory, generally one person gains revenue, accounts, and potential while another person loses them. Often the person who loses customers and potential is a high performer who has generated more business than he or she can handle. The reward for doing well may be perceived as a penalty, causing low morale, loss of enthusiasm, or turnover. If possible, sell the benefits of change: less travel, more time in front of customers for account development, more leisure, and more new challenges from prospecting. Carefully explain why the change is being made and massage the salesperson's ego with lunch or a letter from your boss. To smooth the transition, pay a one-year override to the salesperson on the accounts transferred. Try and transfer a mix of large and small accounts. Take into consideration how your salespeople travel the territories, their route analysis, and where they live. Take into consideration customers' needs and personal relationships.

A refuse removal firm in Baltimore which employees five salespeople represents one extreme in changing territory boundaries. The sales manager rotates salespeople's territories every year. The salespeople and customers enjoy it. Salespeople compete to improve on their peers' performance in the territories. Customers enjoy the variety. All the salespeople share best practices and know all the customers, which prevents bad habits and makes the manager happy. When a salesperson leaves, there is less trauma. Rotating salespeople prevents complacency and plateauing.

Using these analytical, sometimes black-box techniques to establish territory boundaries does not constitute an exact science, but it is a logical approach to improving salespeople's performance. As mentioned, computer software programs exist to assist you in this task.

For a smaller firm, as with channel choice and sales force organization, your salespeople, their needs, and their contacts also require serious consideration in setting territory boundaries. Flexibility represents a competitive advantage for smaller concerns, allowing the sales manager to temper the analytical approach to territories with important human considerations. Smaller firms take into account where salespeople live, their personalities, personal needs, likes and dislikes, and contacts. One salesperson may prefer a territory with smaller accounts; another might do better with majors.

Sizing, deployment, and territory boundaries are also influenced by mountains, bridges, highway systems, and market areas. Although market information on buying power, potential sales, and number of possible accounts is generally available by county, zip code, city, state, or region, sales territory boundaries may not lend themselves to city, county, or state lines. Highway systems, rivers, bridges, subways, and mountains must be considered. Also, major market and trading areas cross state lines.

For example, the highway system connecting Columbus, Dayton, and Cincinnati with Indianapolis is better and shorter than the highway system connecting Columbus, Dayton, and Cincinnati with northern Ohio. The greater Cincinnati, Ohio, trading area also includes counties in Kentucky and Indiana. Therefore, many companies create a territory that includes central and southern Ohio, central and southern Indiana, and northern Kentucky.

TIME MANAGEMENT

Channel choice, sales force architecture, sizing, and deployment have taken us from the macro to the micro of sales force organization. The sales manager's last task in this area involves helping salespeople better plan, use, and track their time within the territory. You must set standards, train, and assist salespeople in call frequency, route analysis, allocation of time between various duties, and time wasters. Time and knowledge represent important resources for salespeople. They must learn how to best utilize a finite amount of time within their geographic territory.

Salespeople resist training in and tracking of time management. Most sales managers hesitate to become involved in these very tactical issues, thinking that mature adults don't need assistance in these areas. But poor time management on the part of salespeople reduces productivity and dilutes the positive affects of proper organization and deployment.

The use of several techniques can make time management training easier for a sales manager. First, ask your salespeople to list their top-ten daily activities in declining order of importance related to meeting sales goals. Then prepare a time log asking salespeople to track the amount of time they spend at each of those activity each day. Activities might include, in declining order of importance, time in front of customers/prospects, time on the phone with customers/prospects, preparing for sales calls, writing proposals, coordinating activities in house with other departments, traveling, waiting, training, sales meetings, administrative work, and conflict resolution. The list will be different for a modified rebuy versus a long, complex new systems sale. Exhibit 5.2 shows an example of a salesperson's time log.

Have the salesperson analyze the amount of time spent in the four most important categories that drive sales versus the four least important. Generally, the most important categories will account for less than 30 percent of a salesperson's time. If salespeople receive performance pay, this time

E x h i b i t   5.2

Time Log.

TIME LOG **TIME MANAGEMENT** **WEEK OF** _____									
FUNCTION/ACTIVITY	SUN	MON	TUE	WED	THU	FRI	SAT	TOTAL ACTUAL	DESIRABLE TOTAL
In front of customer.									
On phone with customer.									
In office preparing proposals.									
Working with other departments.									
Traveling.									
Waiting.									
Conflict resolution.									
In office other.									
TOTAL									
Number of prospect in-person calls.									
Number of customer in-person calls.									

HOW WOULD YOU LIKE TO ALLOCATE YOUR TIME TO IMPROVE RESULTS?

WHAT NEEDS TO BE CHANGED TO ACCOMPLISH THIS?

COMMENTS:
_____
_____
_____
_____
_____

log analysis gets their attention. Solicit their suggestions for increasing the time devoted to activities most important to increasing sales, and agree to a course of action. Often internal administrative changes are needed to free up salespeople's time.

Second, ask the salesperson to prepare a map of his or her territory with account locations color-coded by frequency of visits. Discuss how the salesperson travels the territory and the most efficient schedule/routes for meeting these call requirements. Can accounts be called on in clusters? What overnight trips are necessary? Discuss efficient highways, public transportation, or airline systems for moving between accounts.

Some sales managers organize territories into four quadrants, sections, or slices. A salesperson spends a day per week or a week per month in each quadrant, working it in a cloverleaf pattern, or starting at the farthest point and working back, or working in a line between two overnight stops. Usually one day per week remains for cleaning up unplanned events. Some sales managers further refine this technique by gridding each quadrant and assigning it one day of the week or month. Sales managers may also ask their salespeople to make all planned calls before 2:00 p.m. (prime selling time) and to use the time after 2:00 p.m. to react to customer calls, missed accounts, and other problems. In other words, act in the morning, react in the afternoon. Every product, service, company, and territory requires a customized approach because the problems, opportunities, needs, and customers are different. Again, mapping and scheduling software can assist you in this task.

Experienced salespeople don't enjoy being told how to organize their day. So present your map merely as an aid and let them tell you how they plan to organize their schedule. Provide suggestions and information where you feel they are necessary to accomplish the desired goals.

Some sales managers feel that helping their people schedule calls is not worth their time because it represents a skill possessed by every salesperson. But if your average sales call costs $164, as discussed previously, and if proper scheduling results in one more call a day, or 240 more calls per year per salesperson, then you might be increasing efficiency or lowering expenses per salesperson dramatically. Considered in this light, scheduling deserves and needs your time and attention.

Even the best salespeople sometimes possess poor planning skills or have developed bad scheduling habits. As an objective voice from outside the territory, you can suggest changes.

Third, ask your salespeople how they use day parts to organize their time. What are the best times of day or best days of the week to prospect? What are the best hours to call on a physician or a hospital purchasing agent? Is it better to call on construction sites and restaurants before 8:00 a.m. but on research labs after lunch? In some industries, Friday afternoons and Monday mornings are prime selling hours.

With each salesperson, share your knowledge of how to allocate time as between prospects and established business. You should suggest a different allocation for matured territories with many established accounts than for a newer territory with only a few established customers. Growth occurs not only from opening new accounts but from properly cultivating existing ones.

With each salesperson, share your knowledge of the service versus selling time required for each customer, type of customer, or territory. What allocation produces the best results?

If your company sells more than one product line or has different or distinct markets or customer groups, share your knowledge with each salesperson on how to allocate time between these products, markets, and customers. What allocation produces the best results?

Working smart, or efficiently, is as important as working long and hard. You need to do both. Many salespeople attempt to disguise their ineffectiveness by appearing to work long and hard.

Following are a few tips to maximize efficiency:

- Be sure your salespeople plan their calls at least a week in advance, and that they put their plans into writing. Who will they see and what do they wish to accomplish?

- Be sure your salespeople use available technology to better manage their time. Do all salespeople take full advantage of the contact and calendar management software, cell phones, email, and the Web?

- Be sure your salespeople don't call on unqualified leads that have not been properly screened, analyzed, evaluated, or updated. Selling time is too precious to squander it on low potential prospects or coffee calls.

- Be sure your salespeople use the telephone and email not only to make appointments but also to answer certain questions and write certain reorders. Salespeople often underutilize the phone and email. You can communicate with a lot more customers each day by phone and email than in person.

- Be sure salespeople understand what hours you want worked and how often you want them in the office. Does the day start at 7:00 or 9:00 a.m.? Does it end at 4:00 or 6:00 p.m.? Is lunch to be used for selling or relaxing? Does Friday end at 2:00 or 5:00 p.m.? Set standards, be critical, and sit in judgment.

- Be sure your salespeople don't bury themselves in paperwork then use that as an excuse for not selling. Analyze their paperwork load and help them to reduce it. Work with top management on reducing administrative work and improving communications with other departments.

- Be sure your salespeople prioritize their day, listing their tasks by importance. Salespeople have a tendency to do the easy work, which may not be the most important work, first.

- Encourage your salespeople to set daily objectives and deadlines, to focus on results, and to develop alternatives. Encourage your salespeople to avoid procrastinating, to concentrate their efforts on one thing at a time, and to consider delegating by using available resources intelligently. Remind them of their schedules, but when unplanned events occur, encourage them to be flexible. Remind them that to maintain their priorities, they must occasionally say no to customers, fellow employees, and even you. Help them to anticipate problems and to develop contingency plans, in order to manage the continual flow of daily interruptions. Lack of persistence and poor communication with fellow employees can also be time wasters.

• Use ride-withs and sales meetings to train salespeople in time management. At the end of each day of field coaching, discuss the number of calls, time in front of customers, miles traveled between accounts, and allocation of time between various markets, activities, and products. At sales meetings have salespeople discuss best practices and time wasters. Let the salesperson who is best at time management lead the discussion.

In addition to helping salespeople plan their time, you need to efficiently allocate *your* precious resource—time. For one month keep a time log. What percent of your time was spent training salespeople in the field, in front of customers, traveling, at sales meetings, handling conflict resolution, on the phone answering questions or following up on orders, doing paperwork, at management meetings, or preparing bids, proposals, budgets, or plans? Make a list of your duties. Prioritize activities in terms of driving revenues. Keep track of how you spend your time. Analyze whether a different allocation would produce better results, and if so, what action is required to produce that different allocation.

The object of all this information is to have salespeople economically make the optimum number of effective calls on the right customers and prospects. The emphasis is on helping the salesperson work smarter, thus creating a more productive and efficient sales force. Do salespeople control their territories or do the territories control them? Knowledge is power, and time is money.

QUESTIONS AND EXERCISES

• Have each of your salespeople fill out a Time Allocation Planner. Based on this information, what deployment action will you take?

• What metrics can your firm use to measure potential revenues and margins in each territory?

• How often does your firm analyze channel choice, the number of salespeople, and territory boundaries?

- What percentage of your salespeople's time is spent in the activities that drive results? What are those activities? How can more time be spent there?

SALES MANAGERS' MAJOR MISTAKES/WEAKNESSES
TIME AND TERRITORY/ORGANIZATION

- Not measuring salespeople's use of time with time logs and time wasters
- Creating territories based on equal geography
- Creating territories based on present sales and actual number of accounts rather than potential versus salesperson's call rate
- Not coaching salespeople on travel routes, time allocation, sequence, frequency of visits to A, B, and C accounts; strategic issues
- Not realizing and showing the cost of putting a salesperson on the road
- Not analyzing alternative distribution channels and alternative ways of organizing the sales force; strategic issues
- Not reviewing territory boundaries annually
- Lack of personal organization and time management skills

CHAPTER 6

Sales Forecasting and Sales Planning

Planning makes good things happen. Bad things happen by themselves. Forecasting and planning puts your head in front of your job and creates quiet time. As discussed in Chapter 1, planning, forecasting, job descriptions, candidate profiles, training checklists, development plans, deployment, targeting, and performance evaluations all represent key control points for sales force management. When you correctly use present knowledge, forecasts accurately estimate future sales. You use sales plans to list the action necessary to generate those future sales.

All management involves goal setting, measurement, objectives, and strategy. Sales forecasts and plans are used to set the goals. The performance evaluation, discussed in Chapter 8, measures and compares actual results and action to these goals. We manage what we monitor.

Financial management and sales management meet each other through the sales forecast. If done correctly, the sales forecast helps operating management schedule production, procurement, and staffing. It also helps financial management establish inventory levels, set expense budgets, estimate cash flow, and project banking requirements.

Accurate, effective sales forecasts and plans involve a blending of objective and subjective material and a balance of top-down and bubble-up input. The salespeople and their manager create a micro forecast and plan based on (1) past and present territorial sales trends, (2) changes inside the firm, (3) changes at competitors,(4) changes at customers, and (5) changes in the general business environment/market. Top management creates a macro sales forecast/plan based on past and present sales trends for the company and market assessment metrics. These will be discussed later in this chapter.

BENEFITS OF A BUBBLE-UP SALES FORECAST/PLAN

Asking salespeople to prepare their own sales forecast and plan has many benefits—as well as a few problems. Reaping the benefits and mitigating the problems requires proper structure and process.

Salespeople who prepare and agree to their own forecast/plan have ownership of and involvement in the process. If a salesperson's actual results underperform a forecast he or she had little influence on, then the forecast was unrealistic. If a salesperson's actual results underperform a forecast he or she created, it is his or her responsibility. Bubble-up forecasts prepared and agreed to by salespeople make them feel useful, important, and worthwhile. Management cares about them and their input.

Since salespeople are closest to customers, their involvement in forecasting should improve accuracy and create more realistic goals. The figures were arrived at through a rational process, not just plucked out of the air. The bubble-up process should not force salespeople to accept unreasonable objectives. Bubble-up forecasts level the playing field by allowing each salesperson to evaluate the factors that drive sales in his or her territory. This prevents management from applying the same percentage or dollar increase to all territories without allowing for individual differences.

Bubble-up forecasts involve collecting a great deal of objective and subjective qualitative and quantitative information on sales trends by territory, customer, and product; changes within the company, at customers, and at competitors; and changes in general market conditions that impact sales at the territory level. This micro approach collects many pieces of information from diverse sources, then aggregates them into modules and models which should result in more accurate, more rational sales forecasts. The totals from these micro territory forecasts are then compared to the macro top-down numbers from management, which reflect metrics such as market share and return on investment. If done correctly, these two building blocks produce an even more accurate sales forecast.

Many sales managers claim that the major benefit of a bubble-up forecast is it forces the manager and the salesperson to periodically have a meaningful dialog about the salesperson's entire job. It forces the salesperson and manager to look at past and present sales trends, and to evaluate the factors inside and outside the firm which drive sales. Asking salespeople to forecast their sales without the proper format, discussion process, models, modules, numbers, information, and management input creates frustration and inaccuracy. You can't ask salespeople to forecast from a blank piece of paper.

Bubble-up sales forecasts and plans operate as a reality check and early warning system for sales managers and salespeople. If a salesperson cannot discuss changes occurring at customers and competition, the sales manager may have a problem salesperson.

Brokers, distributors, and outside indirect sales representatives, or channel partners, should prepare a bubble-up forecast using the same techniques and format as direct full-time salespeople. The sales manager should meet with channel partners to have a meaningful dialog on inside and outside factors which drive their numbers. By making quarterly or annual sales forecasts and plans part of their contract, you will get more of their commitment and involvement. Channel partners who forecast sales and get committed give you more of their time and resources. The accuracy of their numbers is also important for the operational and financial management of your company.

PROBLEMS WITH A BUBBLE-UP SALES FORECAST/PLAN

Salespeople may intentionally underestimate or overestimate their sales. When a bonus is based on meeting the forecast, when the forecast becomes a quota, or if a salesperson wants to look like a hero by beating forecast, he or she may underestimate sales. On the other hand, a salesperson who wants to please his or her sales manager, keep his or her job, or be unrealistically enthusiastic may overestimate sales. Also, when salespeople don't understand or aren't given the proper forecasting tools, over- and underestimates occur.

In Hewitt Associates' survey of Fortune 1000 firms, of the 120 respondents, two-thirds used a quota-based component in their sales incentive plan. Of these, 79 percent felt their quota-setting process was moderately effective and two-thirds used a top-down quota-setting process. In another Hewitt survey of fourteen companies, with at least 1000 salespeople each, sales managers ranked their satisfaction with the quota-setting process at 2.3 on a five-point scale. The most common obstacles cited in setting quotas were inability to obtain market-potential data (64 percent) and inaccurate or insufficient product forecasts (62 percent). Market research available through the Web and databases created through customer relationship management software may correct some of this.

Often salespeople resist forecasting and planning because this creates a standard against which they can be measured. Some salespeople dislike being held accountable. Forecasts can be time-consuming and confusing. Many firms include forecasting skills and accuracy on the salesperson's and sales manager's performance evaluation. As mentioned, many firms use sales forecasts to create quotas and pay bonuses to salespeople and sales managers based on reaching or exceeding quota, although, as noted earlier, many firms are moving away from quota-based compensation.

Sometimes sales managers resist bubble-up forecasts because it requires them to set standards with their salespeople, then sit in judgment and be critical. When a salesperson misses his or her bubble-up forecast, both the salesperson and manager are responsible. A sales force is no better than its management.

Many sales managers dislike sales forecasts and plans because they either misunderstand or mistrust the mechanics and because they also fear the results. When a sales manager's forecast or plan turns out to be incorrect, it reflects on his or her ability and performance. Many businesses prepare no forecast, but that is akin to sailing without a rudder—or a map.

These problems can be overcome by using the techniques, models, modules, formats, and processes described in this chapter. To improve accuracy and increase the comfort level, many firms ask salespeople to prepare a best- and worst-case forecast, the probability of each, factors which create the variance, critical risks, and contingency plans. For example, let's assume that a salesperson for a computer manufacturing subcontractor forecasts next quarter's best case at $5 million and the worst at $4 million. The $4 million forecast has a 100 percent probability of success, the $5 million forecast an 80 percent probability of success. The salesperson claims she will meet the $5 million forecast if her largest account does not go on a credit hold, if her company can meet their delivery schedule, if another customer successfully launches its new product, and if her friend does not retire as the decision maker at yet another customer. The sales manager asks the salesperson for her contingency plan should these negative events or critical risks occur and if there are any other reasons that might prevent her from making the $5 million. Contingency plans allow salespeople to anticipate problems and their solutions. This removes some emotion from disappointing events.

This process allows the manager and the salesperson to discuss all the excuses thirty days before the quarter rather than afterward. Salespeople who are reluctant to forecast generally feel comfortable with the best/worst-case method. This bracketing process mitigates the fear of forecasting. As the year progresses and more of the "what ifs" become reality, the salesperson can make revisions to produce a more precise forecast.

Another problem with bubble-up forecasts occurs when management will not accept them or when management does not use them. Imagine that your seven salespeople have forecasted an 8 percent increase for the region. Some territories will rise substantially above 8 percent, some less. However, top management also has prepared their sales forecast, which reflects return on investment and market share metrics. Based on these metrics, top management wants a 12 percent increase from the region.

Salespeople must understand that although management wants and values their bubble-up forecast, management will prepare their own using different criteria. Salespeople and management must understand there can be differences which may be negotiated.

When differences occur, analyze what caused them. Examine each party's assumptions and resources. Did the salespeople evaluate their individual territorial forecasts against market assessment tools, such as hospital admissions, buying power indexes, or semiconductor purchases? Did management evaluate the effect of a new competitor and also the loss of a major account on their company forecast?

What compromises are possible? Is the top-down forecast doable with more resources, such as another customer service person, a Web site, cell phones, or laptops? Can territory boundaries be changed or other products or services sold? Top-down management and bottom-up salespeople/sales management must be willing to negotiate and compromise or the model will not work. If salespeople continually lose, then the bubble-up forecast loses its many benefits. If the forecast becomes a quota on which salespeople receive performance pay, and it is viewed as unrealistic, then salespeople will lose their motivation to exceed quota.

Management also must commit to comparing forecast numbers to actual on a monthly or quarterly basis. Some firms ask for the forecast but never use it, which demotivates salespeople and the sales manager.

FORMAT AND PROCESS FOR SALES FORECAST

Thirty to ninety days before the start of your company's accounting year, quarter, or selling season, send snail mail or email to each salesperson, agent, representative, or distributor who sells your product or service a forecast form for his or her territory. On this form, ask the sales force to forecast orders by month or quarter for each customer or industry, as well as for each product/service/style or product/service/style group. You may ask for this information in terms of dollars or units or both. Request information that the sales force finds easiest to work with and that proves most helpful in meeting the forecast's objectives. If the sales force thinks in terms of dollar sales per customer and if the objective of your sales forecast is cash flow projections, not inventory control, then ask each salesperson to forecast dollar sales per appropriate period by customer. Don't ask for unit sales by product/service.

If your company takes orders for future rather than immediate delivery, then the salesperson must identify what months orders are to be shipped. If 90 percent of all orders are shipped within forty-five days, you can use a standard factor to translate orders into shipments. Similarly, you can translate any unit forecasts into dollars using standards or averages.

If your industry has selling seasons, as the apparel industry does, you may ask for a forecast by season rather than by month or quarter. You may also ask salespeople to update their forecasts each month or quarter to reflect the changing dynamics of the marketplace.

Once you have established the format for your forecast and sent it to your salespeople, it is important to meet with them to discuss the factors which drive the numbers. With new salespeople or those not familiar with the process, help them prepare the numbers. With established salespeople and those familiar with the process, review the numbers. Issues common to all salespeople may be addressed at a sales meeting.

When discussing the forecast, the sales manager has a meaningful dialog with each salesperson on past and present sales trends in the territory, along with changes taking place at competitors, customers, in general business conditions, and at your firm. The sales forecast can be prepared and updated online using function-specific software, which saves time and improves communication.

Each salesperson starts their bottom-up forecast by analyzing past and present sales trends in their territory. The salesperson may do this in total, by customer, or by product, depending on what historical data is available. If next year or next quarter looks like the past quarter or past year, what will sales be? Obviously, companies that don't prepare customer and product analyses by territory cannot do this and can only work with territorial totals.

Here's an example. A marketing consulting company which provides temporary expert help to Fortune 1000 firms asks its salespeople to prepare quarterly sales forecasts. The San Francisco salesperson looks at her total quarterly sales for the last two years. From the first to the last quarter (eight quarters), total sales doubled from $100,000 to $200,000, an average of $12,500 a quarter, or 12 percent. Price increases accounted for 20 percent of the total increase over this two-year period. More of the unit/hourly sales growth came in year two than year one. She considers just using the last four quarters' growth trend to predict next quarter. (Averages computed by removing the oldest period and adding the newest are called *moving averages*.) She notes that growth has accelerated each quarter in the last year and considers giving the last quarter's growth rate more weight. She also notes that growth in Web-based services far exceeds growth in direct marketing and media advertising services. Most of last year's growth came from three large accounts.

Based on these past and present quarterly sales trends for the territory, product lines, and customers, assuming no price increases and using moving and weighted averages, she decides on initially forecasting a 20 percent total sales increase from this quarter to next. She then uses these same techniques to forecast sales for next quarter by customer and product line. She assigns a probability of 85 percent to meeting her forecast, lists several reasons which could cause her to miss it, as well as critical risks, and notes contingency plans.

The forecast process begins with the assumption that the future will look like the past, so we extrapolate next quarter's sales based on past trends. But the future is a moving target and business is a dynamic process, so next the salesperson must analyze how changes within her company, at competitors, and in the market place will impact future revenues. To understand these changes, the salesperson again must have a meaningful dialog with the sales manager. The sales manager presents changes within the company, the salesperson presents changes at customers and competitors, and together they decide on changes in the marketplace and general business conditions.

In our example, the sales manager for the marketing consulting firm asks each salesperson to quantify how the following changes within the firm will impact their territorial sales for the next quarter.

1. Prices on all ecommerce services will be raised 10 percent.
2. A strategic sales alliance has been signed with a major ecommerce software provider.
3. The salespeople will receive laptops and new cell phones.
4. Salespeople will receive a $2000 bonus for exceeding their revenue goal, plus a $1000 incentive for each new account with revenues exceeding $10,000 in the quarter.
5. More marketing consultants, product specialists, and customer support people are being hired.
6. A new Web design service will be offered.
7. Some territory boundaries are being changed.
8. Participation in trade shows and trade publication advertising will be increased.
9. Payment terms will be changed from net 60 to 2 percent 30 days, and the minimum size acceptable assignment increased from 40 to 50 hours.

For firms using channel partners rather than direct salespeople, the sales manager shares the same pertinent information. The sales forecast presents an opportunity for the sales manager to discuss with each salesperson anticipated changes within the company. Salespeople must understand that these changes require sales increases to justify their cost. Changes also must include sharing any negative news, such as capacity restraints, discontinuing a product/service, tighter credit restrictions, or reduced sales support and marketing.

Next, the salesperson and the sales manager discuss changes outside the company which will impact next quarter's sales. These include changes at competitors, customers, and in the general business environment over which the sales staff has little control. For instance, does the competitor plan to add or delete products/services, raise or lower prices, hire more sales-people, improve technology, increase or decrease sales support, change terms, change personnel, or change compensation or policy? Essentially, sales managers and salespeople need to know everything about the competitor that they know about their own company. Knowledge is power if you use it.

The marketing consulting firm sales manager and salesperson discuss changes at three competitors and quantify the impact on next quarter's sales. First, a large brand-name management consulting firm has hired consultants to provide Web-based marketing services. Second, a regional temporary help firm has added marketing personnel to its roster. Third, several regional marketing consulting firms have lowered prices for database and direct marketing services. All these firms have high turnover among their salespeople.

The sales manager has the primary responsibility to explain changes within the company, but the salesperson has a primary responsibility to explain changes at customers. As mentioned earlier, a salesperson who cannot identify changes at key customers and how these changes impact sales represents a potential problem. Salespeople have received training in obtaining customer knowledge and keeping profiles, and they should be aware of changes that could affect their forecast.

Consider asking your key customers to forecast their purchases or use of your services. Sell the benefits of their partnering with your salesperson to create a forecast. For key accounts, a forecast of their needs will allow your firm to better serve them. Deliveries and quality of service should improve. Many large customers insist on participating in their vendors' forecasts. Such partnering creates a barrier to entry for competition.

The San Francisco salesperson in our example feels that her largest customer, a sportswear manufacturer, may be reducing its budget for consulting services and that her key champion may be changing jobs. However, this potential loss may be compensated for by a major computer company in her territory expanding their online sales effort. Some smaller accounts may have credit problems. A potential strike by hourly employees at another customer would reduce their need for direct-mail marketing. Another firm has new ownership and has decided to bring all consulting work inside.

The sales manager and salesperson discuss changes at the top twenty accounts which represent 75 percent of the territory's revenues. The salesperson prepares a dollar forecast for each of these top twenty accounts and compares the number to last quarter and last year. The salesperson also notes the percentage of her total quarterly business each of these accounts represent (see Exhibit 6.1).

The salesperson presents a list, shown in Exhibit 6.2, of her top ten growth accounts for the quarter. These represent present customers with the highest dollar or percentage growth potential. There may be an over-

Exhibit 6.1

Top twenty accounts ranked by volume.

Account Representative: _____   Date: _____

Account Name	Estimated Revenues— Past Quarter and/or Past Quarter Previous Year	Estimated Revenues— Next Quarter	Percentage of Accounts' Business Given to Us	Percent of Territory Total Revenues	Changes at Customer Which May or Have Already Positively or Negatively Impacted Dollars of Revenue or Gross Profit
1.					
2.					
3.					
4.					
5.					
6.					
7.					
8.					
9.					
10.					
11.					
12.					
13.					
14.					
15.					
16.					
19.					
20.					

E x h i b i t   6.2

Ten present accounts with highest growth potential.

Account Representative: _____ Date: _____				
	Customer Name, Location, Decision Makers	**Target Product, Service or Program Problems/ Needs**	**Competition**	**Strategy**	**Potential Volume**
1.					
2.					
3.					
4.					
5.					
6.					
7.					
8.					
9.					
10.					

lap with the top twenty volume accounts. The list includes some reality checks, such as the decision maker's name, product/service to be added, competitors, strategy, and projected revenue increase.

The salesperson also presents a list, shown in Exhibit 6.3, of her top ten prospects, including the decision maker, targeted service, competition, strategy, and potential volume. This level of detail separates prospects from suspects and again acts as a reality check.

Next, the sales manager and salesperson discuss changes in market demand trends and business conditions that will impact next quarter's forecasted sales. For some firms such changes might include interest rates, government regulations, gross domestic product, unemployment, personal income, retail sales, exchange rates, or oil prices. This discussion includes the macros and micros which drive demand for your products or services and your customer's products or services. Your customer's success drives your firm's revenues. In our example, the San Francisco salesperson and her sales

E x h i b i t 6.3

Top ten prospects in terretory.

Account Representative: _____ Date: _____				
Customer Name, Location, Decision Makers	**Target Product, Service or Program Problems/ Needs**	**Competition**	**Strategy**	**Potential Volume**
1.				
2.				
3.				
4.				
5.				
6.				
7.				
8.				
9.				
10.				

manager believe next quarter's revenues will be impacted by a labor scarcity in the Bay Area and by increased demand for high-tech products.

After considering past and present sales trends, anticipated changes within the company, and anticipated changes at the competition, customers, and in-demand trends, the San Francisco salesperson arrives at a best- and worst-case sales forecast for the next quarter of $230,000 to $250,000. She assigns a probability of 100 percent to the worst case and 80 percent to the best. Critical risks and contingency plans reflect the changes inside and outside the firm.

After discussing and agreeing to all the salespeople's bubble-up forecasts, the sales manager aggregates them into a company or regional forecast. He or she might want to add or subtract for a new territory, salesperson, acquisition, management accounts, or other factors outside or in addition to the present salespeople. Online forecasting makes aggregating and adjusting easier.

Now the sales manager must evaluate whether this aggregated national or regional sales forecast meets market assessment and corporate growth requirements. Before the sales manager has a meaningful dialog with each salesperson, he or she should know what growth rates and market assessment tools will shape the top-down forecast. The sales manager will use the dialog to help each salesperson arrive at an acceptable number. The sales manager should know what total sales revenue will prove acceptable. This reduces the need to revise individual bubble-up forecasts and forces communication between the sales manager and top management.

The sales manager also should evaluate each salesperson's forecast against available market assessment tools for that territory and acceptable growth rates for the territory. A smaller, newer territory should grow at a faster percentage rate than a matured one, which may grow at a slower rate but result in larger dollar increases. Apply top management's metrics and market assessment tools to each territory, but also develop your own. How can you measure market potential and market share for each territory? Hopefully, in establishing territories of equal potential, you have decided on proper market assessment metrics. As discussed previously, these will be different for different industries. They can range from buying power indexes by city or region for different SIC (Standard Industrial Classification) codes to the number of prescriptions written by physician by medication.

For products or services with longer, more complex sales cycles, you must modify the sales forecast process. For each product or service, the forecast period would be lengthened from a quarter to six months or more, and the forecast format would include not only sales, but tracking the steps leading to these sales. Each customer's/project's probability of success would depend on moving from one step to another in a timely manner. The meaningful dialog between sales manager and salesperson continues, as does the bubble-up process.

The sales manager would ask salespeople for a list of their customers/prospects ranked by probability of success and organized by potential closing dates and status between search and purchase. The meaningful dialog would again include changes inside and outside the company, but it also would include where each major customer/prospect is in the sales/buying cycle, issues affecting probability of success, and closing dates. The forecast discussion would include dates, probabilities, and strategies for moving customers from need qualification to benefit quantification to betas and final presentation.

After asking salespeople to invest considerable time in the forecasting process, the firm must compare this information to actual results. Actual monthly and year-to-date results by salesperson, distributor, outside sales representative organization, or another channel partner should be compared to the previous year and forecast. Depending on the level of forecast detail, comparisons can be made for each salesperson by account and product line.

The sales manager and salesperson should discuss the causes of variances each month between actual and forecast, and the impact this might have on the forecast for next month or next quarter. Variances might indicate a salesperson's training needs, which would be included in his or her development plan or stressed on the next ride-with. Variances which persist quarter after quarter could indicate a need to replace a salesperson. Performance evaluations also offer an opportunity to discuss these issues.

Similarly, you must compare the national or regional forecast to actual results. Did the national or regional forecast accurately project actual sales? Was your forecast correct in units but wrong in dollars? Was it correct as to direction of sales but wrong as to the magnitude of that direction? Was it accurate for one product line or customer group but inaccurate for another? Analyze the reasons for these variances, and take appropriate corrective action on your next forecast. Perhaps you should put less emphasis on general economic indicators and sales trends and give more emphasis to changes in industry demand, pricing, new accounts, and competitors' new products.

Under what circumstances should a forecast be revised, especially if salespeople receive performance pay based on actual results versus forecast? What if the firm can't provide the product or service, if a major account announces bankruptcy or is acquired, or if customer demand declines because of changes in exchange rates.

Most companies have a sales forecast and a sales budget. One can be changed, the other cannot. One is used for procurement, scheduling, and financial management; the other is used as a benchmark for salespeople. Circumstances that should have been anticipated do not constitute grounds for changing the salesperson's forecast. These represent the critical risks for which the salesperson should have a contingency plan. However, circumstances that could not have been anticipated constitute grounds for changing the salesperson's forecast.

TOP-DOWN FORECASTS

As a sales manager, your total sales force bubble-up forecast must meet the needs of top management and corporate goals. As discussed, one objective of forecasting is to integrate the top-down and bubble-up processes. Understanding the mechanics of top-down forecasts will help you accomplish this.

Like bubble-up, top-down forecasting uses objective and subjective methods to accumulate and analyze quantitaive and qualitative data. However, the top-down process starts with national economic conditions and industry market potential to generate company potential sales and a sales forecast, which becomes allocated by region, district, territory, and then by account. The top-down number must satisfy corporate goals for shareholder value, growth, market share, cash flow (EBITDA), profit (EBIT), and return on investment.

Statistical modeling is used to extrapolate historic data into future forecasts. Regression models rely on information and factors such as the number of calls that "cause" the sale. Time series models rely on observed changes in sales trends and may use moving averages, which average dollars and percentage changes in sales over a number of months, quarters, or years. Time series models may use exponential smoothing, which gives more weight to more recent or older changes in sales over a number of months, quarters, or years. Adoptive filtering and time series extrapolation represent variations and refinements of moving averages and exponential filtering.

The top-down total company forecast must be allocated by region, district, or territory based on the previous year's sales and future potential for that region, district, or territory as a percentage of total company sales or potential. This macroallocation will be measured against each region's, district's, or territory's micromarket potential and market share.

The sales manager and top management must use the same or similar metrics for measuring market potential, such as buying power indices (BPI) and data by SIC code, which correlate to demand for your firm's products/services. BPI combines consumer income, population, and retail sales to arrive at buying power by zip code, city, county, and state. What data tracks, drives, or matches market potential for your company's products or services: number of employees, number of telephones, number of hospitals (input/output models)? As mentioned, some firms will survey the buying intentions of their top accounts. Many firms use outside consultants to obtain and prepare this top-down information, which may also involve economic models and leading indicators.

The top-down forecast is presented to a management committee for approval. The committee should consist of a representative from operations, finance, sales, and marketing, plus the CEO. This same committee will analyze and approve the bubble-up forecast. The key to successful forecasting is using a variety of techniques that combine top-down, bubble-up, quantitative, qualitative, and objective and subjective approaches and then running the results through a variety of judges.

If your company relies on a constant stream of new products or services to drive sales, then top-down forecasting requires more customer surveys and focus groups. Based on these surveys and focus groups, management estimates the number and type of customers likely to buy and rebuy this new product or service. The number of customers for this new product will be multiplied by their estimated initial order and reorders to arrive at total dollar sales.

THE SALES PLAN

The sales forecast is a number. The sales plan is the tactical and strategic action on the part of each salesperson and sales manager to reach that number. The sales forecast says, "I want to get from point A to point B." The sales plan says, "This is how I am going to do it." Sales plans and forecasts overlap and interrelate. The Top Ten Prospect List (Exhibit 6.3) and Ten Present Accounts with the Highest Growth Potential (Exhibit 6.2) contain both forecast numbers and sales plan action. The sales plan, as the sales forecast, represents a joint effort between salesperson and sales manager involving the meaningful sharing of information. The sales plan, as the sales forecast, should be prepared not only by direct company employed salespeople but by your channel partners (independent distributors, brokers, and sales rep organizations).

The sales plan starts by breaking down each salesperson's sales forecast into bite-size pieces. If a salesperson's annual sales forecast is $1,650,000, he or she must analyze how that breaks down by product line, market, new accounts, old accounts, present account growth, customer group, gross margin contribution, and sales by month and week.

For example, the salespeople at a Midwest wholesale commercial paper distributor divide the $1.65 million by 48 selling weeks and 240 working days. The salesperson knows that to meet forecast, he or she must produce $34,370 of revenue a week, or $6874 a day. The rule is no lunch until daily revenues reach $6000. Each day the sales manager posts each salesperson's dollar results and percent of forecast to a secure Web site.

The $34,370 a week or $137,500 a month has product line, customer group, and pricing goals. The dollar forecast and specific goals vary by territory and salesperson. For one salesperson the monthly goal is 50 percent coated paper, 30 percent copy machine paper, and 30 percent fine paper. Her monthly customer group goal is 40 percent commercial printers, 30 percent offices, 15 percent fast print shops, and 15 percent in-house captive company printing departments.

In addition, each salesperson has pricing or gross margin goals, because a great deal of negotiation occurs in setting customer prices for each order. One salesperson has a pricing or gross margin goal of 30 percent and another of 20 percent, because one territory has far more competitors than the other.

Each salesperson has a dollar goal for generating new business versus maintaining or expanding existing accounts. For example, $200,000 of the $1,650,000 is forecast to come from twenty new accounts. Since the closing ratio is nine to one, it will take 180 prospecting/new account calls, or four a week, to open these twenty accounts. Each salesperson's plan includes a list of target accounts ranked by probability of opening them and their potential dollar volume. Each salesperson's plan includes a list of present high-growth accounts ranked by probability of success and potential dollars of volume.

Once the bite-sized pieces are agreed to, the salesperson and manager can agree on the specific action necessary to obtain the sales forecast. Generally, the action involves number of calls a day, number of prospect calls a week, allocation of calls and time between various type customers, product lines and markets, call frequency for A, B, C accounts, targeting, training development programs, customer service issues, account receivable collections, call reports, customer profiles, inactive and lost accounts, time management, and reporting requirements (see Exhibit 6.4). The job description lists most of these activities as duties.

The call allocation goals for the wholesale commercial paper distributor we discussed are based on each salesperson's present and potential accounts, their density, the dollar forecast for new business versus retention or penetration, and the dollar forecast by product line and customer group. The wholesale commercial paper distributor assigns the Milwaukee salesperson a daily call goal of twelve, broken down into one new account call, one service call, and ten penetration/retention calls. Of those ten daily penetration calls, five should be on A accounts, three on B accounts, and two on C accounts. The call goals might also be broken down by end-user type and product line.

The sales plan for products/services with long, complex sales cycles will be less focused on the number of calls and more focused on the strategic and tactical action necessary to move major prospects/customers from one step in the sales cycle to the next. Training, development, time management, and time allocation issues remain important. It is important to determine how this salesperson will allocate her time between the field and the office, between working with customers and working with in-house engineering on proposals.

In addition to the salespeople's plans, the sales manager must prepare his or her own sales plan. The sales manager must determine what strategic and tactical action on his part is necessary to make the region's numbers. The sales manager's plan should include action related to hiring, training, compensating, staffing, deploying, motivating, evaluating, and automating the sales force. Proposed dates and agendas for sales meetings,

E x h i b i t 6.4

Sales forecast and sales plan. Quarter ending _____

TERRITORY: _____

TERRITORY MANAGER: _____

DOLLAR SALES BY PRODUCT LINE

	Month	Chronic	Acute	Staffing	Totals	Percent
1.						
2.						
3.						
TOTAL						

Necessary sales per week each month: _____

Necessary sales per day each month: _____

Factors that might prevent you from reaching quarterly forecast/goals:

_____

_____

_____

Effect of lost or inactive customers versus previous quarter:

_____

_____

_____

Changes you will make in geographic coverage, customer coverage, and product line emphasis:

_____

_____

_____

Number of account calls you plan to make a week: _____

Number of prospect calls you plan to make a week: _____

What assistance would you like from your manager in this quarter to reach your goals?:

Training: _____

Ride-Withs: _____

Accounts: _____

Other: _____

new territory boundaries, field coaching schedules, telemarketing programs, and software for laptops would be included in this plan. For the sales manager, as opposed to the salesperson, his or her sales plan is a simplified microcosm of this book. The sales manager's plan should include critical risks and contingencies. What is the sales manager's contingency plan if a top salesperson leaves or becomes disabled? How will training change if a new competitor enters the market? How will deployment and staffing change if a major customer chooses a competitor?

SALES MANAGERS' MAJOR WEAKNESSES/MISTAKES FORECASTING/PLANNING

- Top-down versus bubble-up
- Annual versus quarterly
- Asking for a number—not a plan, not a model
- No meaningful dialog
- Not prioritizing necessary action
- Not using information, not comparing actual versus goal
- Only forecasting on trends, not future changes or events
- Lack of personal planning

CHAPTER 7

Motivating Salespeople

A sales manager's job is getting work done through other people. His or her success depends on the success of the salespeople. You must hire the best, terminate the rest; train them in product, customer, competitor knowledge, and sales skills; deploy, organize, and staff correctly. To fully capitalize on a salesperson's potential, you must motivate that person. Successful sales managers are agents of change. They take advantage of change, and they modify people's behavior.

Each salesperson has different needs, goals, aspirations, and problems. The sales manager's job involves uncovering these areas, and then helping each salesperson satisfy the needs, reach the goals, and solve the problems. You should have a profile on each salesperson, similar to the one salespeople keep for each customer. The profile might include information on family, interests, hobbies, professional experience, education, strengths, weaknesses, developmental plans, decision-making quadrant, personal goals, needs, aspiration, problems, and motivational hot buttons. The salespeople are the sales manager's internal customer.

Different sparks light different salespeople's fires. You can't mass-produce motivation. For example, overly competitive salespeople want to beat competition and colleagues, high achievers want to better their last year's results, superstars with large egos feel they are the best, service-oriented salespeople use empathy to build lasting relationships with customers and colleagues, and plateauing salespeople reach their "career level" well below their level of competence or may just have stopped learning and growing. The sales manager must create a motivational plan with time frames for each salesperson and for the group.

For example, the sales manager for a regional telecommunication firm offering DSL services to businesses had six salespeople. One had been a history major in college, had no children, and her husband worked. She had grown up in a small town in Iowa. Her major interest was helping existing customers solve their problems, not opening new accounts, even though financial incentives rewarded new business.

Another salesperson had flunked out of college trying to pursue his father's career as a physician. He had grown up in sumptuous surroundings on Long Island and wanted to maintain that standard of living and social status for himself, his wife, and their three children. He needed and wanted to be the best salesperson. Most years he ended up number one in new business and total revenue.

A third salesperson had grown up in Eastern Europe under extreme poverty. Each year she worked long, hard, and smart, not to be number one but to exceed her previous year's figures.

The fourth salesperson was in his mid-fifties, had grown children, had considerable savings, and was in a rut. He has been with his present employer for fifteen years in various positions. He had done it all, knew it all, and felt comfortable.

The fifth salesperson wanted to move up the career ladder into management and had all the necessary experience and education. However, the company had no available positions, and so he had turned complacent.

The sixth salesperson, a young college graduate, was still a mystery. As a recent hire, results met standards, but he did not talk about himself.

During field visits, the sales manager developed personal relationships with these people to find out what they most wanted from their job and from their life. At dinner after the ride-with or between calls in the car, he involved the salesperson in some relaxing, self-revealing conversation. He asked what working environment promoted the best job satisfaction. What did the salesperson most need to be satisfied in his or her job: security, good wages, appreciation, feeling "in" on things, interesting work, pleasant conditions, growth, tactful discipline, sympathy, or loyalty? Each salesperson ranked these criteria differently, which gave the sales manager insight into their needs, goals, and problems. Often, his perception of each salesperson's job satisfaction needs ranked very differently from theirs. Out of this meaningful dialog came each salesperson's monthly motivational program.

Most salespeople want to be successful and enjoy working hard at something; yet that something is often not their job. The sales manager's challenge involves transferring more of their efforts into sales. A salesperson selling B2B ecommerce services produced great results when he worked, but he did not work often or hard enough. On a field visit, the salesperson invited the sales manager to his home for dinner. The sales manager noticed several motorcycles in the garage. At dinner the salesperson spoke about his passion for off-road motorcycle rallies but complained about his lack of funds to support this pastime.

The next day between calls, the sales manager asked how much money the motorcycles required. He then showed the salesperson that by selling one more major contract a month he would generate sufficient commission income to pay for more off-road rallies. That year, the salesperson's sales increased by one contract a month. In subsequent years, the salesperson and sales manager agreed on a bubble-up sales forecast which met both the salesperson's need for income to support his passion and the sales manager's need for growth.

BENEFITS

Our objective is to motivate salespeople not just to reach goal or plan but to fully capitalize on their potential. To accomplish this, we must convert a salesperson's complacency, which drives sales managers mad, into the salesperson's elixir—enthusiasm.

As discussed in Chapter 2, salesperson turnover proves very expensive. You can reduce turnover with proper hiring and training. Properly hired, trained, and motivated salespeople perform better, earn more, have better job satisfaction, and resign less often.

In earlier chapters, we learned that salespeople represent an expensive and important human resource. The annual cost of putting a salesperson on the road, including direct compensation, fringe benefits, and reimbursed expenses, ranges from $60,000 to several hundred thousand dollars. Highly motivated salespeople increase revenues, productivity, and capacity, lowering their cost per sales dollar. Motivated salespeople produce more dollars of output for each dollar of input.

We also discussed how the candidate profile calls for an enthusiastic and confident salesperson. Proper training and motivation maintains and creates enthusiasm and confidence.

Most companies employ some career salespeople who have no desire to move into management. Conversely, many companies have no opportunities for salespeople to move into management. For a smaller firm the career ladder might be closed. In both situations, a major motivator of salespeople, the career ladder, has been removed. In both these situations nonmonetary motivation must to some extent replace the career ladder.

Money represents an important motivator of salespeople. Hopefully, your compensation system rewards positive salesperson action and superior results important to the success of your firm, and reflects the salesperson's influence on the sale, the type of salesperson you desire, and the type of product your firm sells. But money is not a universal incentive. Salespeople reach comfort zones and complacency plateaus. A salesperson's motivation can depend on whether he or she is service-driven, an achiever, or, maybe, ego-driven. The compensation system requires proper structure but represents only one factor in driving salesperson behavior.

An employer deserves a day's work for a day's pay, but motivated salespeople can give you a day and a half's work for a day's pay. A motivated sales force costs no more than an unmotivated sales force, but it does require more of the sale manager's time and energy. Once you have created an environment that encourages self-motivation, it is much easier to sell new ideas to the sales force, whether this involves correcting a salesperson's bad habits or suggesting some new direction.

You need a motivational plan or program for each of your salespeople and the group, just as you do a training plan. Many managers consider motivation silly and unnecessary, thinking perhaps, "My boss doesn't have to motivate me. Why should I have to motivate the salespeople working under me?" Keep in mind, however, that a manager's lack of personal motivation can filter down to salespeople.

Although we can't force salespeople to be successful, we can help them to solve motivational problems and meet motivational needs. To motivate salespeople, you must first understand the specific needs and desires driving individuals and then find the activities and rewards that satisfy those needs. Each salesperson has a particular package of needs and goals, and these are not necessarily rational. Most salespeople, for instance, need varying degrees of recognition, a sense of achievement, a feeling of usefulness, and consistent leadership. In addition, some salespeople have a strong need to belong; many others require job or financial security.

Needs create tensions, and to relieve these tensions, salespeople engage in goal-directed, motivated behavior. When they achieve their goals, the tension is reduced. Other individuals and social groups influence people's needs and the goals they choose to satisfy these needs. A salesperson might desire certain positive results such as leisure, recognition, security, more money, or better use of time. Achieving these results creates a peace of mind and prestige. Not achieving them leads to a sense of failure, humiliation, or rejection and creates anxiety and depression.

As sales manager, your job is both to pinpoint the needs and to encourage the goal-directed actions that lead to the satisfaction of those needs. By using the individual's needs and goals, you thus motivate the salesperson to optimum performance. Of course, the results of this action also increase sales. And, eventually, salespeople obtain enough pleasure from their goal-directed activities to become self-motivated.

Positive incentives produce better results than using rank, punishment, and threats. Of course, you must use negative motivation in some situations with certain people, but it tends to lose its effectiveness when used more than once. Before you threaten a salesperson with probation, use up all of your positive tools.

Motivation represents an internal process of need satisfaction. Again, we can't force salespeople to be successful. However, this internal process is greatly influenced by external factors. You, the boss, represent one of the most important external factors. Consider how you feel when your boss does not return a phone call or fails to congratulate you in front of the president. How does it affect your personal motivation?

Salespeople's needs, goals, and motivation can be classified as those related to:

- Praise and recognition
- Feelings of usefulness
- Challenge and achievement
- Authority and freedom
- Self-realization and fulfillment through personal growth
- Esteem and status
- A sense of belonging
- Pleasant interpersonal relationships with management and peers
- Consistent, competent leadership
- Fair company policy and administration
- Job security
- Compensation, and advancement

These are the external factors that influence internal motivation. No one of these factors alone is terribly important, but taken together they create a powerful interrelated motivational force that requires a delicate, ever-changing balance.

In addition, these factors, needs, and goals not only motivate salespeople but any employee. Although this book deals with salespeople, you need to motivate all your employees using these techniques.

The motivational ideas and techniques described in this chapter are not only appropriate for direct full-time salespeople but also for channel partners, such as distributors, brokers, independent sales representatives, and value-added retailers (VARs). These same ideas and techniques can be successfully applied to telesales and customer support people.

RECOGNITION

Salespeople want to be noticed, praised, and appreciated for their performance, and as sales manager you should reinforce and reward positive action and results with recognition. Recognition involves anything from a casual thank-you over the phone to a formal awards dinner. Salespeople possess an insatiable appetite for recognition, which goes with the territory.

Salespeople must understand exactly which positive results will be rewarded with recognition: for example, more new accounts, more calls per day, better retention of existing business, selling price increases, shorter sales cycles, increased net sales, or better collections. The required results and the form of recognition—for example, a plaque, membership in a sales club, or a prize—should be different for different salespeople. Moreover, you must create different levels of recognition for varying levels of performance. The salesperson who visits a customer on Saturday to handle a service complaint deserves your thank-you. The salesperson who doubles his quarterly new account quota deserves to be nominated for salesperson of the month.

Also, lack of recognition—the silent treatment—can be a powerful tool. Make sure the person you choose not to recognize knows why. Otherwise, they will become frustrated and angry. Remember, positive motivation works better than negative.

Recognition becomes a more effective motivational tool when it is sincere, receives publicity, is recorded, and involves top management. Insincere praise has a negative effect on the recipient. Say it as if you mean it or don't say it at all. Save praise for the appropriate occasion. You can't praise all the people all the time.

Where appropriate, as when someone has won a sales contest, publicize the recognition in the company newsletter, in a bulletin, or in an email sent to all salespeople. If the recognition involves an award or civic involvement, consider sending press releases with pictures to the local papers. Community, suburban, and small town newspapers often need this type of material.

When a salesperson opens a major new account or places a new product or service with an important customer, have the other salespeople sign a copy of the order with a congratulatory note and send it to the appropriate salesperson. Peer recognition is a powerful tool and creates peer pressure to emulate the performance.

Where appropriate, record recognition with plaques, sales club memberships, certificates, or annual awards. For example, if a salesperson goes 50 percent over annual quota, issue a plaque or certificate inscribed with his or her name to commemorate the results.

Here's a more specific example: A leading dairy products firm has ten regional sales managers, each responsible for ten salespeople. Each month, each sales manager must send the company president the name of a salesperson from his or her region who has accomplished something above and beyond the expected. Each month, the president sends a letter to the ten selected salespeople thanking each one for the particular activity or result. The cost is minimal, but the motivational effect is tremendous. The letter goes home so that it can be shared with a spouse, and a copy of the letter goes into the employee's file. Salespeople need to feel that someone at the top knows and cares. Also, this program keeps pressure on the regional managers to create, identify, and track key results and activity for all salespeople. A regional manager who does not have a salesperson with an outstanding accomplishment must answer for it.

In another example, the sales manager of a telecommunication firm inaugurated a salesperson-of-the-month award. The criteria changed from month to month. The sales manager established criteria that fit her marketing/ sales plan and that were important to the company's success: calls per day, new accounts per month, net revenue increases, percentage above quota, dollars of overdue accounts, gross margin contributions, list price maintenance, new product placements, product mix, number of presentations, number of trials, and closing ratios. The salesperson who did the worst each month got to choose the criterion for the next month. Every fourth month the sales manager chose a winner based on extra effort, improved results, or some outstanding performance related to solving a problem. The goal was for everyone to be a winner at least once a year.

The salesperson of the month used a reserved parking place with gold lines, got a day off (with the sales manager covering the territory), had his or her picture hung in the reception room, and received a trophy that rotated each month among winners, as well as a bouquet of flowers. In addition, the sales manager established a salesperson of the year based on her criteria. Winners received a ring, a watch, a clock, or a pin commemorating the award and had their pictures hung in the reception room for the next twelve months. The salesperson-of-the-month award was given at a weekly sales meeting. The salesperson of the year was awarded at the annual sales dinner. Each salesperson of the month and salesperson of the year recorded a fifteen minute audio tape on how he or she accomplished the results. Copies of the audio tape were sent to the other salespeople to share best practices and further reinforce motivation.

In yet another example, the sales manager for a B2B desktop computer manufacturer created an honor society for any salesperson whose cumulative shipments exceeded $10 million. This generally took three years and was called the Circle of Excellence. Members of the Circle of Excellence had a calling card with their picture and the Circle emblem. Salespeople's calling cards represent them in the marketplace and influence their self-image. Circle of Excellence members occasionally had dinner with the company president, and all served on various advisory committees that reviewed new products and service and set agendas for sales meetings. Salespeople worked extra long and hard for this honor.

Since this B2B desktop computer firm hired many salespeople each year to open new territories, they also had a rookie-of-the-year award. That award was based on actual performance versus goal.

As mentioned in Chapter 3, many companies engage in scoreboarding salespeople on a quarterly, monthly, and sometimes weekly basis. These firms publish salespeople's rankings from best to worst, generally based on percent above or below quota. Depending on the marketing strategy, these firms rank salespeople based on cumulative revenue, gross margin, new business, product mix, or some combination. Rankings appear for each region and the company as a whole. Knowing the status of those salespeople just above and below them makes the top performers run faster. No one wants to be in the bottom 10 percent. Everyone wants to improve. Competitive, ego-driven, and high-achieving salespeople respond more positively to scoreboarding than service-oriented salespeople. Some firms that emphasize team selling don't use scoreboarding. Some firms just list those salespeople in the top 50 percent. If you don't scoreboard, consider it. Many successful sales managers recommend it.

In motivation, little things mean a lot. The salespeople for a hospital supply firm deal with an immense amount of conflict resolution because of broad product lines and lack of customer organization. Each month the sales manager presents the Lifesaver award to a salesperson for quickly and economically resolving a customer problem. A pack of three Lifesaver candy rolls are tied together with fancy ribbon.

A telesales firm asks any salesperson who opens a new account or surpasses the daily quota to ring a bell. People enjoy this, and it creates peer pressure.

A cruise line with a sales force calling on travel agents has created a career ladder of titles. Entry-level salespeople start as sales representatives. After two years and after the attainment of certain sales goals, skills, and knowledge levels, they become eligible for the title of territory manager and a small increase in compensation. After four years and the attainment of higher goals, skills, and knowledge, they become eligible for the title of senior territory manager and another small increase in compensation. At each level they receive some managerial responsibilities for interviewing new salespeople, mentoring, or assisting at sales meetings. This company has limited management opportunities and attracts career salespeople. People work extra hard and smart to put that new title on their calling card.

When considering motivation, ask yourself these questions: What do you and your firm do to recognize salespeople? Should you do more?

FEELING USEFUL, IMPORTANT, AND WORTHWHILE

Salespeople need to feel that their work serves a useful purpose and contributes significantly to the company's success and well-being. A salesperson's motivation can be destroyed overnight by a feeling of worthlessness. Training programs, management's attitudes, good communications, appreciation of their work, and sensitivity to their problems all contribute to their sense of feeling useful, important, and worthwhile.

Although they hide it, many salespeople approach their jobs with feelings of insecurity and inferiority. They live with customer rejection every day. Their skills are intangible and difficult to describe, and non-selling coworkers—even family members—often don't respect or understand them.

The sales manager's investment of time and the company's investment of money in initial training, field coaching, performance evaluations, development plans, continuing education, and sales meetings makes salespeople feel useful, important, and worthwhile. During the initial training period and in periodic field visits and sales meetings, management should make it clear that the company could not exist without its salespeople. Without a sales force, there would be no orders, shipments, or revenues to employ anyone else. Management's positive attitude will in turn influence that of its nonselling employees, which will further reinforce the salesperson's sense of worth. Management's lead in recognizing the centrality of its sales force proves particularly important in technology and operationally based firms.

Unfortunately, many manufacturing-, technology-, design-, engineering-, or operations-driven firms look at salespeople as a necessary evil: jokers with company cars and expense accounts. This attitude makes salespeople feel useless, worthless, and unmotivated. Often this attitude starts at the top and filters down. Such an atmosphere negates other attempts to motivate salespeople and reduces sales force productivity. In a fast-changing world where technology, design, and engineering quickly commoditize products and services, many top managers realize their sales force remains a key differentiater.

When top management travels with salespeople, meets them at sales meetings, and shares their corporate vision, this creates a feeling of usefulness. Words and action which make salespeople feel part of the team help them to feel important and worthwhile.

Good communication, especially timeliness in responding to their efforts or to their particular problems, helps make salespeople feel useful, important, and worthwhile. For example, when a salesperson has invested effort in opening a new account, placing a new product, or meeting the key decision maker, respond to the situation with the attention it deserves. Follow up on credit approval and delivery dates or write a letter to the decision maker. If a credit or delivery problem develops, get back to the salesperson quickly. Lack of communication, attention, and follow-up tell the salesperson that he or she is useless: it communicates the message that new business, progress in long sales cycles, and the salesperson's efforts don't count. Such instances demoralize the sales staff.

In some firms salespeople are the last to know about price increases, management changes, design alterations, new policy, and shipping delays. As a result, they feel useless, worthless, and unimportant.

When you raise prices or a new competitor enters the market, let your salespeople know that you sympathize with the problems this causes them. Help them with your knowledge. Don't say, "That's part of your job. Now get it done."

In-house customer service representatives, sales coordinators, product managers, and engineers who provide sales support can help to motivate salespeople in the field. The message is "We care; you are important."

As sales manager, you should promptly answer all correspondence, emails, and phone calls from your people. Make sure they receive samples, catalogs, emails, bulletins, sales aids, and software on time. When you wait days or weeks to answer a call, email, or letters from your people, you place their usefulness in question. Always return salespeople's calls, even if only to report, "I am very busy this afternoon but will call back tomorrow." How do you feel when your boss or one of your customers does not return your calls? Similarly, when a salesperson unexpectedly pops into your office and you are swamped, don't say, "I don't have time to see you," but rather, "I am busy right now, but let's set a time to talk tomorrow."

Some smaller companies, especially those using commission compensation or expense reimbursement, do not pay their salespeople promptly. They may send checks out late or defer payments until the following month. The message conveyed by such action is that the salesperson's work contributes little, and this quickly destroys motivation.

Lack of training can also destroy motivation. For instance, when the sales manager does the salesperson's job, it makes him or her feel useless and unimportant. It also wastes the sales manager's time. If you can't train salespeople to do their job, terminate them. Admit a hiring mistake and cut your losses.

For instance, the Philadelphia salesman for a men's clothing company called on a number of major accounts who preferred to review his line at the company's New York showroom. The Philadelphia salesman asked his sales manager, who ran the New York showroom, if he could come to New York to work with these major accounts. The sales manager replied that this was not necessary, because he, the sales manager, would work with these accounts himself. The sales manager assured the salesman that all commissions on such sales would be credited to the salesperson. The sales manager felt the Philadelphia salesman had plenty to do calling on the many smaller retailers in his territory, but the implication was that the salesman wasn't needed in New York.

These major accounts did purchase clothing through the New York office, and the salesman did receive his commission. He nevertheless continued to complain that he wanted to participate in the selling, even though he received a commission for putting forth no effort. Management refused to let him participate, and after two years, this top salesman joined a competitor. At his previous job he had felt useless.

Climate or employee surveys make salespeople feel useful, important and worthwhile. They also represent an effective vehicle for communication. Climate surveys called *90° surveys* allow employees to evaluate those above them, management, and their firm; *180° climate surveys* allow employees to evaluate those above them, management, their firm, and their peers; and *360° climate surveys* allow salespeople to not only evaluate management, their firm, and their peers, but the people below them. In a 180° and 360° climate survey, salespeople and sales managers evaluate each other and are evaluated by peers. The degrees refer to the organization as a circle with peers at your side and management above you.

Exhibit 7.1 is an example of a customized climate survey for salespeople to evaluate management and the firm. The climate survey, which should be anonymous but coded by region, can be filled out in a group or individual setting. The coding tells you who a particular group of salespeople report to. Human resources or an outside consulting group can administer and score the surveys, aggregate results, accumulate narrative answers, and conduct follow-up meetings. Any question where 25 percent of the respondents are "somewhat dissatisfied" or "very dissatisfied" needs to be discussed with the group for further clarification.

Within thirty days of doing a climate survey, a person from human resources or an outside consulting firm should meet with appropriate groups of salespeople. To encourage candid conversations, the sales manager should not be present. Even the best sales managers have trouble remaining neutral during climate surveys. Confidentiality is critical for the success of a climate survey.

The facilitator asks probing questions about areas of salesperson concern. The facilitator first explains why certain changes cannot be made. The facilitator then discusses areas where changes can be made and looks for consensus, for example, "We can use EDI for order entry; we can't accept collect calls from customers," or "We can increase the amount of performance pay in salesperson compensation. We cannot increase the amount of fixed pay."

Few firms customize climate surveys for salespeople. Generally, salespeople become included in a total company generic format. Keep in mind, however, that generic formats generate generic results. Customized formats (Exhibit 7.1) allow salespeople to make suggestions on increasing

E x h i b i t   7.1

Salesperson climate survey.

1. The degree of overall satisfaction with your position as a territory manager.
   - ❑ Completely Satisfied
   - ❑ Mostly Satisfied
   - ❑ Somewhat Dissatisfied
   - ❑ Very Dissatisfied

2. The degree to which you feel motivated to perform the responsibilities of a territory manager.
   - ❑ Completely Satisfied
   - ❑ Mostly Satisfied
   - ❑ Somewhat Dissatisfied
   - ❑ Very Dissatisfied

3. Top management's appreciation of your job.
   - ❑ Completely Satisfied
   - ❑ Mostly Satisfied
   - ❑ Somewhat Dissatisfied
   - ❑ Very Dissatisfied

4. Your regional manager's perception of the importance of your position.
   - ❑ Completely Satisfied
   - ❑ Mostly Satisfied
   - ❑ Somewhat Dissatisfied
   - ❑ Very Dissatisfied

5. The degree to which you feel that the training needs of your position are being met. Training includes knowledge of products, customers, competition, and selling skills. Training includes ride-withs, sales meetings, and classroom sessions.
   - ❑ Completely Satisfied
   - ❑ Mostly Satisfied
   - ❑ Somewhat Dissatisfied
   - ❑ Very Dissatisfied

6. What additional training would you like? Please list specific topics and general format (ride-with, sales meeting, classroom session). _____
   _____
   _____

7. Your satisfaction with the performance evaluation process and criteria.
   - ❑ Completely Satisfied
   - ❑ Mostly Satisfied
   - ❑ Somewhat Dissatisfied
   - ❑ Very Dissatisfied

8. The level of your understanding of your goals and performance expectations.
   - ❑ Completely Understood
   - ❑ Mostly Understood
   - ❑ Somewhat Understood
   - ❑ Seldom Understood

9. The level of your understanding of corporate philosophy and guaranteed fair treatment policy.
   - ❑ Completely Understood
   - ❑ Mostly Understood
   - ❑ Somewhat Understood
   - ❑ Seldom Understood

E x h i b i t 7.1 (continued)

10. Management's responsiveness to your ideas as to company policy and performance.
    - ❑ Completely Responsive
    - ❑ Mostly Responsive
    - ❑ Often Unresponsive
    - ❑ Usually Unresponsive

11. Your regional manager's responsiveness to your ideas as to company policy and performance.
    - ❑ Completely Responsive
    - ❑ Mostly Responsive
    - ❑ Often Unresponsive
    - ❑ Usually Unresponsive

12. The degree to which you feel your relationship with your regional manager supports or hinders the accomplishment of your goals.
    - ❑ Completely Supports
    - ❑ Mostly Supports
    - ❑ Often Hinders
    - ❑ Usually Hinders

13. The level of importance of your compensation package in motivating you to greater accomplishments.
    - ❑ Very Important
    - ❑ Somewhat Important
    - ❑ Seldom Important
    - ❑ Not Important

14. Are you satisified with how your current compensation package is structured?
    - ❑ Completely Satisfied
    - ❑ Mostly Satisfied
    - ❑ Somewhat Dissatisfied
    - ❑ Very Dissatisfied

    Why or why not? _____

15. Employee policies for the most part are clearly articulated and fair.
    - ❑ Completely Satisfied
    - ❑ Mostly Satisfied
    - ❑ Somewhat Dissatisfied
    - ❑ Very Dissatisfied

16. Customer policies are for the most part clearly articulated and fair.
    - ❑ Completely Satisfied
    - ❑ Mostly Satisfied
    - ❑ Somewhat Dissatisfied
    - ❑ Very Dissatisfied

17. In the last year has your job satisfaction improved or deteriorated? (If you have been with us less than a year, then in the last quarter.)
    - ❑ Improved Greatly
    - ❑ Improved Somewhat
    - ❑ Deteriorated Somewhat
    - ❑ Deteriorated Greatly

    Why? _____

What areas of the company or your region are better?

What areas of the company or your region are worse?

E x h i b i t   7.1 (continued)

---

18. The people in your region are cooperative and ❑ Completely Satisfied
work with a team spirit. ❑ Mostly Satisfied
❑ Somewhat Dissatisfied
❑ Very Dissatisfied

Any ideas for improvement?

19. The people in the company are cooperative and work ❑ Completely Satisfied
with a team spirit. ❑ Mostly Satisfied
❑ Somewhat Dissatisfied
❑ Very Dissatisfied

Any ideas for improvement?

20. The level of effective communication between you and the following:

	Completely Satisfied	Mostly Satisfied	Somewhat Dissatisfied	Very Dissatisfied
Regional Manager	❑	❑	❑	❑
Corporate Management	❑	❑	❑	❑
Customer Service	❑	❑	❑	❑
Warehouse/Distribution	❑	❑	❑	❑
Engineering	❑	❑	❑	❑
Telesales	❑	❑	❑	❑
Credit	❑	❑	❑	❑
Marketing	❑	❑	❑	❑
_____	❑	❑	❑	❑

21. How can our company help you to be more effective and more productive in the future?

22. What constructive criticism would you make of your region's functions?

23. How can communications be improved?

24. What are your ideas for better serving customers' needs?

25. What are your ideas for reducing costs in any area?

---

sales, lowering costs, serving customers better, and increasing sales force productivity. After all, they are closest to the customers.

Salesperson climate surveys should contain the following elements:

- The degree to which each salesperson feels his or her sales manager supports or hinders the accomplishment of his or her goals and why.

- Any suggested changes to the compensation package, training program, and performance evaluation.

- Whether job satisfaction has improved or deteriorated in the last year. This benchmarking forces firms to do climate surveys on a continuous basis.
- The level of effective communication between salespeople and other departments. Salespeople stand at the vortex of any organization. The ability to communicate and coordinate with other departments reflects the importance of seamless service.
- Ideas on how the salesperson and the firm can better serve the customer, increase sales, and lower costs.

As a sales manager, keep in mind that salespeople must feel useful; they must feel a sense of worth in relation to the company. Temper your words and actions with knowledge of this need and treat salespeople as mature professionals who are performing significant work. What do you do to make your salespeople feel useful, important, and worthwhile? Equally important, do some of your actions turn salespeople off?

CHALLENGE AND ACHIEVEMENT

Different sparks light different salespeople's fires. Most salespeople need recognition, but many salespeople thrive on the challenge of opening new accounts and increasing the volume of existing ones. They possess a high need to achieve that exceeds any monetary rewards they may gain. Long after they have satisfied their financial needs, these achievers continue going the extra mile to do better. For high achievers—that is, ego-driven salespeople—money represents table stakes, and beating last year provides the challenge.

Can you pick out the superstars in your organization—the 30 percent who produce 70 percent of your sales? The people with no complacency plateau or comfort level? Often we concentrate on motivating underperformers when in fact motivating the superstars could produce better results. Would you rather obtain a 10 percent increase on 70 percent or 30 percent of your region's sales? The superstars, who often have large egos, have their own set of needs. Being independent and successful, they appear not to need motivation, training, or management. But without nonmonetary motivation, training, and management, their flame can go out.

Generally, such high achievers enjoy taking personal responsibility for problem solving, are willing to take calculated risks, enjoy participating in management decisions, and need constant feedback on their performance. Because they are your best performers, you must continue to motivate them by providing outlets for their achievement-related needs. Assign such people difficult customers, possibly expand their territory, and let them participate in management decisions. These assignments motivate them, and their participation can benefit the company. One note of caution, however: These people will accept whatever challenge you assign them, so beware of overloading them. They have boundless energy.

A Denver company which erects cellular phone and television transmission towers knows how to motivate high achievers. Its California salesperson has an insatiable appetite for achievement and challenge. When its largest national customer threatened to take its business elsewhere, the sales manager asked the California salesperson to accompany him on a visit to the customer's national headquarters in Washington. Together, they won the business back, and the salesman talked about his participation in this success for the next year.

When a Chicago insurance agency had an opportunity to bid on a large group program in Dallas, it sent its highest-achieving salesperson to make the presentation. He failed to obtain that business, but he enjoyed the opportunity, appreciated the recognition, and worked even harder on his return

Because many high achievers enjoy participating in management decisions, you should develop vehicles for accommodating this need. For instance, invite these people to participate in the committees that set the agendas for sales meetings, approve new products or services, discuss field problems and new technology with management, or develop new sales techniques and compensation programs. Let them interview, ride with, and evaluate potential new hires. Let them mentor and train new hires. Let them lead sales meetings or make presentations as knowledge experts. Encourage them to make positive suggestions for change. Seek their advice. Let them know you consider their recommendations seriously. When you take a vacation, put them in charge. From this participation they gain a special sense of achievement and self-worth, and you get a job well done. Delegating to high achievers frees your time for other tasks and motivates them to even greater excellence.

Sales managers can also have a negative impact on top performers. For example, reducing a high achiever's territory can severely damage his or her motivation. Such people need to perceive unlimited challenges and opportunities for achievement. Often they outrun their ability to service all the new accounts they open. But by reducing their territory, you are relaying a message that can only be interpreted as "Thanks for the great job; your reward is a demotion, a penalty." The Salesperson's Time Allocation Planner, discussed in Chapter 5, might indicate that a high achiever has grown the territory to a point where accounts cannot be called on at the correct frequency.

For instance, a large Atlanta conglomerate acquired a storm window manufacturer in Tennessee. The storm window company's New York salesperson also covered Boston and Philadelphia. He worked six days a week, never took a vacation, and produced 25 percent of his company's sales. The conglomerate reduced his territory to New York City, so that less traveling would be involved and so that Philadelphia and Boston could each have a resident salesperson. His compensation remained at the same high levels because of overrides on the territories he gave up. His total compensation equaled that of the storm window firm's president.

However, after six months he quit and went to work for a competitor. Because he sold every major account in New York City, no challenge remained, and he lost interest in the job. This unfortunate situation might have been avoided by giving the salesperson part of New Jersey or Connecticut, which were underdeveloped. He also might have received a title, such as national accounts sales manager or assistant sales manager. Possibly explaining the benefits of a smaller territory, less travel expense, and more time off the road for customer development and leisure would have proved helpful.

In addition, high achievers want constant feedback on their results. Be sure these people receive weekly, if not daily, comparisons of their results to forecast, quota, and previous year. They respond to and understand gross margin and profit contribution numbers. Discuss this material with them.

Eventually, you may wish to promote the high achiever to assistant manager for the region or to the sales manager for another region. However, sometimes high achievers prefer to remain career salespeople or don't have the appropriate skill set for management. What are you doing to motivate your superstars with a high need for challenge and achievement?

FREEDOM AND AUTHORITY

Many salespeople prize the freedom and authority available to them through selling. They thrive on planning their own day, on not going to an office, on representing the company to a customer, and on making their own decisions. Many salespeople even feel that they are in business for themselves and enjoy managing their own territories. This is why they chose a career in sales to begin with. Can you pick these people out in your organization?

To satisfy such people's needs, you can remove some of the controls, allowing them more freedom and authority. Also, you can allow them to work directly with customers on certain nonselling activities, hold them accountable for performance results, and issue them titles, as discussed in the "Recognition" section earlier in the chapter.

You might, for instance, let them make certain decisions on their own that previously had required your approval. As an example, if an account met volume and credit requirements, you might let the salesperson vary prices, terms, freight, and advertising allowances within certain limits. They generally accept this new freedom by pricing at the higher end. If an account met certain operational requirements, you might let the salesperson customize features, within limits, to meet customer needs. If you normally require weekly call and route reporting from your salespeople, you might consider requiring them only biweekly from this person. You must measure what impact these changes might have on the morale of other salespeople. Will other salespeople consider these changes playing favorites? You might assign this person more responsibility for forecasting monthly sales and dollars of gross margin in his or her territory.

Such a person often enjoys working directly with the customer on nonselling, service-related projects. Depending on the product or service, this might involve advertising, promotions, recycling, plant layout, design, safety issues, formulas, markups, total quality management, perpetual inventories, estate planning, displays, Web page design, total quality management, testing, or reengineering. Allow this person the time and authority to get involved with these sorts of activities. What are you doing to motivate your salespeople with a high need for freedom and authority?

SELF-REALIZATION AND FULFILLMENT THROUGH PERSONAL GROWTH

Do you have salespeople working for you who are over forty or have been with the same firm for more than ten years? These people may require special attention. Older salespeople, especially those who have been with the same firm over ten years, have a stronger need for self-realization and fulfillment through personal growth. These people enjoy change, fear being in a rut, and want to feel more skilled and knowledgeable this year than last year. If you don't attend to these needs, such salespeople may reach positioning or contribution plateaus or stagnate in comfort zones.

Your responsibility as sales manager includes creating an environment conducive to productive change and personal growth so salespeople don't get burned out. Continual training helps to satisfy this need and can take many forms, including sales meetings, field visits, workshops, seminars, continuing education programs, industry conferences, and trade shows. Trained salespeople produce greater sales not only because of improved knowledge but also because of improved motivation.

The sales manager of a successful company selling highway safety devices to various government agencies detected growing dissatisfaction among his three best salespeople. All three individuals were well compensated, received adequate recognition, and were allowed considerable authority. Each had been with the company more than fifteen years and was over fifty. Their dissatisfaction puzzled the sales manager until he realized that these three salespeople had stopped growing personally, that they felt burned out, and that they had developed bad self-images.

The sales manager decided to send one salesman to a conference in Washington, DC, on highway safety, another to a marketing association three-day seminar on selling municipal customers, and the third to view a new European safety system being installed in Mexico City. The next two years he repeated this type of experience, but rotated each salesperson's activity. The salesmen learned and grew, and a feeling of self-realization and fulfillment replaced that of dissatisfaction. When the salespeople returned from their conference, association, or site visit, they had to present their experience, findings, and conclusions at a sales meeting.

In another example, the sales manager for a national giftware company had a plateaued salesperson who had represented the company for ten years. Paul had long been an above-average performer, had handled the largest territory in terms of dollar sales, and was respected and liked by customers and prospects. But ever since his two children's graduation from college and his wife's promotion at her firm, Paul's attitude and performance had been disappointing. His calls per day fell, along with his number of new accounts and total sales dollars.

The final blow came when Paul started losing a significant number of accounts because of a price increase. To make matters worse, the sales manager and Paul had become personal friends. She could not live with the situation but wanted to avoid terminating Paul, who had just reached fifty. (If you haven't had this problem, you will. Only the names will change.)

Calling Paul into her office, the sales manager explained how she perceived the problem. She then asked Paul what his goals were, what he would do to solve the problem, and if their roles were reversed, what action he would take. Together, they came up with a specific remedial plan and the time frame for its execution. She reminded Paul of his excellent past performance, but they both agreed that Paul was unmotivated and felt left behind, and that he had a bruised ego that needed pumping. She realized Paul was neither angel nor devil and that fear and love were needed to correct the problem.

They looked at a number of possible causes and alternative solutions, such as changing the territory, providing more training, giving Paul some special projects, making him an inside customer service representative, putting him in charge of trade shows and a national account, and using him for training new people.

The sales manager gave Paul a title, sent him to several seminars, let him represent the company at trade shows, and assigned specific performance goals/metrics. They met every two weeks for five months and even discussed the possibility of termination. At one meeting Paul's wife was present; at another the vice-president of marketing participated; at a third Paul watched a video on motivation. Slowly Paul started to feel better and once again became an above-average performer.

Many sales managers would prefer to complain about the Pauls in their departments than to confront the issues squarely. Most sales managers procrastinate in dealing with this type of employee. Unfortunately, the problem only gets worse unless you take the bull by the horns and actually offer to help the unmotivated salesperson. The Quarterly Performance Evaluation discussed in Chapter 8 creates early detection of motivational problems and forces corrective action.

Sometimes older salespeople become intimidated by computers, sales force automation, and customer relationship management software. If handled correctly, this situation offers a wonderful opportunity for the salesperson's personal growth. If handled incorrectly, it can destroy an older salesperson's self-worth. Most sales managers suggest giving salespeople who did not grow up with a computer some special off-site training. They also suggest teaming a computer-proficient salesperson with someone who is not as proficient. This represents a nonthreatening way to share best practices for the entire sales process, a form of mentoring. Computer use and skills can be on performance evaluations and part of bonus compensation. Salespeople with weaker computer skills can be asked to present new software features at sales meetings. This forces them to get up to speed.

ESTEEM, STATUS, AND RESPECT

Most salespeople want the esteem of their fellow salespeople and of other company employees, management, customers, friends, and family. This helps build their self-esteem. For some, esteem comes in the shape of praise, recognition, or money. For others, it is associated with status within the organization and is represented by a job title. Still others need more direct expressions of esteem.

Little items such as impressive calling cards help establish self-esteem and status every day. When an auto parts distributor stopped issuing embossed calling cards to his salespeople and substituted cheaper offset cards to save money, several of his salespeople paid for the printing of the old personalized embossed cards out of their own pockets.

A successful steel products salesperson did a great deal of customer entertaining with his wife at company expense. They wined and dined customers twice a week, played golf with many, and even took a few on vacations. When industry sales declined because of imports and a recession, the sales manager cut back on these entertainment expenses. The salesman asked for the expense allowance to be continued even if it meant a decrease in his salary. The lifestyle made available by the expense account was critical to this man's status in the company and to his personal self-esteem.

The salesperson with a high need for self-esteem and status requires special treatment. Special treatment may demotivate other salespeople who feel it is not deserved or warranted. However, budget permitting, consider special privileges such as a company credit card, subscriptions to trade publications, better car, first choice on vacation time, airline or hotel room upgrades, bigger desk, cellular phone, laptop, membership in a private club, entertainment allowance, or fancy calling card. Often, additional expenses can be traded for reductions in other areas, or these perks can be used to reward superior performance. Most important, as sales manager, you should enhance every salesperson's esteem with your respect.

SENSE OF BELONGING

Many salespeople have a strong need to belong and participate in their work organization where they spend forty or more hours a week. After all, most salespeople belong to a family, a community, some clubs, and probably a religious organization. Within the work organization, any group activities, such as sales meetings, conferences, social events, training seminars, teleconferencing, and athletic teams, can satisfy this need to belong. If the sales force lives within a day's drive of your office, scheduling frequent group activities proves more practical than if they live far away. If the sales force sells out of one central office, the everyday personal social contact creates a sense of belonging. In addition, the sales manager's field visits remind salespeople that they belong to an organization. Satisfying the need to belong for a national field sales force spread from Boston to Los Angeles proves the most difficult, yet because these people are physically separated from each other, their need is the greatest. A salesperson who works far from the home office can get very lonely.

Newsletters, email, and bulletins that contain information about other salespeople or employees remind salespeople that they belong to an organization. Both personal news (concerning births, new houses, birthdays, anniversaries of employment, vacations, graduations, children, illness, and retirement) and business news (concerning contests, competition, customers, programs, products, services, promotions, quotas, results, and new accounts) prove effective. Have salespeople contribute articles and information. Have a contest to name your newsletter. Make it warm and folksy. Many firms use part of the newsletter to scoreboard salespeople, as described earlier in this chapter. These newsletters can be published on a regional, district, divisional, or companywide basis, or some combination. Each regional manager may want to email his or her own letter of news in addition to the company newsletter. Newsletters may be online or hard copy.

In addition, once or twice a year, resources permitting, a well-planned sales meeting can provide a productive means of communication, motivation, and training. As discussed earlier, the sales meeting is of particular importance because it offers a prime opportunity for one-to-one human interaction within the sales force and between management and the sales organization. Regional companies and regional offices of national firms with local salespeople can hold shorter but more frequent—monthly or even weekly—sales meetings. All this satisfies a salesperson's need to belong.

As good corporate citizens and responsible human beings, the sales manager's sincere expressions of concern for salespeople's well-being creates a feeling of belonging. Salespeople want to know that management at all levels cares about them and their families. Congratulate your salespeople on events of joy such as births, graduation, or marriage. Express your sympathies on events of sorrow such as illness or death. Remember how you felt when your boss and your boss's boss expressed these concerns. People never forget it, which creates bonding and loyalty.

The president of a national software company sends and personally signs birthday cards to all employees. The sales manager of a small garbage disposal company has a birthday cake and brief party for his people. A financial services company gives salespeople a day off on their birthday. Many companies have similar programs to celebrate anniversaries of employment. A wholesale seed company sends flowers to its people on the anniversary of their employment. In addition, many companies send birthday cards to employees' children and spouses. The cost is nominal, and the motivational results are excellent. Salespeople receive a feeling of belonging and a sense that the company cares about them. Once you start such a program, salespeople will remind you should a date be missed.

We send birthday cards to customers. Why not send cards to our salespeople? As mentioned previously, just as salespeople maintain customer profiles, sales managers should maintain profiles on their salespeople. These profiles should include birthdays, anniversaries, children's and spouses' names, events of joy and sorrow, hobbies, education, work experience, training, and how they use and filter information. To communicate effectively with the salespeople, you need insight on how each person makes decisions and the best technique to persuade them. Again, we ask salespeople to keep this information on customers (see Exhibit 3.7), and we must maintain such information on them. Is the salesperson logical and concrete (aim, aim, aim), conceptual (ready, fire, aim), people-oriented (how will the decision impact those around me?), or big-picture-oriented (fire, fire, fire)?

The sales manager of an international consulting company visited each of sixteen field sales representatives twice a year. The first question salespeople asked concerned news of their colleagues in other territories. The company could afford only one international sales meeting a year, but the sales manager sensed a strong feeling for or need for belonging. He decided to have shorter, less expensive regional sales meetings six months after each international meeting. Then between regional meetings each salesperson received videotapes featuring one of their colleagues discussing selling skills and product knowledge. Each month the tapes were rotated.

He also asked his administrative assistant to write an online newsletter for the sales force. Each salesperson submitted information. Each month salespeople received a bouquet with one carnation for every new account opened. A nice spirit developed, and the sales force seemed even more willing to put forth that extra effort.

Apparel with discreet company logos gives salespeople a feeling of belonging. Use apparel, briefcases, luggage, and golf balls with a discreet company logo as rewards for short incentive programs. And, again, all these techniques prove equally effective for motivating channel partners.

Last, consider a salesperson or channel partner council to advise management on topics for sales meetings, new product ideas, and ways to better serve customers, increase revenues, and lower costs. Rotate the membership so all salespeople have an opportunity to serve. This satisfies many motivational needs, including a need to belong.

POSITIVE INTERPERSONAL RELATIONSHIPS

Pleasant personal relationships with management and peers represent a positive motivational force for salespeople and also foster a feeling of belonging. Unpleasant relationships represent a negative motivational force, which reduces a salesperson's productivity.

The Los Angeles representative for a data storage company did a satisfactory selling job in his territory, but he had a personality clash with the sales manager. The sales manager was an authoritarian, a high-powered generalist, and the salesperson was a low-key detail man. The sales manager recognized their difference in styles as a problem, and he knew that his salesman would do better if their relationship improved.

Over the next few months, the sales manager showed more flexibility toward, and applied less pressure on, the Los Angeles salesperson. He also provided this salesman with more detailed information on his territory. The relationship improved, and so did sales in that area.

In dealing with motivational problems, such as plateauing and disruptive behavior, most sales managers procrastinate, which exacerbates the situation. Have a meeting with the salesperson earlier rather than later. Explain and agree on the problems and issues. You can't solve the problem until you have defined it. Discuss the problem's causes. Ask the salesperson for alternative solutions and corrective action. Agree on implementation and put it in a time frame. What represents the benefit for positive results? What represents the consequence if positive change and results do not occur? Set performance standards. What metrics will you use to measure change: success or failure? Have follow-up meetings to monitor progress.

A Detroit automotive after-market company employed five excellent salespeople for the greater metropolitan area. However, one of the people annoyed the other four to the point where sales were affected. This member of the sales organization always had the right answers, told his colleagues what to do and how to do it, monopolized sales meetings, and bragged a great deal. His ideas were right, and everyone else's were wrong. He was a superstar with a giant ego. He consistently told the sales manager how to do her job and seldom listened to her suggestions.

Because this salesperson represented 40 percent of the sales manager's revenues, he felt free to call the vice president of marketing with questions and the district warehouse for inventory information. One action violated the chain of command; the other action violated company policy. Several saleswoman and female customer service representatives accused him of being abusive. (You've probably met this person. If you have not, you will.)

The sales manager realized that this dissident salesman's problem probably stemmed from lack of self-esteem and self-discipline. She realized he was neither angel nor devil and that both fear and love were needed to correct the problem. One day at lunch, the sales manager expressed her respect for the salesman's performance, skills, and judgment, but noted that the salesman must also respect his colleague's opinions. She explained that he was becoming a problem. She asked a number of questions to stimulate self-analysis and discussion, such as "What do you feel is causing the problem?", "What would you do if you were the sales manager?", and "What are your career goals?" She mentioned that he was a role model for younger salespeople.

At that meeting she discovered he wanted her job and had time on his hands. They agreed on a program: If his behavior improved, he would make certain presentations at sales meetings, attend several sales management workshops or seminars, take responsibility for several large inactive accounts, represent the company at several trade shows, and read a book on getting along with people, and each month they would meet to discuss progress toward their goal. She was careful not to upset the other four salespeople with her program. The sales manager also stated very firmly that unless his behavior improved, other less pleasant action would be necessary. She set the metrics for measuring improved behavior. Thereafter, the two had many discussions concerning this matter, and although the problem never disappeared, it subsided. As a result, the performance of all five people improved.

CONSISTENT, MOTIVATED, COMPETENT LEADERSHIP

Salespeople require consistent, motivated, and competent leadership in order to maintain their own motivation. A sales force is seldom more motivated or competent than its sales manager.

Successful sales managers vary greatly in style, from autocratic to democratic, from sales- or task-oriented to employee-oriented, from persuasive to consultive. However, successful sales managers do have five common traits:

1. They realize that their job is getting work done through others; their success depends on the success of the people who work for them.
2. Their styles, techniques, and policies are consistent. They don't switch between autocratic and democratic, or persuasive and consultive.
3. They believe in what they do, which creates strong, contagious personal motivation, and they communicate this strong personal motivation to the sales force, who display it to customers.
4. They realize they are agents of change, and they manage change, take advantage of change, and modify people's behavior.
5. They set standards, are critical, and sit in judgment.

If asked, most sales managers would say they feel motivated. Yet, when asked how they communicate this personal motivation to the sales force, they stumble and hesitate. In addition, when these same sales managers' salespeople are asked if their sales manager is motivated, most reply no. Most sales managers do a poor job of communicating strong personal motivation to their sales force.

When asked how they know if a sales manager has strong personal motivation, salespeople reply because he or she appears organized, prepared, focused, confident, enthusiastic, emotional, passionate, excitable, and is a good presenter. In addition, tone of voice, eye contact, being hardworking, having high energy, asking for more work, being volunteer-oriented, and the fact that he or she loves Mondays are often mentioned.

Ask your salespeople to anonymously evaluate your personal motivation and leadership skills. Each year ask for suggestions for improvement. The answers may enlighten you.

At the very least, evaluate yourself quarterly asking the following questions:

1. How motivated do I appear to the sales force? Do I believe in what I am doing?
2. Am I consistent in my style of management and my techniques and policies? Am I consistent in the use of love and fear. Am I consistent in perceiving a salesperson as angel or devil?
3. Do I attempt to get work done through other people, or do I just do it myself?
4. How much time do I spend training salespeople?
5. Do salespeople have difficulty understanding what I want from them?
6. How often do salespeople turn over in my division?
7. Is each salesperson showing net revenue increases?
8. Are the salespeople self-motivated or must I always prod them?
9. What percent of my time do I spend each month on administrative duties? Personal selling? Time with salespeople? Other responsibilities?

The following are examples of poor sales manager leadership qualities. The sales manager for a DVD company asked his salespeople to call on certain specific retail accounts. If they didn't call on the accounts within ten days, the sales manager would make an appointment to see the retailer. Soon the sales manager was calling on more accounts and the sales force on fewer accounts. As a result, company sales declined. This sales manager had failed to realized that his job depended on getting work done through other people.

When the United States Surgeon General issued his initial warning on smoking, an entrepreneur started marketing no-tobacco lettuce-leaf cigarettes. The sales manager for this new product continued smoking his old brand, and this contributed to his sales force's lack of motivation. The manager didn't recognize that sales managers must believe in what they are doing.

In another example, a regional sales manager for a credit card company told the sales force not to call on smaller restaurants because of credit problems. Then, the next month, he introduced a special program just for that market. One week this sales manager would use persuasion to implement policy. The next week, he used threats. During the credit card company's second-busiest month, August, he took a three-week vacation. The salespeople responded by losing their motivation. This sales manager was not competent, consistent, or motivated.

COMPANY POLICY AND ADMINISTRATION

Company policies and administration that promote an open, constructive, and relaxed environment and embody trust, faith, consistency, and fairness will promote job satisfaction and positive motivation. Likewise, company policies and administration that promote inefficiency, ineffectiveness, and frustration within the organization and do not embody trust, consistency, and fairness will cause job dissatisfaction and damage salespeople's motivation.

For example, a company policy that prohibits salespeople from calling or emailing the factory to check on delivery dates or outstanding customer balances can create frustration and job dissatisfaction, as can a company policy that prohibits salespeople from communicating directly with engineering and design. A less rigid policy that allows salespeople to call or communicate once a week would satisfy both management's need to limit the time and expense involved and the sales force's need for information.

A company policy that prohibits salespeople from making credit card calls to the sales manager or using the 800 number or asks salespeople to pay their own cell phone charges can cause frustration and unhappiness. A company policy that asks people to share these costs would be more equitable. The latter policy embodies trust but prevents salespeople from abusing a privilege.

An administrative policy requiring a company officer to review each order can unnecessarily delay order processing and thus shipping. Such a policy might cause job dissatisfaction and damage salespeople's motivation. A more moderate policy requiring officer review only of new-account orders would be less likely to damage either salespeople's morale or delivery schedules.

In one small family-owned company, salespeople were not allowed to park in the company lot, and the president/owner opened all incoming mail and occasionally listened to phone conversations. Sales force turnover was 50 percent a year.

An information technology policy which does not give salespeople access to customer credit records, Electronic Data Interchange (EDI), past purchases, gross margin numbers, or certain new product specifications might cause sales force frustration and unhappiness and seriously damage motivation. A company policy giving limited access would be fairer.

A company policy establishing certain national house accounts on which salespeople receive no income certainly dulls motivation. A policy that splits national accounts among a number of salespeople, who then share the income, would improve motivation. A policy which gives salespeople whose territories have been reduced an override on transferred accounts would improve motivation.

In the twenty-first century, company policy concerning channel conflicts will have a major impact on motivation. Create a committee that includes salespeople to clearly define how performance pay is split on ecommerce or Web-generated orders.

JOB SECURITY AND COMPENSATION

A salesperson who feels underpaid or on the verge of termination will not put forth that extra effort you are looking for. In fact, all other motivational techniques fail when salespeople sense that their jobs are threatened or believe that their remuneration, including expense reimbursements and fringe benefits, is inadequate. Corporate downsizing, right-sizing, reorganizations, automation, mergers, acquisitions, liquidity, and personal probation all threaten salespeople's job security.

A St. Louis regional securities firm employed forty "retail" brokers to handle its individual investors. When the firm's major partner passed away, the brokers (salespeople) became concerned about their jobs. Unnerved by persistent rumors concerning the firm's imminent liquidation or sale, they became much less aggressive in pursuing new business. To offset this concern, the other partners increased the brokers' commissions, called them account representatives, and held weekly sales meetings—all to no avail. Only after a year did the brokers realize that their fears were unfounded and once again start producing additional business.

Similarly, an international aerospace firm announced a corporate downsizing and reorganization because of reduced government defense spending. It took six months for a group of consultants and management to agree on a downsizing plan. During that period, salespeople hung around headquarters and made few customer visits. After 25 percent of the salespeople were terminated, the remaining 75 percent lost their motivation and the firm lost market share.

In 2000, a specialty shoe importer lowered its sales force's commission rate from 10 percent to 6 percent because inflation and exchange rates had raised the price of its line by 40 percent. The sales manager never fully explained the reason for lowering the commission rate to his people. Even though their dollars of commission income rose slightly, because dollars of sales increased over 40 percent, the salespeople failed to produce that extra effort. They felt underpaid.

A temporary employment agency hired a top salesperson at a salary considerably lower than his most recent position had paid. The salesperson arrived at work late, left early, showed little interest in his job, and had to be terminated. He obviously felt underpaid and was not motivated.

Occasionally, we must threaten salespeople with termination or put them on probation. Once you do this, the probability of improvement narrows, so start looking for a replacement. A salesperson whose job is threatened generally loses rather than gains personal motivation.

To motivate a salesperson, you must satisfy many interrelated needs—not just one. The sales manager requires a written customized motivational program for each salesperson similar to the training or developmental plan. Different salespeople have different needs, goals, and problems, so you must motivate them as individuals. Each motivational idea presented here represents a spark to light the fire; putting them all together provides the sales manager with a powerful tool.

QUESTIONS AND EXERCISES

- What programs does your firm have to recognize salespeople?
- As sales manager, how do you make salespeople feel useful, important, and worthwhile?
- Do you have a written motivational program for each salesperson?
- How do you motivate top performers?
- How do you communicate personal motivation to the sales force?

SALES MANAGERS' MAJOR MISTAKES/WEAKNESSES MOTIVATING SALESPEOPLE

- Having one motivation program for all salespeople
- Using negative motivation more than positive
- Not planning motivation; letting it happen
- Blaming other functions for sales-related problems
- Fear or love; Lack of empathy
- Lack of personal motivation or inability to communicate it
- Lack of consistent style
- Not being a leader; lacking personal discipline
- Doing salesperson's job
- Not asking salespeople for input or sharing ideas
- Having house accounts
- Not delegating; not developing a successor; micromanaging

PART THREE

PERFECTING THE PROGRAM

CHAPTER 8

Performance Evaluations

Each quarter a sales manager must not only formally evaluate his or her salespeople's results, but the activities, skills, knowledge, and personal characteristics that drive those results. Generally, you and the salespeople informally review results on a continuous basis, possibly monthly or weekly. The performance evaluation and resulting development plan, along with the job description, candidate profile, training checklist, deployment, targeting, and sales forecast/plan, represent the key control points for sales force management.

Your job as a sales manager is to get work done through other people. Your success depends on their success. To increase sales force productivity, this book recommends sales managers spend more time dealing with people, process, and technology. Each quarter the sales manager must stop and ask, "How are my people doing?" "How am I doing?" "Is my extra effort and time bearing results?" "Which of the new ideas, tools, and techniques work best?"

Performance evaluations force sales managers to manage their salespeople. Many sales managers abdicate their responsibility to a performance-based compensation program and operate as little more than traffic managers. In some firms, human resources takes a major role in hiring and training salespeople, and compensation and deployment issues are decided at management levels above the sales manager. However, performance evaluations can still give such sales managers an important tool to increase sales force productivity. Performance evaluations force sales managers to set standards, be critical, and sit in judgment.

Many sales managers would rather complain about a salesperson than analyze the underlying problems and attempt to solve them through a formal evaluation process. They dislike setting standards, being critical, and sitting in judgment, which are traits that separate the best from the not-so-good sales managers. When sales managers give a salesperson a poor appraisal, they are in effect evaluating their own performance as managers.

Many sales managers prefer being evaluated by their superior to evaluating the salespeople who work for them. Many dislike the possible confrontations when their evaluation of a salesperson falls below the salesperson's expectations. Successful sales managers deal with these confrontations by concentrating on a salesperson's goals/development plans and through the salesperson self-evaluation process. When asked to formally evaluate their own results, activities, skills, knowledge, and personal characteristics, most salespeople will be more critical than their manager.

Many sales managers dislike performance evaluations because of the time involved. It takes an hour to properly prepare for a performance evaluation and ninety minutes for the actual meeting. Multiply two and one-half hours times seven salespeople, four times a year, and you realize this process requires seventy hours, or two weeks each year. However, because of the many benefits, which we will explain later, performance evaluations actually save the sales manager's time and make their job easier in the long run.

A major complaint from salespeople concerning evaluations involves their boss not understanding the job or not being qualified to evaluate their performance of the job. With all the downsizings, right-sizings, and corporate reorganizations, salespeople complain their constantly changing sales managers have not had the proper opportunity to observe their skills, knowledge, and personal characteristics.

To obtain the information necessary to evaluate salespeople, the sales manager must ride with them and read the call reports. Field coaching, as we discussed in Chapter 3, also provides the sales manager necessary insights into a salesperson's activities, skills, knowledge, and personal characteristics. A sales manager must ride with salespeople to understand their selling skills, customer, product, and competitive knowledge.

As a sales manager, you are always evaluating your salespeople: on field visits, weekly sales results, sales forecasts, sales plans, call reports, phone calls, or hallway conferences. The quarterly performance evaluation represents a summary of each of these less formal encounters. It also formalizes the process into some planned quiet time, where both parties can get their heads in front of their jobs. Planning makes good things happen; bad things happen by themselves. Because the formal quarterly performance evaluation is a summary of past discussions, it should seldom contain any surprises, which makes both participants more comfortable. The performance review evaluates a salesperson's results, activities, skills, knowledge, and personal characteristics against the goals expressed in the sales forecast and sales plan.

To efficiently do these rather time-consuming quarterly performance evaluations, sales managers must keep a current log on each salesperson. As suggested in Chapter 3, use the Field Coaching Salesperson Evaluation

Form for each ride-with. After you and a salesperson discuss a customer call or competitive knowledge over the phone or in the hallway, write a follow-up note for discussion at the next performance review. After you and the salesperson discuss quantifying benefits at a sales meeting, or after you send the salesperson an email based on a call report, write a follow-up note for discussion at the next performance review. With this material at hand, preparation for the performance review is easier and specific information to substantiate evaluations is readily available.

BENEFITS

Salespeople have a need and a right to know what the sales manager expects from them, if those expectations are being met, and if not, what corrective action is necessary. They can't read your mind. The salesperson who started out well but has since gone downhill and now must be dismissed might well have been rehabilitated along the way through regular performance evaluations. Companies that regularly evaluate salespeople and hold them accountable outperform those that do not.

Regular performance evaluations motivate salespeople through recognizing positive action and results. Recognition of positive performance motivates a salesperson to do even better, and anticipation of such recognition stimulates self-motivation. Quarterly performance evaluations make salespeople feel useful, important, and worthwhile. Management cares about them.

From a legal standpoint, regular performance appraisals can document and justify termination, leave an audit trail, and avoid lawsuits by ex-employees. Terminations should never be a surprise. Too often, performance evaluations of recently terminated salespeople are not critical enough. The manager has not set standards and sat in judgment.

Quarterly evaluations prove more beneficial than annual evaluations. Sales managers cannot realistically evaluate an entire year at one sitting, and salespeople know this. In an annual review, the last quarter receives most of the attention. Quarterly evaluations allow you and the salesperson to set quarterly goals and development plans, which are more meaningful than annual goals and annual development plans. Annual reviews place too much pressure on the salesperson and manager. Quarterly reviews remove some of the emotion and allow room for disagreement, because next quarter can show improvement. On a quarterly basis, you have a continuous process for improvement—a helpful dialog, not a dreaded event. Salespeople don't feel you are using the evaluation as an excuse for reducing their compensation.

Most sales managers claim the major benefit of performance evaluations, like sales forecasts/ plans, lies in the meaningful dialog generated between the sales manager and the salesperson. It forces the sales manager and salesperson to discuss not only results but the activities, skills, knowledge, and personal characteristics that drive results. It forces the sales manager and each salesperson to agree on individualized objectives, goals, corrective action, and a development plan. Both parties commit to a time frame for accomplishing these performance standards and set metrics for measuring them. Performance evaluations make the sales manager's job easier. You can't afford to waste your most important resource—people.

For these reasons, sales managers also use performance evaluations for channel partners, customer service people, and sales administrators. Just as you have channel partners submit a sales forecast/plan, you want to engage them in formal quarterly performance evaluations. The categories you review may differ, but the process remains powerful. Companies which contractually insist on performance reviews, forecasts, and plans from independent sales representatives, distributors, brokers, and other channel partners receive more of their time, energy, and commitment.

Most companies try to separate performance evaluations from compensation reviews even though one strongly influences the other. If salespeople feel the purpose of a performance evaluation is to justify a change in compensation, they become very resistant to constructive criticism and development plans. Emotional issues overwhelm the process of continuous improvement. In companies with compensation programs heavily weighted by performance pay, these concerns remain less important. Quarterly evaluations help to disconnect this process from compensation. Many companies complete this task by having either a separate compensation review or replacing one of the quarterly performance evaluations with a compensation review. Then the compensation review topics, although related, are different from the topics in the performance evaluation. Many companies have customized performance evaluations for each functional area including sales. These appraisals evaluate tasks specific to each function or position. However, these companies use a more general universal generic format for compensation reviews.

The evaluation process involves the following:

- Deciding what you wish to appraise
- Developing metrics and performance standards for these categories
- Creating a rating system
- Holding an evaluation review meeting with each salesperson

Most important, using the appraisal form, ratings, and discussion, you agree on future objectives and obtain a commitment from each salesperson to a plan and time frame for achieving these goals.

WHAT TO APPRAISE

The evaluation process starts by deciding what you wish to appraise. Prepare a list of activities, actions, personal characteristics, knowledge, skills, and results critical to the successful performance of a salesperson for your particular company. This will differ greatly from company to company and may even differ from salesperson to salesperson within the same organization. Performance appraisals are meant to be flexible. Start by reviewing the job description and candidate profile used to hire each salesperson. The job description lists a salesperson's anticipated duties, the candidate profile his or her personal characteristics. Next, review the format of your training program, which lists the skills and knowledge necessary for success. Then add any other items not mentioned in the job description, candidate profile, or training format that contribute to effective performance.

The appraisal list will contain quantitative issues such as sales results, quality of results, and activities, as well as qualitative issues such as skills, knowledge, self-organization, time management, reporting, administrative, expense control, personal characteristics, and company and customer relations. Divide the appraisal list into twelve major categories:

1. Sales results
2. Sales quality
3. Sales activity
4. Selling skills
5. Job knowledge
6. Self-organization and planning
7. Participation
8. Administrative and monitoring
9. Expense control
10. Customer relations
11. Company relations
12. Personal characteristics

Whether your sales force sells soft goods or durables, or products or services to consumer, industrial, or government users, these twelve interrelated categories should prove helpful in deciding what to evaluate. These categories apply to both long, complex sales cycles and modified rebuys, to both relationship and consultative sales, to direct salespeople and channel partners, to ecommerce, bakery products, motherboards, fiber optics, and telcos.

Sales results should include such items as market share compared to forecast/goal and previous year or period, total dollar and unit sales volume, sales volume as a percentage of quota or forecast, sales volume compared with previous year or month, number of new accounts opened, number of new product placements, number of existing customers lost, and total number of active accounts. Did market share, total sales, total revenues, and total number of customers grow or decline, and how does that compare with the forecast? If a salesperson had responsibility for collections, then results would also include days of sales outstanding or account receivable aging. For longer, more complex sales cycles, results might include the status of major prospects from search to purchase.

The metrics for measuring sales quality would include such items as dollars and unit sales by product or service group, area coverage, pricing, credit losses, territory gross margin, average revenue per account or order, and customer mix. Did the salesperson sell the entire range of products/services or just a few? Did he or she concentrate on selling the least expensive or least profitable? Did he or she maintain list prices or sell off price? Did the Ohio salesperson saturate the Cleveland market but neglect Dayton, Columbus, and Cincinnati? Did the Illinois salesperson call on appliance companies but not on printed circuit board manufacturers? Did the California salesperson call on chain and discount stores but not pharmacies and garden shops? How many new and existing accounts pay slowly?

The metrics for sales activities would include such items as number of calls per day or week on present accounts versus prospects, on one market segment versus another, and on targeted A accounts versus lower potential C accounts. For longer, more complex sales cycles, sales activities might include number of proposals, trials, demos, betas, appointments with key decision makers, and contracts. The sales manager knows that certain activities lead to increased sales. As part of the performance evaluation, you need to measure these metrics against predetermined standards or objectives.

Selling skills would include such items as:

- Finding prospects
- Qualifying leads
- Asking for referrals
- Selling laterally to different departments within the same firm
- Calling on inactive accounts
- Upgrading accounts
- Making conversions
- Creating empathy
- Using probing questions to identify customer needs and problems
- Presenting features, benefits, and proof
- Quantifying benefits
- Answering objections
- Shortening the sales cycle
- Identifying decision makers and influencers
- Handling price increases
- Resolving conflicts
- Handling complaints
- Planning each call
- Closing
- Using sales aids
- Displaying written and verbal presentation skills

You base your evaluation of selling skills on observations made during field visits. Part of each ride-with is spent observing the salesperson's selling skills and how he or she relates to customers and prospects. Part of each post-call critique and end-of-day summary involves a discussion of selling skills. The performance evaluation summarizes these post-call critiques.

The metrics for measuring job knowledge would include knowledge of your company, its customers, the competition, competitive advantages, product/service features and applications, pricing, programs, market and industry information, and company policy. During a customer visit, could the salesperson answer questions on product performance, competitive pricing, industry sales trends, or new applications? Customer knowledge metrics would include knowledge of decision makers, the decision-making process, key drivers of the customer's business, and past history with your company. Information exchanged in emails, call reports, phone calls, sales forecasts/plans, sales meetings, and individual meetings would influence your evaluations, along with actual observations in the field. Did the salesperson know all the decision makers' names and roles at each customer and understand the steps from search to purchase in the sales cycle? Did the salesperson make suggestions to increase the customer's sales or lower their expenses? Some companies also use tests to measure job knowledge.

Self-organization and planning would include the following:

- The salesperson's efficient use of time in traveling the territory
- Allocating time correctly between different activities, functions, type accounts and different geographic areas
- Keeping accurate records and profiles on customers
- Setting up appointments
- Planning each day and week; planning each presentation
- Keeping samples and sales literature neat

Does the salesperson call on clusters of customers or spend many hours traveling between accounts? Does the salesperson use his or her cell phone and email to communicate between customer visits and reduce unscheduled visits? On Monday morning does he or she call ahead for a week from Friday's appointments? Does the salesperson have an objective for each sales call and know what happened on the last visit? Does the salesperson spend too much time at his or her office? Again, you base your evaluations on observations made during field visits, as well as on information obtained from call reports, phone calls, emails, sales meetings, and individual meetings.

Participation would include prompt attendance at and involvement in sales meetings, trade shows, seminars, outside workshops, advisory groups, and new product committees, as well as prompt response to company questionnaires. A salesperson who continually misses or arrives late to training sessions or fails to return memos/emails on what new services received the best customer response would receive a poor rating in this category. A salesperson who does mentoring, interviews new candidates, and actively contributes to climate surveys would receive a superior rating.

Administrative, planning, and monitoring the sales effort refers to the prompt submission of accurate route sheets, call reports, orders, service agreements, expense accounts, customer credit information, requests for advertising material, requests for return permission, sales forecasts, sales plans, customer profiles and status reports, market assessment analysis, and any other required written material. A salesperson who submits call reports once a month when you require them once a week or who submits requests for advertising material after the customer has run an unauthorized ad would not rate well in this category. Does the salesperson properly update customer profiles and account files? Are orders or service agreements filled out correctly in legible handwriting? A salesperson who submits the required customer decision-making steps, as well as names and roles of decision makers, and who tracks the monthly status would rate well in this category.

Expense control refers to maintaining reimbursable travel/entertainment costs, samples, betas, in-service training, customer terms, discounts, promotions, freight, and advertising allowances at an agreed-upon budgeted level. If a salesperson's reimbursed annual travel expense is budgeted at $20,000 but actually amounts to $30,000, or if annual territorial cooperative advertising and freight allowances are budgeted at $15,000 but actually amount to $20,000, the salesperson would probably receive a "needs improvement" evaluation in this category.

You may wish to carry the sales quality and expense control evaluation one step further by evaluating territorial profits. Using the territorial profit-and-loss analysis discussed in the section on the salesperson break-even point and contribution margin in Chapter 5, you can rate each salesperson's profitability in total dollars and as a percentage of sales.

Some firms use annual customer satisfaction surveys to measure a salesperson's customer relations. Other firms evaluate the salesperson's ability to solve customer problems and satisfy needs, timeliness in responding to complaints and service calls, conflict resolution, providing technical knowledge, merchandising, or engineering skills, stock counting, order expediting, and post-sale follow-up services. Does the salesperson call on different type customers frequently enough, provide the necessary service and assistance, and develop positive relationships with correct customer personnel? A salesperson who avoids target customers which require conflict resolution would need improvement in this category.

Company relations involve abiding by company policies and procedures, and cooperating with other company personnel. Proper cooperation with other company personnel/functions in engineering, design, credit, customer service, warehouse, distribution, operations, marketing, and billing create seamless service for customers and improve employee morale. If it is company policy for salespeople to quote a four-week delivery date or not call the warehouse, and a salesperson continually quotes two-week dates and then calls the warehouse, this would affect his or her rating. The salesperson who annoys fellow workers as a know-it-all or yells at customer service about technical support would not rate well in this category.

Personal characteristics might include such items as enthusiasm, self-confidence, assertiveness, aggressiveness, follow-up, persistence, drive, flexibility, judgment, stability, dependability, sense of urgency, imagination, creativity, initiative, responsibility, being a team player, consistency, ethics, integrity, problem-solving abilities, and appearance. The salesperson who fights any change in products, services, prices, procedures, or personnel would not be considered flexible. The salesperson you must remind for six months to call on a specific prospect would rank poorly in initiative. These qualitative soft issues, such as personal characteristics, are important to the success of your salespeople, but are sensitive matters to discuss. Listing these qualities in your appraisal informs salespeople of their importance and forces a discussion of them.

Exhibit 8.1 lists a menu of topics you may wish to include on the salesperson's performance appraisal. Pick those topics most appropriate to the success of your sales organization. Topics can be altered or changed from year to year. The topics and categories contain considerable overlap. Ask salespeople for their input on topics to be added and deleted. Exhibit 8.1 first outlines the major categories you will want to appraise and then the measurable features or metrics relevant to each.

THE RATING SYSTEM

After the sales manager decides what to appraise and what metrics to use for each category, he or she must establish a meaningful rating system. The most recent trends in rating systems for salespeople's performance evaluations involve (1) removing middle ratings, (2) keeping it simple, and (3) eliminating overall ratings. This focuses you and your salespeople on each category's goals, objectives, and development plan.

E x h i b i t   8.1

The twelve categories on which appraisal is based.

SALES RESULTS
- Dollar sales volume
- Unit sales volume
- Percent of quota or forecast
- Compared to previous year or month
- New accounts opened
- Existing customers lost
- Total active accounts

SALES QUALITY
- Dollar sales by product line
- Unit sales by product line
- Area coverage
- Account type coverage
- Credit losses
- Gross margin
- Pricing

SALES ACTIVITY
- Number of calls per week on prospects versus present accounts
- Number of proposals; number of presentations
- Number of appointments

SELLING SKILLS
- Prospecting
- Using referrals
- Calling on inactive accounts
- Upgrading accounts
- Making conversions
- Probing questions
- Using empathy
- Planning each call
- Presenting benefits
- Handling objections, price increases, and complaints
- Use of sales aids
- Closing

KNOWLEDGE OF
- Product features
- Company strengths and policy
- Applications
- Pricing
- Customers
- Prospects
- Market
- Industry
- Competition
- Competitive advantages
- Programs
- Computer software

SELF-ORGANIZATION AND PLANNING
- Traveling efficiently
- Customer records

- Allocation of time between accounts and geographic areas
- Planning each day, week, and presentation
- Condition of samples and sales literature

PARTICIPATION
- Sales meetings
- Trade shows
- Seminars
- Setups
- Questionnaires

ADMINISTRATIVE
- Route sheets
- Call reports
- Expense reports
- Credit reports
- Return requests
- Advertising requests
- Orders

EXPENSES
- Travel and entertainment
- Freight and advertising allowances
- Terms and discounts
- Promotions

CUSTOMER RELATIONS
- Frequency of visits
- Service and assistance
- Personal relationships
- Handling complaints

COMPANY RELATIONS
- Policy and procedures
- Personal relationships

PERSONAL CHARACTERISTICS
- Attitude
- Enthusiasm
- Assertiveness
- Self-confidence
- Aggressiveness
- Follow-up
- Drive
- Flexibility
- Persistence
- Judgment
- Stability
- Dependability
- Sense of urgency
- Imagination
- Initiative
- Dependability
- Appearance

Rating systems that include good, average, and poor (i.e., 1, 2, and 3) encourage managers to select the safer middle ground. Most firms are changing rating systems that involve multiple choices but have middle ground, such as "poor, fair, expected, very good, excellent" or "poor, consistently below average, average, consistently above average, excellent." Performance appraisals ask managers to set standards, be critical, and sit in judgment.

Because of this, many companies have binary rating systems—that is, with only two choices. Such systems use "meets standard" or "below standard," "acceptable" or "not acceptable," "very satisfactory" or "less than very satisfactory," or "very satisfactory" or "needs improvement." Many company presidents insist on such ratings to create continuous improvement of the sales force. They don't want salespeople with mediocre skills, knowledge, and personal characteristics.

Other firms offer more than two choices but also attempt to remove middle ratings. Regional sales managers for a software firm must choose between "outstanding, very satisfactory, fair, and unsatisfactory." "Fair" and "unsatisfactory" ratings require immediate corrective action. Keep it simple and remove emotionally loaded words so you and the salesperson can concentrate on goal setting and development plans.

In an attempt to eliminate emotionally loaded words, some firms use numbers, such as 1 through 4 or 1 through 10, and others use letters, such as A through D. However, at some point the manager must define what these numbers, letters, and words stand for. Salespeople need to know what proficiency level of skills and knowledge result in a rating of C or 3 or "less than satisfactory" or "below standard," as well as what constitutes "satisfactory" and "standard." You need to clearly define whatever terms, letters, and numbers you choose.

The salesperson's appraisal will consist of quantitative issues, such as sales results, quality of results, and activities, along with qualitative issues, such as skills, knowledge, self-organization, time management, reporting, administrative, expense control, personal characteristics, and company/customer relations. Rating the quantitative issues involves comparing current actual numbers to goal or forecast and previous periods. Rating the qualitative issues involves using the terms, letters, and numbers mentioned in the previous paragraph.

Most companies have eliminated overall or total ratings for each salesperson, because it takes the emphasis off a meaningful discussion of goals for each category or topic. Overall or total ratings carry considerable emotional baggage and often are tied to compensation. These ratings create more arguments than meaningful discussions because salespeople obsess over their final score.

For example, the sales manager for an independent regional tele-phone firm uses the following rating system for each category and topic:

Rating 1: Poor. Accomplishment is significantly below acceptable levels.

Rating 2: Fair. Performance is close to but not yet at an acceptable level. Some improvement has been made.

Rating 3: Expected. Performance is at an acceptable level, with accomplishment very satisfactory.

Rating 4: Very good. Performance is above acceptable level, and accomplishments satisfactory.

Rating 5: Excellent: Performance and accomplishments are outstanding.

In contrast, the sales manager for an ecommerce B2B marketplace rates each salesperson's performance for each category and topic only as strong or weak, with a note explaining next quarter's objectives and any necessary corrective action. Both sales managers consider their evaluation methods a successful tool, but the telco manager is considering eliminating overall scores and the middle rating. The ecommerce sales manager will add arrows to indicate changes in ratings from the last evaluation.

Select a rating system that proves most appropriate for your particular sales organization—a rating system that accomplishes the desired results in the simplest, easiest, fairest way possible. Overly complicated rating systems prove hard to administer and understand.

THE EVALUATION INTERVIEW

The ultimate effectiveness of the appraisal process depends on how the sales manager prepares for, organizes, and conducts the salesperson appraisal interviews. Let's assume you currently conduct quarterly performance evaluations. You and the salespeople have some experience with the process. If this is not correct, you must vary the suggested procedure.

Thirty days before the evaluation date, send each salesperson a copy of the appraisal form and fully explain or reexplain the process. Some topics may have changed or another rating system added. Be sure to clearly define any new topics, their measurement metrics, and what each rating means. You may choose to do this in a comprehensive memo or email, but you can also devote time at a sales meeting or during a conference call. Include information on the appraisal's goals, benefits, topics, metrics, definitions, rating system, interview process, time frame, changes, and each party's responsibilities. Also include a copy of the evaluation form noting any new topics, metrics, or ratings.

In addition, encourage questions so that your salespeople know what to expect and can express whatever concerns they may have. Remember, most salespeople have apprehensions concerning appraisals. Explain that your job involves helping the sales force to improve performance, which leads to greater compensation, and that the appraisal form and interview assist in that task. Exhibit 8.2 is an example of a performance evaluation format.

Exhibit 8.2

Account representative quarterly performance evaluation and planner.

Revenue

Product Line	Quarter			Year to Date		
	Actual	Quota Budget	Previous Year	Actual	Quota Budget	Previous Year
Private Home Care						
Pediatrics						
IV						
Rehab						
Institutional Staffing						
TOTAL						

Gross Profit

Product Line	Quarter			Year to Date		
	Actual	Quota Budget	Previous Year	Actual	Quota Budget	Previous Year
Private Home Care						
Pediatrics						
IV						
Rehab						
Institutional Staffing						
TOTAL						

Number of Referrals

Product Line	Quarter			Year to Date		
	Actual	Quota Budget	Previous Year	Actual	Quota Budget	Previous Year
Private Home Care						
Pediatrics						
IV						
Rehab						
Institutional Staffing						
TOTAL						

E x h i b i t   8.2 (continued)

New Contracts Signed

	Quarter			Year to Date		
Product Line	Actual	Quota Budget	Previous Year	Actual	Quota Budget	Previous Year
Private Home Care						
Pediatrics						
IV						
Rehab						
Institutional Staffing						
TOTAL						

Fill Rate/Number of Admissions

	Quarter			Year to Date		
Product Line	Actual	Quota Budget	Previous Year	Actual	Quota Budget	Previous Year
Private Home Care	.					
Pediatrics						
IV						
Rehab						
Institutional Staffing						
TOTAL						

Comments, Goals, Objectives:

Payers

	Quarter			Year to Date		
Product Line	Actual	Quota Budget	Previous Year	Actual	Quota Budget	Previous Year
Medicare						
Insurance						
HMO/PPO						

Comments, Goals, Objectives:

MARKET PENETRATION

Number of active physicians:

- Beginning of quarter: _____
- End of quarter: _____
- Percentage of increase or decrease: _____

Comments, Goals, Objectives:

E x h i b i t   8.2 (continued)

CUSTOMER SATISFACTION

Number of active physicians

• Number of survey respondents that gave an overall rating of "very satisfactory."   ——————

Comments, Goals, Objectives:

SALES ACTIVITIES

	Goal	Actual	Previous Quarter
• Number of referral source in-person calls a week:			
• Existing	—	—	—
• Prospecting	—	—	—
• Frequency of visits to A accounts:	—	—	—
• Frequency of visits to B and C accounts:	—	—	—
• Efficient coverage of managed care:	Very Satisfactory		Less than Very Satisfactory
• Effective targeting	Very Satisfactory		Less than Very Satisfactory

Comments, Goals, Objectives:

WORKING KNOWLEDGE OF:

• Physicians	Very Satisfactory	Less than Very Satisfactory
• Payors/managed care	Very Satisfactory	Less than Very Satisfactory
• Facilities	Very Satisfactory	Less than Very Satisfactory
• Hospitals	Very Satisfactory	Less than Very Satisfactory
• Extended care	Very Satisfactory	Less than Very Satisfactory
• Products	Very Satisfactory	Less than Very Satisfactory
• Nursing services	Very Satisfactory	Less than Very Satisfactory
• Infusion services (acute and chronic)	Very Satisfactory	Less than Very Satisfactory
• Competition	Very Satisfactory	Less than Very Satisfactory
• Competitive advantage	Very Satisfactory	Less than Very Satisfactory
• Disease management programs	Very Satisfactory	Less than Very Satisfactory
• Technical terminology	Very Satisfactory	Less than Very Satisfactory
• Territory management	Very Satisfactory	Less than Very Satisfactory
• Time management	Very Satisfactory	Less than Very Satisfactory
• Company policy	Very Satisfactory	Less than Very Satisfactory

Comments, Goals, Objectives:

SELLING SKILLS

• Making appointments	Very Satisfactory	Less than Very Satisfactory
• Precall planning	Very Satisfactory	Less than Very Satisfactory
• Research on each account	Very Satisfactory	Less than Very Satisfactory
• Building rapport	Very Satisfactory	Less than Very Satisfactory

E x h i b i t 8.2 (continued)

• Probing questions to uncover	Very Satisfactory	Less than Very Satisfactory
• Needs/problems to solve	Very Satisfactory	Less than Very Satisfactory
• Needs analysis	Very Satisfactory	Less than Very Satisfactory
• Value-added proposition	Very Satisfactory	Less than Very Satisfactory
• Benefit statements	Very Satisfactory	Less than Very Satisfactory
• Using referrals	Very Satisfactory	Less than Very Satisfactory
• Overcoming objections	Very Satisfactory	Less than Very Satisfactory
- Pricing	Very Satisfactory	Less than Very Satisfactory
- Happy with current provider	Very Satisfactory	Less than Very Satisfactory
- Service limitations	Very Satisfactory	Less than Very Satisfactory
• Closing	Very Satisfactory	Less than Very Satisfactory
• Negotiating skills	Very Satisfactory	Less than Very Satisfactory
• Post-call analysis	Very Satisfactory	Less than Very Satisfactory

Comments, Goals, Objectives:

PLANNING AND MONITORING SALES EFFORT

• Market assessment analysis	Very Satisfactory	Less than Very Satisfactory
• Sales forecast	Very Satisfactory	Less than Very Satisfactory
• Sales plan	Very Satisfactory	Less than Very Satisfactory
• Weekly activity reports	Very Satisfactory	Less than Very Satisfactory
• Daily call reports	Very Satisfactory	Less than Very Satisfactory
• Key account reports	Very Satisfactory	Less than Very Satisfactory
• Territory management system	Very Satisfactory	Less than Very Satisfactory
• Expense reports	Very Satisfactory	Less than Very Satisfactory

Comments, Goals, Objectives:

PARTICIPATION

• Sales meetings	Very Satisfactory	Less than Very Satisfactory
• Field training	Very Satisfactory	Less than Very Satisfactory
• Trade shows	Very Satisfactory	Less than Very Satisfactory
• Mentoring	Very Satisfactory	Less than Very Satisfactory

Comments, Goals, Objectives:

CUSTOMER/COMPANY RELATIONS

• Use of updated customer files and profiles	Very Satisfactory	Less than Very Satisfactory
• Use of CRM	Very Satisfactory	Less than Very Satisfactory
• Customer satisfaction surveys	Very Satisfactory	Less than Very Satisfactory
• Understanding and usage of company policy	Very Satisfactory	Less than Very Satisfactory

E x h i b i t 8.2 (continued)

• Expense control	Very Satisfactory	Less than Very Satisfactory
• Positive relations with other company personnel	Very Satisfactory	Less than Very Satisfactory

Comments, Goals, Objectives:

PERSONAL CHARACTERISTICS

• Appearance	Very Satisfactory	Less than Very Satisfactory
• Enthusiasm	Very Satisfactory	Less than Very Satisfactory
• Self-organization	Very Satisfactory	Less than Very Satisfactory
• Follow up	Very Satisfactory	Less than Very Satisfactory
• Sense of urgency	Very Satisfactory	Less than Very Satisfactory
• Team player	Very Satisfactory	Less than Very Satisfactory
• Self-confidence	Very Satisfactory	Less than Very Satisfactory
• Assertiveness	Very Satisfactory	Less than Very Satisfactory
• Drive to succeed	Very Satisfactory	Less than Very Satisfactory
• Persistence	Very Satisfactory	Less than Very Satisfactory
• Business judgment	Very Satisfactory	Less than Very Satisfactory
• Consistency	Very Satisfactory	Less than Very Satisfactory
• Creativity/ability to develop new ideas	Very Satisfactory	Less than Very Satisfactory
• Ethics, integrity	Very Satisfactory	Less than Very Satisfactory
• Self-starter	Very Satisfactory	Less than Very Satisfactory
• Initiative in problem solving	Very Satisfactory	Less than Very Satisfactory
• Written and verbal communications	Very Satisfactory	Less than Very Satisfactory

Comments, Goals, Objectives:

SUMMARY PLAN OF ACTION:

_____

_____

_____

_____

_____

_____

_____

_____

_____

I agree to these goals and objectives:

_____   _____
Manager   Representative

If the sales force resides locally, conduct performance reviews at your office. If the sales force resides an airplane ride away, conduct the appraisal interview in your hotel room at the end of a field visit. Set appointments at least a week in advance. The meeting should last one to two hours.

Do not hold appraisal interviews at sales meetings because you cannot devote the proper time and it detracts from the learning/social atmosphere necessary for a successful sales meeting. Combining them confuses and enervates participants. Often, sales managers use sales meetings for individual appraisals because of the convenience. Even though you are pressed for time, don't hold appraisals over the phone. This negates the benefits, insults salespeople, and trivializes the process. Some managers and salespeople prefer to review performance over dinner. Keep in mind the importance of the process.

As stated earlier, schedule performance evaluations away from compensation reviews. Although appraisals certainly influence compensation decisions, the appraisal interview becomes too emotional if held as part of the compensation review. Salespeople may feel that the performance review is being used to justify lower compensation and that attitude would make the appraisal much less effective.

Several weeks before the interview, ask each salesperson to review their past performance, future goals, and objectives. Using the performance evaluation format, ask them to rate themselves on each category and fill in the necessary information on results. Salespeople must have access to the results on which they are being evaluated. Ask them to review their previous evaluation and previous goals. Has anything changed? Did they accomplish goals agreed to on the last evaluation review?

At the same time, you should start rating the salespeople for each item on the appraisal form, making written comments, noting any corrective action you feel is necessary, and suggesting goals and objectives for the next ninety days. Do your homework; don't wing it. Be prepared to discuss each topic. Review the past three quarterly appraisals for recurring problems, trends, and objectives. Review the notes, logs, and files you have prepared for each salesperson, including the field coaching ride-with evaluations. How does this information influence each salesperson's appraisal? What proof does this lend to ratings?

At the appraisal meeting, whether in an office or elsewhere, create a relaxed, positive atmosphere. Don't accept phone calls. Do offer coffee and sit away from your desk in a comfortable chair. If you give your total attention to the salesperson and the evaluation, you add an element of importance and recognition to both.

After some small talk to set the salesperson at ease, review the reasons for the appraisal process and state what you hope to achieve. Restate the agenda. Pose broad opening questions related to last quarter's evaluation and the salesperson's objectives for this quarter. Stress this quarter's overall goal of mutually agreeing on guidelines, objectives, action, and a time frame to improve future performance. Remind the salesperson that you are not here to complain about any substandard performance and that another appraisal will be held in ninety days.

Next and most important, review each section of the appraisal form, asking for his or her assessment and then giving yours. You will be surprised how often salespeople rate themselves lower than you do, admitting the need for improvement and help. This makes your job easier and trains salespeople in self-evaluation. The appraisal form thus becomes a basis or agenda for discussion; it provides a starting point for talking about the job. Deal not only with results but with the knowledge, skills, activities, and personal characteristics that lead to results.

Be positive, straightforward, and helpful. Ask probing questions that encourage talk, such as "How did you determine the decision maker, decision-making process, and budget?" Mix praise with criticism. After all, *appraisal* contains the word *praise*. Reward positive actions and results with recognition—for instance, "Your closing skills have improved" or "You did a great job on new business."

Use positive, nonemotional language. Use "I" statements so that the salesperson knows you are expressing your opinion. Deal with issues and problems, not personalities. Don't criticize people; criticize their work. A salesperson may have an obnoxious personality, but the problem lies in being disruptive. A salesperson may be complacent, but the problem lies in loss of market share. A salesperson may be sloppy, but the issue is their accuracy. When evaluating a friend, ask yourself: "Would the evaluation be similar if I did not like this person?"

Avoid the following pitfall: Don't overemphasize one or two skills, activities, or results that could lead to an unbalanced evaluation of the person's overall contribution. For instance, Alex has weak computer skills but top sales skills. Joan seldom submits required reports but leads the sales organization on new business. Corrective action is still necessary, but keep the larger picture in mind.

Sales managers often view salespeople as angels or devils, when in reality each person has positive and negative traits. One quarter, a salesperson performs well and she is an angel. The next quarter, performance is below expectations and the same person becomes a devil. This type of change confuses and demotivates salespeople and makes performance evaluations very emotional and less useful. This sales manager syndrome is closly related to the fear and love extremes discussed in Chapter 7. Sales managers need to balance fear and love in motivating salespeople.

Don't rely on impressions; rely on fact. When discussing weaknesses, have some examples, facts, and figures to offer as proof. For example, "Do you remember the competitor questions you could not answer when we visited Telex on our June ride-with?", "Your closing ratio for this quarter is half of last quarters", "Your customer profiles don't note the decision-making process", or "The number of target account calls on your reports has halved this quarter."

Don't hold salespeople responsible for the impact of factors beyond their control. Don't compare one salesperson to another. Don't talk too much. Instead, listen to what salespeople tell you, and search for important messages. Restate what the person says to make sure you have understood it. Summarize points along the way to confirm agreement.

As you and the salesperson move through the performance evaluation topics, explain your ratings and justify them, using supportive feedback, but don't argue, complain, threaten, or lose your temper. Where appropriate, commend strong performance, good points, or improvements first before discussing weaknesses. Stressing the positive reduces defensiveness. However, never ignore unsatisfactory performance. Discuss the salesperson's ideas for improvement. Ask how you can be helpful. Develop trust. Be tactful, frank, and fair. Avoid negative words such as *fail*, *neglect*, and *fault*. Be specific, not general. Be flexible. Ask salespeople to discuss their reasons for poor performance. Encourage open-ended answers, not simply *yes* or *no*.

Performance evaluations prove less productive when salespeople become overly defensive. If the techniques previously mentioned don't overcome defensiveness, think about how the salesperson "feels" concerning the discussion. What is causing the defensiveness? Share your feelings, experiences, and personal information. Rephrase statements that become too emotional. Skip over sensitive areas of the evaluation and return to them later. Be empathetic to the salesperson's feelings and concerns. Usually, appropriate doses of empathy, concern, recognition, praise, and understanding will correct defensiveness.

Most important, using the appraisal form, ratings, and discussion, agree on future objectives and obtain a commitment from the salesperson to an action plan and a time frame for achieving these goals. The goals should correct weaknesses and build on strengths. Stress their benefits. The time frame should be long enough to achieve the desired goal, but short enough to maintain motivation. At the next quarterly appraisal, you will discuss whether these objectives were met.

The sales forecast has set the goals for results, and the sales plan has set the goals for activities. Each quarter, you should break the appropriate forecasted revenue, margin, or market share goals into bite-sized pieces. Each quarter, you should break the appropriate sales plan goals for number of calls, prospecting, the sales cycle, and marketing funnel into smaller time frames. The sales forecast and plan represent integral parts of the performance evaluation.

The agreed-to goals for skills, knowledge, and personal characteristics become the salesperson's development plan for training. How does the salesperson improve specific areas of customer or competitor knowledge and sales skills? What training is needed? The performance evaluation pulls together many steps in the sales management process. You should use information gained from appraisals to improve sales force training and update job descriptions. If you find most salespeople are not selling benefits or are not calling on target customers or are not aware of competitive pricing, possibly your training program requires changing. If you find that most salespeople no longer service customers by counting stock or working with design engineers, perhaps the job description requires a change.

Close the interview with an upbeat, supportive summary of strengths, weaknesses, and goals. Ask "Is there anything else you would like to discuss?" Then you and the employee sign the appraisal form, which makes it more of a mutual commitment. The salesperson may not wish to sign the appraisal because he or she disagrees with it. If that happens, accept it, but express the goal of mutually agreeing to and signing the next performance appraisal. In either case, place the jointly discussed and hopefully agreed-to performance evaluation in the salesperson's file and give the salesperson a copy.

Once the performance appraisal discussion has concluded, the sales manager should review any personal commitments he or she has made that require specific action. If you agreed to give the salesperson training audios for the car or videos and CD-ROMs for at home, make sure you do it. Also evaluate how effectively you conducted the session. Was it fair, realistic, and equitable? Did you set standards and sit in judgment? Were you critical? Would you do it differently next time? What did you learn about the salesperson, the job, and yourself? Did you learn that this salesperson would like to be manager or does not have the characteristics required of a salesperson?

Be sure and follow up on whatever operational and developmental plans were agreed to. The entire appraisal process loses its impact without follow-up, because the salesperson then assumes that no one really cares about his or her performance. Your follow-up in fact becomes the initial stage of the next appraisal. For example, at the end of thirty and sixty days, review call reports to see if the salesperson targets agreed to key accounts or calls on agreed-to market segments. In the thirty or sixty days since the last performance evaluation, has the salesperson taken the agreed-to action or produced the desired results?

SALES FORCE PRODUCTIVITY

Overall, this book discusses increasing sales force productivity through improved hiring, training, compensation, deployment, forecasting, evaluations, motivation, and automation. But how should a sales manager measure sales force productivity?

The activities and results which a sales manager uses to measure sales force productivity will vary from one company and industry to another. Some of these activities and results aggregate individual salespeople's activities and results. Some are unique to sales force productivity. Choose the activities and results appropriate for your company, report them quarterly, and compare them to previous quarters and industry standards.

Results might include the following:

- Revenues per salesperson, per order, and per account
- Margins/profits per salesperson in dollars and as a percent of revenues
- Costs per salesperson in dollars and as a percent of revenues
- Costs per order or per call

Aggregated salespeople's results might include the following:

- Closing ratios
- Market share
- Number of new accounts
- Total accounts sold
- Lost accounts
- Product mix

Activities, inputs that create outputs might include the following:

- Number of calls per week on present and potential accounts
- Frequency of calls on A, B, and C accounts
- Identifying decision makers and the decision-making process
- Number of demos, tests, betas, presentations
- Hours per week spent in front of customers/prospects.

QUESTIONS AND EXERCISES

- Does your company use a customized quarterly performance evaluation for salespeople?
- What sales force results, activities, skills, knowledge, and personal characteristics important to the success of your firm should be evaluated?
- What rating system would you use?
- How would you conduct the appraisal interview?

SALES MANAGERS' MAJOR WEAKNESSES/MISTAKES
PERFORMANCE EVALUATION

- Conducting annual rather than quarterly evaluations
- Not having salesperson do self-evaluations
- Forgetting to set goals and standards
- Neglecting meaningful dialog
- Viewing the salesperson as a devil or angel
- Evaluating (concentrating on) only results, not skills, knowledge, activity, and personal characteristics that drive results
- Not recognizing that weak performance reflects weak management
- Not being critical and not sitting in judgment
- Not monitoring results between evaluations
- Not taking action based on evaluations

CHAPTER 9

Sales Force Automation

Sales management involves people, process, performance, and technology. We have discussed the techniques, models, and methodologies for hiring, training, compensating, deploying, motivating, tracking, and evaluating salespeople. This chapter deals with using technology, sales force automation, customer relationship management, ecommerce, and the Internet to assist the people and the process in increasing sales force productivity and capacity. Technology does not replace salespeople or sales managers; it makes them more effective. Computers don't build customer relationships; they enable salespeople to do it. Software does not set standards, act critically, or sit in judgment. Instead, it assists sales managers in performing these tasks. Technology helps sales managers gather and analyze data for forecasting, for evaluating salesperson performance, and for territory alignment. Technology helps manage workflow more efficiently and put information about customers and prospects in one central repository that can be accessed by the sales manager, salespeople, channel partners, and other departments. We manage what we monitor, knowledge is power, and time is a valuable resource.

Shorter product/service life cycles; longer, more complex sales cycles; the need for expert consultative selling; just-in-time deliveries; group buying decisions; global markets; increased competition from "ants" and "gorillas" and less customer loyalty; and the changing landscape—all of these factors accelerate the need for salespeople and sales managers to embrace technology. Much of what we discussed in previous chapters can be improved through computer-generated sales support systems. The use of technology in sales and sales management can give your firm a competitive advantage in a commoditized marketplace. Not staying up-to-date creates a competitive disadvantage.

Computers represent the most exciting advance in selling tools since the invention of the telephone. When used in conjunction with cellular phones, fax machines, and the Internet, benefits expand further. Computers, software, ecommerce, and the Web integrate all the elements of sales and sales force management, satisfy customers' needs for enterprisewide solutions, and help ensure your firm's effective impact in the marketplace. Customer demands for more information, faster deliveries, and total integration with suppliers, along with dramatically lower costs and increased capabilities of hardware, software, networking, ecommerce, and the Web, further fuel sales force and sales management automation.

However, automating a weak sales force or inefficient sales management process will not improve productivity. Therefore, the models, methodologies, and techniques discussed in this book must be in place. Automation alone will not improve a weak sales force or a weak sales management process.

Most firms use sales force automation to increase revenues, lower costs, increase sales force productivity, provide quicker response time to customers, improve communication with the field, and provide more information to field salespeople so they can partner with customers. For a sales automation project to succeed, people at all levels of the organization must understand how they will benefit. What effect will automation have on a salesperson's territory, time, and compensation? What effect will automation have on a sales manager's span of command, duties, and compensation? Will automation eliminate sales support positions or increase the workload for programmers? Will financial people benefit from automated reporting? How can top management measure return on investment or greater productivity produced by sales force automation.?

To increase the probability of success and lower the risk of failure in automating your sales processes, you need metrics for determining success. Set goals for increasing revenues, margins, closing ratios, lowering costs, and improving customer satisfaction. For example, if sales force automation allows your salespeople more time in front of targeted customers, you might assume revenues should increase 10 percent annually for several years. Of course, other factors such as new products or services might also increase revenues.

For example, if sales force automation helps salespeople to better quantify benefits, partner through greater information sharing, and add value to the customers' supply chain, then as you automate, prices should have less importance and value-added features/benefits should have more importance. Therefore, as you automate, you might assume that dollars of margin as a percentage of revenue should increase 1 percent a year for several years. Of course, other factors such as new products/services, higher or lower prices, and changes in manufacturing costs might also impact margins as a percent of revenues.

In addition, you might assume targeting, information sharing, partnering, customer connectivity, and better time management from automation should also improve closing ratios by 5 percent for several years and customer satisfaction by 3 percent. Automation should decrease the amount of time spent in sales administration, thus lowering costs in that area. Again, other factors also impact these areas.

The important point is to set performance standards and metrics on which to measure the effectiveness of your automation program. Since sales force automation represents one step in the sales management process, it can be difficult to quantify benefits. Often, implementing a sales force automation program forces managers to audit and improve other parts of the process. Consider the following universe of activities and metrics in setting goals for using sales force automation to improve sales and sales force management:

- Productivity
- Customer account management
- Communications with the field
- Preparing proposals
- Customer satisfaction
- Professional image
- Order-shipment cycle
- Sales volume
- More selling time
- Budgeting
- Closing ratios
- Product mix
- Prospecting
- After-sales support
- Call reporting
- Number of sales/prospecting calls per week
- Sales expense reporting
- Error reduction
- Lower total sales costs
- Obtaining market and competitive data

Within a year of implementing a sales automation program, the sales manager should see significant improvement in controls and management feedback, sales performance productivity, access to timely and accurate data, faster responses to customers and faster decisions, more selling time, precise customer targeting, communications, professionalism, revenues, and competitive advantage. One company found that productivity increased 10 percent, another that inventories fell 20 percent. One company reports salespeople made 24 percent more calls after automation, another that salesperson meeting time fell from 13 percent to 7 percent of their time. Many firms claim that sales force automation improves their images with customers and allows them to hire better salespeople.

Because of these benefits, the use of computers, software, ecommerce, and the Internet for sales and sales management have become table stakes in the twenty-first century.

SYSTEMS APPLICATIONS

The most common applications of sales force automation are as follows:

- Customer account management
- Communications
- Lead tracking and qualifying
- Targeting
- Market research
- Order checking
- Database activity
- Word processing
- Proposal preparation
- Presentation preparation
- Customer needs analysis
- Account profiles
- Forecasting
- Budgeting
- Analytical spreadsheet preparation
- Order entry
- Pricing
- Prospecting
- Email
- Telemarketing
- Telesales and teleprospecting
- Direct mail
- Product information
- Training
- Inventory checking
- Sales call planning and reporting
- Graphics
- Time management
- Territory alignment
- Reporting of expenses
- Competitive intelligence

The applications will vary by industry, such as service versus manufacturing, as well as the type of selling, such as consultative versus transactional.

Sales force automation tools start with low-end information managers such as Palm Pilots and contact management software, and continue to more complex systems involving group relationship managers, customer relationship management (CRM), partnership relationship management (PRM), and enterprisewide solutions. CRM systems are often enterprisewide applications that integrate sales, marketing, customer service, online activities, and channel partners. PRM focuses on serving and collaborating with channel partners. Enterprise relationship management (ERM) emphasizes sharing information within and across an enterprise.

Order entry and order checking are often the first priority for computerization of sales functions, because they drive customer billing, accounts receivable, inventory, and other general ledger accounting-related functions already on the computer. Although order entry seems like table stakes in automating the sales function, it eliminates errors, improves accuracy, saves time, and reduces shipping time. By having salespeople use laptops to enter orders from the field, they can access real-time information on availability of items, price changes, and shipping dates. Some firms allow major customers to access this information directly using a security code, which saves customers and salespeople time. Automated order entry and inventory checking can reduce costs by eliminating the need for as many customer service representatives and reducing inventory levels.

Contact management software programs are often the first or second automation priority. These programs create a database of customer/ prospect profile information, as discussed in Chapter 3. This database can be accessed by the sales manager and other appropriate people. It can be tracked and aggregated. The information-gathering function is formalized through scripting and formatted look-up windows. Contact management allows quicker responses to customers' requests for information, faster conflict resolution and better follow-up. Acquisition costs of customers are lowered, growth is enhanced, and lifetime value is increased.

These programs contain information on all the salesperson's and the company's contacts and activities with the customer/prospect. Contact management programs provide the sales organization and salesperson with continuity in managing customer relationships. Should a salesperson leave, the information remains.

Calendar management functions allow salespeople to more efficiently plan and use their time through appointment data banks, to-do lists, alarms for important events, full-time search functions, accept or reject meeting invitation functions, and activity tracking. Calendar management can be performed on laptops or palm devices which can be synchronized to central servers.

Document management applications allow salespeople and sales managers to generate form letters, merge documents, automate the generation of presentations, and store documents for easy access. Documents, letters, proposals, presentations, and quotes can be emailed or faxed from laptops in the field. A double-click on a catalog icon will activate literature fulfillment to a customer. These systems provide document templates with embedded fields referenced to the database for the instant generation of correspondence, forms and proposals. This might enable salespeople to generate their own targeted direct mail or email marketing campaigns via batch merges. Document management software allows salespeople to attach related documents or computer files to customer records and also allows other users access to quotes, proposals, presentations, and correspondence. Synchronization allows field files to be transferred to the central database. These functions reduce time spent on administrative matters.

Activity analysis functions allow salespeople and sales managers to view, aggregate, and analyze completed activities such as number and types of calls, time spent with customers, number of presentations, and close ratios. You can also track customer status and company activities in the marketing funnel or sales cycle. With one click, this information can be displayed graphically, allowing salespeople to quickly spot trends and managers to identify best practices.

Computers can track lead generation, follow-up, and closing ratios. What direct mail, email, trade shows, and media produce the most and the best leads? You can compare the cost of a lead to the profit it generates and monitor closing/success ratios. You can determine customer profiles. This type of information helps targeting customers, media, and markets. It gives salespeople confidence in leads, improves closing ratios, and enhances customer profitability.

All leads are entered into a database according to established criteria. Leads are rejected from the database if they have been entered previously or are outside a certain geographical area. Each lead is coded according to zip code, account characteristics (e.g., industry, date of receipt), and the source by which it was generated. Next, a teleprospector calls the lead to ask key qualifying questions and then enters the information in a database. At this point, some leads are purged and some are sent to the sales manager, but most go to the appropriate field salesperson. At the same time, the company produces a direct-mail label or email database and one of several letters following up on the phone call, which is sent along with appropriate sales literature to the prospect.

The computer ranks the leads using target account and ideal candidate criteria. For example, commercial accounts with more than 100 employees located in certain zip codes are ranked as A prospects.

The salesperson must call on the lead within two weeks and report on what transpired. This information is entered into the database, along with the next required call date. Five days before that call date, the computer automatically generates a contact reminder so that viable prospects are not ignored. In addition, each salesperson receives a comprehensive list of all customers and prospects to be seen in the coming week, along with vital background information for the call—that is, the prospect/customer profile data. After the prospect visit, the salesperson transmits a call report to the regional office, detailing the status of the account and any new information on needs, problems, competitors, time frame, and decision makers. The salesperson indicates why and when to follow up on the prospect. All of this data is entered into the database, and the computer automatically follows up on the account, reminding the salesperson a week before the next contact date.

Laptops and software can expedite forecasting by providing easy access to historical data, customer and competitor information, top twenty accounts/prospects, probability of success, and sales cycle stage. This data is not only easily accessible to the salesperson but the sales manager. Forecasting can be accomplished with online software formats, which walks the salesperson through the forecasting process.

Similarly, the databases on customers, competitors, historical sales, closing ratios, territory potential, prospects, sales cycle tracking, and probability of success prove helpful in market research. Here again, marketing and sales management can work together. Sales collects this data. Marketing aggregates and analyzes the data.

Laptops and software automate most sales force reporting functions and eliminate most manual reports. They collect data for the activity analysis function mentioned earlier. Salespeople formalize the information-gathering process with scripting and formatted look-up windows, which saves time and lowers expenses. Call reports, route sheets, daily planners, customer profiles, expense reports, and customer/prospect lists are all prepared and submitted on laptops.

Computers and software can generate a salesperson's daily route sheet of specific customers to be seen by type and prospects by stage. The route sheet should have the customer profile documents and results of the last visit attached.

Remote synchronization of field salespeople's laptops to centralized servers used by management, marketing, and the sales support staff improves communication. Leads provided to salespeople are fresh, as is data available for analysis by management. Customer response time shrinks, and again, field salespeople have more time for sales-related activities.

Remote synchronization allows salespeople, marketing, and accounting access to real-time information on each customer. Access to this data breaks down the information silos within a business and allows the company to better serve customers. All customer-facing departments have access to shared real-time customer data.

In a long, complex sales cycle, software and laptops can automate and track the sales cycle and marketing funnel for each customer. One of the screens contains all the steps between search and purchase: qualifying, needs analysis, demo, trial, proposal, and group presentation. For each customer/prospect, the salesperson inserts the present status in the sales cycle, along with dates, costs, and probability of success for moving to the next steps.

As you can see, these applications work together to increase the percent of a salesperson's time devoted to the most important customer-related activities. Instant access to account information, forms, documents, and correspondence; delegation of administrative tasks; automated sales tracking and reporting; and centralized knowledge sharing all allow salespeople more time for targeted sales activities.

Email represents an efficient way for salespeople and sales managers to communicate with each other, with other departments/functions, and with customers. However, few companies take full advantage of the medium's capabilities for prospecting and customer maintenance. Email marketing obtains higher response rates than traditional direct-mail, offline advertising and Web banner ads at a fraction of their costs. Salespeople need to obtain the customer's or prospect's permission to send email, because "spam" (i.e., unsolicited email) creates customer hostility and results in low response rates. Customers prefer to "opt in" or proactively give permission by checking a box online. By giving permission, customers agree to allow your company or salesperson to email programs, promotions, special events, and usage updates. Limit these messages to one a week, possibly two, and mix the topics. Keep the length to 150 words, and limit each email to one topic.

As mentioned in Chapter 7, email can be used for sending newsletters to the sales force. It can also be used for inexpensively sending newsletters to customers about industry issues, best practices for improving profits, and product announcements.

The salesperson's calendar management software can remind him or her of a decision maker's birthday or business-related event. The salesperson can use email to send a birthday greeting or a reminder about a business activity such as a reorder, trial, or benefit analysis.

The more often a salesperson can serve a customer, the stronger their relationship. Email can be used to update the appropriate decision maker on order status and shipping information. The same email might present and suggest other related products or services. These emails can be sent direct from the company or from the salesperson. Similarly, use emails to follow up after a trade show, customer seminar, or meeting with additional product information.

The customer service function can use email to answer inbound customer inquiries and do cross-selling of related products or services. Customer service people reluctantly do cross-selling in a person-to-person phone call but have no problem using the less personal email for suggestive selling.

Email marketing allows the salesperson and the company to customize customer messages depending on needs, which improves response rates. Customer replies to emails should be tracked and response rates measured and compared.

Emails to customers/prospects should always contain a button for "Send this to a friend." This represents an inexpensive form of referral and viral marketing. Consider having a related firm with a similar customer base attach your email to one of their emails. Strategic partners, channel partners, and suppliers often do this. Certainly use email to communicate efficiently with your channel partners and help them use email to communicate with their customers.

Computers and software can also make direct mail more efficient through targeting and tracking. By using selection criteria and coding names (by industry, size, number of employees, purchasing potential, title, and location) to target mailings, results improve and costs decline. The process eliminates inappropriate names. Salespeople can assist in continually updating names, addresses, titles, and other appropriate database information. As mentioned earlier, computers should track direct-mail campaigns from response to order entry, and the sales or marketing manager should analyze these results.

Mapping technology, another application of sales force automation, helps sales managers decide the most effective deployment of the sales and service forces to balance account loads and achieve the highest margins. As discussed in Chapter 5, to optimize sales, territories should contain equal potential based on present and potential number of accounts and dollars of revenue balanced against the salesperson's call capacity or workload. Mapping software quickly analyzes all this data and suggests how many salespeople you need, and then graphically displays their territory boundaries on a map. By changing the inputs, the sales manager can look at alternative boundaries. Mapping technology can recommend which accounts a salesperson should cover each day and estimate travel time between accounts. The use of software to validate territory size makes boundary changes easier to sell to direct salespeople and channel partners.

In this century, mapping technology also will be used to track advertising responses, customer buying behavior, target accounts, and of course, market potential. Analyzing spreadsheets and statistics can be enhanced by displaying the data graphically on a map. All you need to accomplish this are the customers'/prospects' addresses or locations.

Call center automation represents a major application of customer relationship management and sales force automation. Telemarketing, telesales, customer service centers, and inbound and outbound calls all benefit from computet-integrated phone systems. The telesales or customer service person who receives an inbound call has all the pertinent customer information on a screen before he or she picks up the phone. The salesperson's screen shows the customer's purchase history, credit issues, outstanding orders, pricing, decision-making information, decision-maker's personal preferences, and inventory of key items. Outbound telemarketers receive daily reminders on events, who to call, and follow-up issues. Telesales people continually input new information into the database and customer profile, which, if appropriate, can be accessed by a field salesperson and the manager.

PowerPoint and similar applications allow salespeople to make powerful, professional, and flexible customer presentations. Spreadsheets allow salespeople to quantify benefits and then display them graphically. When a customer does not agree with the spreadsheet assumptions, the salesperson changes them, generating new dollars of benefits. Complex pricing and product information can be accessed quickly in the customer's office from CD ROMs containing product catalogs. Accurate and current ship dates, product availability, and inventory levels all reduce customer response time, compress the sales cycle, and create a professional image and uniformity of approach, satisfying both customer's and salesperson's needs for accurate timely information.

ECOMMERCE AND THE INTERNET

Traditionally, sales and marketing software has been installed on a company's server. Increasingly, however, those existing applications and most new ones, are available via the Web. There are a host of benefits to Web-based applications:

- The system is not installed at your site, which saves time and improves flexibility.
- A system hosted by an application service provider (ASP) offers small and medium-sized companies access to technology they could not otherwise afford.
- Salespeople in any location can access the most current real-time information online.

Solutions now exist to move all sales-related business functions to the Web. Implementing this kind of technology enhances an enterprise's ability to attract and retain customers and supports its existing structure. The Web helps to open the lines of communication and facilitate the flow of information inside and outside the enterprise.

Self-service represents one of the Web's greatest assets. Customers, salespeople, and support staff can find consistent answers to many questions on the firm's Web site. Answers to simple, routine questions no longer require a specialist's time. However, customers and salespeople also require easy access to a call center where the customized human touch can enhance self-service. Therefore, your Web site should include an 800 number. This merges old and new technologies, allowing people to reap the benefits of both. Melding EDI into your Web strategy presents another example of blending the old with the new.

Many of the tasks and service functions salespeople traditionally handle can be pushed to the Web. This allows salespeople to focus less on transactions and more on relationship and consultative selling. Salespeople have more time to customize solutions for present customers and target new business. For example, while customers may need to negotiate prices with a salesperson, allowing them to go to the Web to research products, place orders, or check the status of an order can improve customer loyalty and give salespeople more time to focus on high-value activities. This means blending ecommerce with offline channels and requires people who touch your customer, salespeople, channel partners, call center personnel, marketing, and the Web team to create a seamless buying experience that allows customers to choose the channels that best suit their needs. This saves customers' time and money and compresses the sales cycle.

The Internet also is helping with secondary and primary market research. Information that you can obtain on the Web ranges from SEC filings to the national trade databank. Your market research staff can spend hours surfing this ocean of information. Also, companies can survey prospects and customers concerning purchases and buying habits online.

Salespeople and sales managers also use the Web for gathering customer and competitive information, advertising, lead generation, online customer service, email marketing, and brand building. In addition, salespeople and sales managers use the Internet for email, reading business news, and making travel arrangements.

Ecommerce Web sites are being used to generate new sales to new customers, and by converting existing customers to Web-based ordering, they produce incremental sales to existing customers. An ecommerce Web site immediately makes your company global. To a much lesser extent, these sites replace catalog sales, third-party sales, third-party sales forces, direct-mail, and trade show sales. Because it involves the direct sales of products and services over the Internet, ecommerce still requires salespeople in the field at channel partners or at call centers. For example, Cisco requires new customers to work with a dealer before purchasing online. Ecommerce must offer the customer the flexibility to work online or with the assigned salesperson, since customers' needs and technical capabilities vary. A customer may wish to use the online catalog or ask for a paper copy. Ecommerce lends itself to homogeneous products or services with short sales cycles and modified rebuys, as well as to easily differentiated and easily understood products or services. B2B exchanges help to automate larger, more complex sales cycles, but they still require salespeople to reach strategic partners. B2B Web sites create enterprisewide partnerships between sellers and buyers, but someone must still sell the concept to potential users. In 1998 B2B ecommerce accounted for $43 billion of transactions, compared to $7.8 billion in business to consumer transactions. The Department of Commerce estimates that the online B2B market will grow to $1.3 trillion by 2003.

Ecommerce allows firms to provide their largest customers with customized, private extranets. These extranets allow the largest customers to browse a catalog, which includes their negotiated prices, or to look at their purchases over the past two years. They can also track the delivery status of a product or service on order.

Ecommerce, along with telesales, also allows firms to efficiently serve the smallest customers who do not warrant a salesperson visit. In the past, these accounts were called on infrequently or handed off to a channel partner. Now these accounts can receive information and service through the Web site and order online.

Many people influence the customer's buying decision, and they all have different online needs. Who are the influencers, decision makers, gate keepers, and users at your customers? They might include purchasing, design engineers, and finance. Many firms provide customized links for each group. For instance, design engineers would have easy access to product specifications and purchasing agents' easy access to quantity pricing discounts.

Ecommerce fails when firms don't involve the salespeople, focus only on selling, require customers to have the latest software, and force customers online. Salespeople are frightened by the Web and sales force automation, because it threatens their customer relationships, compensation, and job security. If salespeople don't support your firm's ecommerce endeavors, they will fail. You must sell salespeople on the benefits of greater sales, more customer loyalty, and less administrative work.

Customers want not only to order online but to be able to obtain product information, ask questions, and solve service problems. Successful Web sites must offer more than order entry. Some sites provide communities of interest for customers by listing trade show dates and industry statistics.

Not all your customers have the fastest Internet connection or all of the software necessary to view certain types of video or graphic files. Therefore, for these customers, consider a reduced bandwith or text-only option for your site.

Customers want to use communication channels that are easiest for them. One week they may wish to order over the Web; the next week they may wish to order through a salesperson or call center. You must offer customers this option.

Some users claim that adding ebusiness capabilities to existing sales force automation applications allows salespeople to open 40 percent more new accounts, to increase their customer load by 15 percent, to increase annual sales volume by 40 percent and to reduce sales cycle time by 15 percent. This trend could have a major impact on channel choice. If proper sales management processes, as described in this book, along with proper sales force automation and proper use of the Web, as described in this chapter, can significantly increase sales force productivity, customer loyalty, and reduce costs, more companies may reduce their use of channel partners and increase their use of direct salespeople. Also, higher productivity through automation and the Internet might allow salespeople to handle larger territories.

Channel partners are becoming alarmed by this data and are threatened by ecommerce and the Web. As discussed previously, channel partners represent an important part of many firms' marketing strategies. Therefore, include channel partners in your automation, online, and ecommerce plans to strengthen their capabilities. Link your site to their site. Allow channel partners' customers to access your site for product data and to ask questions online. Refer new or existing customers to the appropriate channel partner's site or sales representatives for placing orders. List your firm's distributors, phone numbers, Web site addresses and links, and fax numbers on your Web sites. List contact names at the distributor and their geographic territories. Your firm will benefit from direct contact with your channel partner's customers, and the customers will benefit from having access to your entire product line, not just the segment carried by the channel partner. Rather than using the Web to compete with channel partners, use it to create a seamless organization.

So far, you have heard the good news—the promise of the Web. Most sales force automation (SFA), CRM, and PRM programs underperform their potential, which is the bad news. From contact management software to Web-based data centers, execution is the key to success.

IMPLEMENTATION

Most businesses can benefit from some combination of palm organizers, contact management, ecommerce, or customer relationship management programs. The tools exist and they work. Your job as a manager involves increasing the probability of success and reducing the risk of failure in implementing these programs.

To accomplish this, you must first decide on your company's goals and objectives for sales force automation. How will salespeople, sales management, top management, and other departments/functions benefit? What metrics can be used to measure these benefits and during what time frame? Tie the objectives to business goals, along with the individual goals, needs, problems, and opportunities of the users.

For each application—contact, relationship, calendar, and document management—articulate three or four objectives. The objective for relationship management software might include improving closing ratios, customer connectivity, or reducing the sales cycle time. The objective for mapping might be to reduce salesperson turnover. The more specific and measurable the objectives or problems to be solved or opportunities the better. These might include orders getting lost or containing incorrect information, the unprofitability of calling on smaller customers, salespeople refusing to follow up on leads generated by advertising, direct mail being returned, salespeople spending only 25 percent of their time with customers, or salespeople and customers ordering products that are out of stock or discontinued.

Specific opportunities available to increase sales force productivity and to better serve customers through automation might include increasing the number of quality salesperson calls per day from five to six, reducing the time between order receipt and shipping from seven days to five, reducing the customer service staff from five to four people, allowing customers immediate access to information on availability and pricing, knowing how many leads and sales are generated by each ad, improving lead quality and closing ratios through email marketing, telemarketing, and better direct-mail responses.

Prioritize and rank the problems and opportunities. Which are the musts, which are the wants, which are the easiest to accomplish, and which the most difficult? Which will increase sales the most and which will decrease costs the most? Which will require the greatest investment and highest operating costs? Which can be done the quickest? What are the risks and rewards of each? In what order would you like to solve the problems and realize the opportunities? Because of their complexity, automation and ecommerce must be implemented in prioritized bite-size pieces. Knowing the specific goals, opportunities, needs, problems, and priorities will help you properly select software features, define users, and determine types of necessary data.

Second, based on reading the chapters of this book, what underlying sales processes need to be improved before automation? Automation alone will not improve poor sales or a poor sales process. Sales force automation and ecommerce do little to improve a poorly hired, trained, and deployed sales organization. Assuming you have reengineered the sales process, your sales automation programs must reinforce and support these methodologies. Don't expect software vendors to be sales management consultants, but do ask software vendors for references from firms with methodologies and processes similar to yours.

Next, consider the type of selling your salespeople perform, what portion of the sales process requires automating, and what people will be involved? Software which performs well for modified rebuys may prove less functional for long, complex sales cycles, for new product sales, or for commoditized transactional selling. Software which performs well for inside call center sales may prove less functional for an outside direct field sales force or channel partners. Automation vendors have specialties, strengths, and weaknesses, so make sure your needs match their specialties.

Next, what data do your salespeople and managers need to perform their jobs more efficiently? Do your salespeople need fast access to decision makers' names and interests, product specifications, prices, competitor knowledge, or historical shipment data? Do sales managers need fast access to territory potential, forecasts, market research, and salespeople's activities? Types of data to be accessed influences system's requirements and features.

Conduct a needs analysis by distributing questionnaires to field salespeople, sales support personnel, call center personnel, sales managers, marketing personnel, executives, and channel partners. Ask them what data they require and what functions need automation? Select a representative sample of salespeople for the survey and make sure they constitute 50 percent of the total participants. Have participants rank data requirements and features as follows: not required, not required at this stage, would like it, required in the future, and required now. Include categories such as contact management, personal calendar management, work group functionality, document management, reporting, lead tracking, opportunity tracking, marketing, data synchronization, communications, Internet connectivity, ecommerce, data collection, automated processes, and customizable feature buttons. Once you accomplish the needs analysis, make sure your firm's current or planned information systems will support the business functions that the survey indicates require automation.

Create a representative multifunctional task force to choose, develop, implement, and manage the sales automation and ecommerce system. The task force should include participants from information systems, sales management, salespeople, marketing management, customer service, sales support, call center, accounting, finance, sales training, human resources, and channel partners. The task force provides valuable input from the people that will use the systems and starts the critical process of buy-in and commitment. Each department expresses its concerns, needs, problems, opportunities, and expected benefits.

The task force chairperson should be from sales—not information systems—since success depends most on understanding sales/marketing processes, not hardware and software. The chairperson needs the attention and respect of top management to obtain the necessary human and financial resources for a successful project. Every member of the task force can say no to a proposal, but implicitly only sales/marketing people can say yes. Include one or two members from outside the company, knowledge experts who have experience in selecting and implementing an automation system. This brings balance and prospective to the task force. Finally, each member should be assigned specific tasks, which might include needs analysis, budget, software, or training.

Before the task force begins analyzing the value of specific software programs and systems, it needs to establish a realistic budget for each component of the sales automation project: software, hardware, and services, including training and upgrades. In the year 2001, a firm can expect to spend $5000 per salesperson to become fully automated, excluding costs related to ecommerce. Actual costs depending on the size of your sales force and the number of functions involved can vary from $3000 to $10,000 per sales person.

The detailed budget should include estimated costs for the initial investment in software, hardware, consultants, programming, installation, and training, as well as estimates for the annual operating/maintenance costs, which might include additional personnel. The budgeting process will force you to look for hidden costs and hard-to-quantify benefits. For instance, during the first two months after rollout, sales force productivity falls off as salespeople learn to use the system. You must consider the cost of a backup system or contingency plan or lost time when the system malfunctions. The budget process forces you to seek the advice of hardware and software vendors, consultants, and independent programmers.

Once the task force has established goals, needs, opportunities, and a budget, it should identify the required software, hardware, and services, along with the possible vendors to supply them. The first task involves deciding what portion of the work and software will be done internally and what portion will be contracted out or bought. In making this decision consider the following:

- *The human resources.* Does your firm have enough capable systems engineers and programmers available to write and implement the programs/systems? Often the information systems department wants to own this project, but past experience indicates they seldom deliver as promised.
- *The cost of time.* How much longer will it take to develop a system internally than to buy one on the outside? Multiply that estimate times two or three. How important is time to this project?
- *The cost and cash flow difference.* It may cost more to develop a system internally, but marginal cash flow will be less because you are already employing the necessary systems engineers and programmers.
- *Your information system's people versus an outside software vendor.* Who has more experience with the sales management process,

automation, and company culture? Information systems people and sales/marketing people seldom speak the same language. Sales and marketing managers think about sales force productivity, while information systems people focus on technical considerations. What mixture of outside vendors and inside system engineers can best bridge this gap and produce the optimum solutions. Which group can do a better job of keeping the system running, preventing malfunctions, and quickly correcting problems?

- *The risks involved.* What are the risks if a vendor fails? Who has the source code and knowledge?

In 1990, three-fourths of companies with operational sales support systems developed those systems in-house. By 2000, many more experienced vendors offered proven sales force automation, ecommerce, and customer relationship management programs, and costs per function or activity had declined. In 2000, 65 percent of companies with operational sales support, ecommerce, and customer relationship management systems used outside vendors for all or some part of their process.

Many firms split the responsibility between in-house capabilities and outside contractors. For example, you could use inside people to automate functions such as order entry, order processing, pricing, inventory status, and direct mail, but use vendor software and services for mapping, contact, calendar, relationship, and document management. Sophisticated online, Web-based applications involving ecommerce, enterprisewide solutions, or customer relationship management require proven, experienced outside vendors. An acceptable turnkey system can save development time, create an operational system sooner, take advantage of the vendor's prior experience with similar installations, provide more reliable cost estimates, and avoid costly surprises.

Early in the software selection process you should obtain evaluation copies of each program and, if possible, run a limited trial. Demonstration copies represent selling aids, but evaluation copies, which you pay for, are full-blown versions of the product that allow you to gain hands-on experience.

Always check with software providers' previous customers whose requirements are similar to yours. Ask the vendor for a list of customers in your industry using functions, features, applications, and activities similar to your firm's. Talk to known users who were not referrals, ask for accounts who were not satisfied, and talk to the vendor's competitors' customers. Look for comparables, visit customers' sites, and ask tough questions. How was follow-up service, training, and conflict resolution? What features and functions met expectations and which did not? Would you choose this vendor again and why? Be sure to talk with a variety of people from sales, sales management, and information systems. Tell them your requirements. Do they match theirs? Ask questions concerning total costs and number of users.

In choosing a vendor, consider price points, technology, customization, interfacing, and viability. Understand all the costs associated with using a package, including software, hardware, consultants, training, services, in-house support and development, seat licenses, server licenses, reports, third-party add-ons, and vendor maintenance. It is difficult to compare vendor prices because solutions, features, benefits, and applications are seldom comparable. Also, vendors make price comparisons difficult by quoting modules and per-user prices, plus add-ons for custom features. Understand all the costs associated with each vendor, package, and solution, then arrive at and compare the total dollar figure.

Software products have five key technologies: development language, client database, operating system, synchronization engine, and server database. Make sure each of these mesh with your firm's standards and infrastructure. Let the task force members from information systems handle this analysis. Watch out for proprietary or older technologies which may not interface well with your firm's systems, may have no support outside the vendor, and because of obsolescence, are subject to replacement by open systems and new standards. Identify the information technology standards and infrastructure strategic to your firm and have vendors prove that their software supports your database, operating system, and network.

What differentiates many software packages are the tools required to easily customize them. In some cases, vendors offer only development environments or authoring languages specific to their software package. Most users prefer more flexibility in customization tools, because their needs change over time and might differ for various divisions. In choosing a software vendor, consider whether your firm's information systems organization has the tools and the people to customize. Will the vendor or a third party do customization or are customers responsible for this? Also, who has responsibility for upgrades and maintenance?

Because many sales force automation firms are privately held, smaller companies, ask for or use third parties to obtain data on each vendor's financial strength and viability. Software vendors require substantial capital to invest in development and add functionality. Therefore, a vendor's financial strength should influence your choice.

The software selection criteria will be influenced by the project's size, so the number of salespeople that you plan to automate will impact the type of software needed. Smaller projects involving up to ten salespeople don't require data synchronization or integration with existing technology.

Projects involving up to 100 people do require system integration and data synchronization. Projects involving over 100 people require data warehousing functions.

As the task force proceeds through the implementation process, communicate with top management to confirm their agreement and support. Don't surprise them with a final report before obtaining their agreement on goals, applications, budgets, and vendors. When possible, quantify the top and bottom line implications of your decisions. Identify at least three top management champions. Keep them informed on critical risks and contingency plans. The software selection process requires three months, and task force members should schedule their time to meet this requirement.

Sales force automation represents a journey—a continuous process, rather than a destination. A successful implementation of sales automation keeps advancing the system's functionality over time and in phases. The users can only absorb so much information and training at one time. In addition, new beneficial technology such as ecommerce, wireless, and customer relationship management is always being introduced. The system is no better than the user's skill set, which must always be advanced. Also, ever-changing bottlenecks require reengineering.

Because of this, launching a full-scale program from scratch seldom succeeds, so most firms start with a pilot program, which is then rolled out in phases by region, segment, or function. Pilot programs allow firms to test the results, take corrective action, and then proceed. Establishing a realistic pilot program requires many decisions. You must choose what functions to test, how long to test them (usually two to six months), what people to include, and how to measure results.

First, choose representative salespeople, managers, customer service, sales support, call center people, and channel partners to participate in the pilot program. Start by automating one function at a time, but make sure that eventually the test includes automating all proposed functions for a territory, region, product, person, or department, so that you can evaluate the total system's complexities, problems, and effectiveness. Critical performance results and limitations may remain hidden unless the complexity and scale of the tests parallel the system's actual use.

You may choose to test lead tracking first, because it can show the greatest results and contain the least risk. You might then add contact, calendar, relationship, and document management, then forecasting, mapping, and activity tracking, and finally, remote synchronization, ecommerce, customer relationship management, and Web-based programs. You will have an easier time selling and training the entire sales organization on automation if these tests go well. The salespeople involved in testing the various automated functions should enthusiastically sell it to their colleagues, because they have experienced the many benefits. Test programs quickly identify problems and implement solutions. Making and correcting small mistakes saves money.

As with sales force automation in general, setting metrics and time frames for measuring the pilot program's success is necessary but difficult. Is proof of success faster order turnaround time, a better closing ratio, more time with customers, more new accounts, fewer pricing mistakes, lower cost per call, greater dollar sales per call, more calls per week, or some other criterion?

Salespeople and management may resist technology and automation because it invades their privacy, challenges their abilities and authority, quantifies an amorphous skill set, causes concern about more administrative work, requires changes, makes them feel insecure, and raises the fear of replacement. Technology itself does not drive success. Therefore, user buy-in, motivation, and training represent key elements for successful implementation of sales force automation.

To overcome this resistance, salespeople and management must understand how the system personally benefits them and have confidence in using it. These issues require change management and training. The best hardware and software will not produce your desired results without training the users. Identify critical risks and barriers to success, and then create training programs to remove them.

Develop a formal training program to assist not only salespeople, but customer support and customer service people, call center personnel, management, and channel partners. Make computer and software training part of a new hire's initial training, add it to the job description and training checklist, and include it as a topic at sales meetings. An automation training program requires classroom and online presentations, videos, mentoring, hands-on drills, exercises, a telephone hot line, a user's guide, field training, and follow-up evaluation.

Assess salespeople's, management's, and all users' technology skills before designing the training program. First, train salespeople on using their laptops or desktops. Next, train them on using individual software programs. Finally, train them on integrating the programs with remote synchronization, the Web, ecommerce, and customer relationship management. For every dollar of software and hardware, budget $1.50 for training over the life of the project. If the sales force automation software and hardware cost a total of $666,000, budget $1 million for training, or $200,000 a year over a five-year life span.

In training salespeople, remember each person's needs, skills, and concerns are different. Train users by establishing groups with common skill levels and concerns. Do training in segments or steps, because information overload can impede implementation. Training should be structured in a very task-oriented, protocol-based manner, covering those activities most essential to using the automation tools in performing a salesperson's or other user's job. Don't use generic or generalized training, because it causes confusion. All training programs should continually sell users the benefits of sales force automation and leave time for questions. Let more skilled people assist and mentor those with fewer skills. Systems which management and nonsales departments don't access often fail. Therefore, train not only the sales organization in using the system but also management, marketing, finance, and related departments.

Do you need to hire or use a contract trainer who has expertise in automation and use of your software, or do you have present employees capable of providing the knowledge? The task force needs a human resource representative to evaluate these issues.

Help desks and continuing support prove important for implementing and training salespeople and other users in automation. Be sure a knowledgeable person is available during evening hours when the field salespeople use their computers at home.

Training creates successful automation systems which boost salespeople's self-image, morale, and motivation. They are proud to be part of a forward-thinking organization. In addition, the sales force's use of computers enhances its credibility, professionalism, and image with customers.

During the long, complex process of designing, testing, and implementing an automated sales system, responsibilities and project accountability may become blurred. Every few months, have the task force define or redefine who has responsibility for each area in the start-up and continuing operation of this system. Every month, have a member of the task force monitor the project's status versus certain milestones, and if necessary, recommend corrective action. Also, during this long, complex process, keep all participants, including top management, informed on the status of each component through online bulletins or individual email.

Finally, remember that successful implementation of an automated sales system involves not only altering technology to accommodate the sales/marketing environment but also altering your organization to fit the technology. If your salespeople work out of their homes, far from each other and any company office, laptops, remote synchronization, and online programs become essential. With the availability of these tools, a sales manager may start asking salespeople for customer activity and status reports. Top management may decide these tools will allow regional sales managers to supervise nine salespeople rather than seven.

QUESTIONS AND EXERCISES

- What functions in your sales management process are automated?
- What functions in your sales management process need to be automated?
- Does your firm have a sales force automation task force with representative members?
- What training do you give salespeople in the use of computers, software, and the Web?

SALES MANAGERS' MAJOR WEAKNESSES/MISTAKES
SALES FORCE AUTOMATION

- Not devoting proper resources to implementing sales force automation and training salespeople in it
- Not personally using the automation tools and software
- Not properly selling the benefits of automation, customer relation management, and ecommerce to the sales force
- Letting information systems and technology issues drive important decisions rather than sales and marketing issues

INDEX

ABOUT THE AUTHOR

Robert J. Calvin is president of Management Dimensions, Inc., an international consulting firm specializing in sales management training, sales training, marketing, and strategy for clients ranging from the Fortune 500 to the Inc. 100. Calvin is an adjunct professor at the University of Chicago Graduate School of Business, where he teaches sales force management in the MBA and executive education programs. As a teacher, busy consultant, successful entrepreneur, salesperson, sales manager, and executive, Calvin has rebuilt many sales forces. His previous books include the award-winning *Managing Sales for Business Growth* and *Profitable Sales Management and Marketing for Growing Businesses.*